A Science
of
Consciousness

PNEUMATOLOGY FOR A NEW MILLENNIUM

Shiva C. A. D. Shankaran

BALBOA.
PRESS

A DIVISION OF HAY HOUSE

Balboa Press books may be ordered through booksellers or by contacting:

Balboa Press
A Division of Hay House
1663 Liberty Drive
Bloomington, IN 47403
www.balboapress.com
1 (877) 407-4847

Because of the dynamic nature of the Internet, any web addresses or links contained in this book may have changed since publication and may no longer be valid. The views expressed in this work are solely those of the author and do not necessarily reflect the views of the publisher, and the publisher hereby disclaims any responsibility for them.

The author of this book does not dispense medical advice or prescribe the use of any technique as a form of treatment for physical, emotional, or medical problems without the advice of a physician, either directly or indirectly. The intent of the author is only to offer information of a general nature to help you in your quest for emotional and spiritual well-being. In the event you use any of the information in this book for yourself, which is your constitutional right, the author and the publisher assume no responsibility for your actions.

Any people depicted in stock imagery provided by Thinkstock are models, and such images are being used for illustrative purposes only. Certain stock imagery © Thinkstock.

Print information available on the last page.

ISBN: 978-1-5043-4349-7 (sc)
ISBN: 978-1-5043-4351-0 (hc)
ISBN: 978-1-5043-4350-3 (e)

Library of Congress Control Number: 2015918707

Balboa Press rev. date: 11/28/2016

Table of Contents

Introduction

When we begin a discussion about Consciousness, what it is, its relevance to us in our lives today and all the other facets of how we are influenced and made by our own Essence, we find we are drawn into a discussion about ourselves that quickly becomes more broad and larger than we may have ever before imagined. I am reminded of a concept of myself I had once held as a child where I had wondered how it had come to be that I found myself in this or any particular physical body. Of all the people in the world or for that matter all the animals and plants and elements present in our world, how could it have come to be that this awareness that I seemed to be identified with had found itself not only in any bodily form at all, but also in this one in particular.

This was a question that I pondered upon and remembered for many years growing up and I believe has influenced me profoundly throughout my life since. To be sure it has been a major sub-conscious motivator in my personal spiritual quest to discover the answer to the fundamental question of "Who am I", and clearly in retrospect for the yearning for a reunification with That ultimate Being that I must have even then known innately I was always a part of. This eternal quest for Yoga, Union with the Divine is such a deeply set condition within this Thing that we call Essence that there is simply no escaping it in any ultimate sense. It can be suppressed, put off and procrastinated, even denied and betrayed in the short term, but ultimately we are irresistibly returned to it, like a river that can meander about for thousands of miles but eventually must return to the ocean from which it originally came, as evaporation that formed into clouds that rained down upon the highlands that collected into streams and found its long slow trek back to the sea.

So it has been and so it will be, for these are patterns of evolution that are reflected above and below from the metaphysical plains of Being through the natural physical worlds of nature and all the layers of spirit and mind and feeling in between.

As we embark upon a new millennium, in which first our own Universe is being opened to us and then even the existence of other Universes as well, all the marvels of an entire Creation in which we Live and Breath and Have Our Being, we are to come to a series of great awakening in answer to that question of "Who we really are" and with them also to an unbounded knowing of what this Creation is and Its Creator as well. This new century is just the beginning of a quest that will take us through at least the next thousand years to a new level of Being that we might only guess at now and could not even begin to imagine.

Let us begin to take our first steps; it is the right time for us to do so, and what better beginning than a renewal of the age old study of Consciousness itself the Essence of who and what we are revisited, refreshed and reawakened.

Come with me upon a journey of Body, Soul and Spirit, Soma, Psyche, Pneuma, as St. Paul called us so long ago; this study of Spirit, Pneumatology, this study of Consciousness, as I call it for our scientific age, and let us see where it leads.

Preface

At the outset certain terms need to be defined. Ideas in this volume will be new to many and certainly I will present concepts of my own which, although I believe to be based in antiquity, they are not the common usage of today. It is the hope of this author that with the help of this book they soon will be and a new scientific approach to Pneumatology can emerge more befitting the spiritual needs and development of our new century and millennium.

My own background makes me something of a student of world religions and spiritual traditions. Yet first and foremost I am a student of Truth. That at the offset is a controversial statement to some traditions that hold there is no big "T" Truth. I beg to differ. If you hold this belief, I simply ask you to suspend your disbelief long enough to consider the concepts and meanings and insights of this work. I am not out to convince or convert, only to promote a Cosmology that can only be of great help to humanity in maturing spiritually at a time of impasse in the development of our civilization that requires in the most desperate terms the maturing of our spiritual energies for the sake of our very survival as a species upon this Earth and within this solar system. Our Earth deserves and requires nothing less of us as well, not only for its own survival also, but for its spiritual success as a fully balanced mono-polar and fifth dimensional world. Not to be overly ambitious yet this work attempts to outline and promote a view of humanity in this solar system beginning here with Earth of course, that will place us in a genuinely healthy and sustainable relationship with our environment, our technology and ourselves, that will enable us to move forward in the present, with all our capacity for good and ill, in a way that is True to our Spirit of goodness and loving tenderness, and that will keep us firmly planted in the Good in all ways and ventures for all foreseeable generations to come. An admirable goal I propose yet not nearly as unattainable as it may have been in times past; for now at last we are on the cusp as it were; we are ready to listen to learn to hear and give it our God's honest try for the love of Humanity our world and the Truth; whatever that may be.

For many reasons I prefer not to discuss my own identity; the greatest of which is that it might tend to limit the views of those seeking to interpret this information for themselves or to seek to pigeon hole me into a class or set that would explain away important ideas as if not applicable to all. That would be a great mistake. These ideas represent a Truth that is bigger than me or anything I could say about myself. The real author here is the Cosmic Mind Itself, the True Universal Self to which we all belong. I am able to present this material only in as much as I maintain a clear open connection to That which I recognize as my True Self, beyond this mind that thinks and identifies with me. In short I am writing this thru what I call genuine Knowing that I do in fact know to be the True Me, what I really Am and can therefore know as such. I do not consider this book channeled therefore, but rather a cognition, a recognition of that which simply and purely Is and is hence the birthright of every human being and also living thing to the extent that their God given Consciousness can reflect and express the Totality of what Is.

So here goes; I will say it; I call myself at this phase of life a Christian Yogi. I say this because it is the closest term to the Truth I can come to in our spoken language given the Reality as I have come to know it thus far. I do not say it out of any connection to any church or dogma and this I must make clear. I call myself Christian out of the pure love for Christ and everything that represents to me and as Reality, and that thru That I have gained some degree of Yoga or Union with the divine, that gives meaning and goodness and power and life to whatever It is that I Am. In this life I have been blessed to have had several enlightened teachers, some of whom are Hindus and from them have learned what I know about Yoga. Not merely the physical yoga that too often passes for yoga in the West but also mental and spiritual yoga, meditation and breathing and the great gifts of wisdom and understanding that are a part of so many practices, which enable us to benefit from them as we are meant to. I have also learned from many western teachers who have themselves learned in similar ways and have shared the Grace freely and widely and have made their teachers proud. For them All, living and Ascended I offer my deepest Heart felt Gratitude and pray this book may in some way prove worthy of them.

Part I

CONSCIOUSNESS AND THE NATURE OF SPIRIT

The term Pneuma in ancient usage is translated as Spirit. Thus often Pnuematology is used to mean a Theology or Study of Holy Spirit. The word holy is demystified by the mystery schools to simply mean whole. Thus the Whole Spirit is implied by the orthodox Holy Spirit. In the Cosmic sense of Divinity, this Whole Spirit therefore rightly refers to the very Spirit or Consciousness of Creation. This is a vital recognition to arrive at; that Creation as a Whole has or rather is Consciousness Itself, and that everything within that Creation, including ourselves and all things animate and inanimate must be part of and included in That Whole. For anything whatever to be left out, even the tiniest particle of matter or energy, the Whole would be lacking and thus less than itself: a fundamental absurdity. That said, let us sit for a moment with the idea of the Consciousness of Creation.

1

Put simply and completely, the Consciousness of all living things, plant, animal, human, angelic and beyond and the physical and energetic structure of all that makes up all the nine kingdoms taken together in all of this Creation comprised of this Universe and any others that may be a part of this whole Creation, all that combined into One Whole and Unified Consciousness is what the Holy Spirit Is.

Modern science as in Quantum and Unified Field Theory claims to have identified ten distinct dimensions of energy-matter-time, as this fundamental process of Creation gives rise to what we call Universe. [1] In fact these dimensions themselves represent ten distinct universes together comprising what we think of as Creation. Yet it is all One Unified Field that this whole Creation of ten Universes emerges from. Still this scientific study is by no means finished or conclusive, for all we know there could in reality be more yet to be discovered. And still there is One Whole Consciousness that encapsulates it all and is in Reality the very Essence of All of This That Is. This is how I define Holy Spirit, the One Whole Consciousness of All That is. In scientific terms It is the Unified Field of Existence through and through all manifestation of Being and Existence everywhere present and on all levels of expression.

This is in itself an attempt to demystify Holy Spirit from its concept as a religious and theological entity into a truly scientific reality in the field of Consciousness that not only makes it more comprehensible but at the same time enhances our appreciation of the divinity and Oneness of this massive Reality. For me the cognition of this Whole Consciousness of Creation opens awareness to a recognition of Creation Itself as a living, breathing, Being, One and entirely complete within Itself, of Which we are all members and parts within That. This is the direct cognition of a Unifying factor, the Oneness of all Being, that is the genuine Reality of the Creation in which we find ourselves as Its own intimate expression. Holy Spirit is defined as Divine; It can be what we might call God or Supreme. We now know that the Consciousness that we are cannot in any way be apart and separate from the Whole Consciousness of That. It is through this that we are both participants and members of the Divine. Consciousness makes us Whole; Consciousness makes us One; there is nothing else but That, as we also are That.

When we look at Creation with all its possibilities of multiple universes and the huge potential for different worlds, environments, patterns of evolution and life forms, intelligences of innumerable kinds, we can now appreciate how It is all unified as One entity and Being within a single Consciousness of the Whole.

If I seem to be repeating myself here, it is just that this cannot be overstated either in its importance nor realized from too many angles, because as I propose and will attempt to show over and over that as we can look at this reality from infinite sides, all angles of observation will reveal in growing richness the same Truth in myriad and endless ways like a hologram of infinite diversity that always points back to a single point of Unity containing within Itself the expression of all possibilities.

This is not some wild and hair brained speculation; rather it is a Truth so beautiful as to boggle the mind and fulfill the mind's need to understand both at once. Can Infinity be brought into Awareness any more clearly or more understandably than this? If it can, I am waiting with baited breathe to see it, for I know this is standing at the threshold of any such Awareness growing out of it into deeper insight into such Divine Unity.

(At this point if you are still reading this, you are either with me or wondering what I am going off about so excitedly. For those who are wondering this may be a good time to backtrack a bit and perhaps fill in a few gaps in where I am coming from.)

Traditionally western Mystery Schools have postulated the existence of 12 dimensions. Recently a 13th dimension has been suggested by at least one such School as a birthing process collectively of the activity of the first 12. [2] This may give us some insight into what the Unified Field scientists are uncovering as they peer into the tiniest particle life and discern the 10 dimensions they have come to recognize thus far. Perhaps as they continue to look deeper still, they will uncover yet even more. That will be interesting to see. Yet we are speaking of something so far beyond our present comprehension that for all we know at this point there could in Reality be many more than 13. The point being made here, is that what was once assumed to be one universe and one Creation, is in fact much more and bigger than that, and with that far more complex and unknown to us than we ever imagined. We are just now at the threshold of coming into an awareness of how great and varied and immense it might All Be.

Some Greater Thoughts of Implications

My first Guru, Maharishi Mahesh Yogi, is well known among his followers for saying that everything is interconnected. By everything he truly meant everything; that nothing in existence either existed in isolation and also that every part of existence is somehow influencing in each moment every other part. [3] All of Creation is One vast interconnected Whole on a truly magnificent and grand scale. A simple Truth that bares pondering and reflection for its power and implications and depth of meaning, all of which could fill many volumes as well. The one great implication that is the subject of this book is this Reality: that the entire Creation no matter how vast and how many universes it may entail, is still One great cohesive Whole in which every single particle is somehow in communication with and influencing and being influenced by every other particle, even as they may be present between universes. That this common influence must as well cross not only all of space but also all of time. Remember, Creation is a living, breathing, entity with a life of Its own and a Consciousness that is fully aware and conscious of Itself. That as a living Being, It maintains the functions that all living beings do and cares for Itself as any Self-aware Being would by Its own Nature.

The ancient Mystery Schools tend to define anything that may exist outside of the realm of this Creation or anything not held within the attention of the Creator as Unknowable. This simply means unknowable for us, because we can know only what is within the sphere of the Creation as we are each a part of That. And as such as we are a part of That, it is within our ultimate capacity to know and consciously connect to anything within this Creation. It is within this context and because of it, that we have the capacity to know It as Creator or Supreme Being. This is so precisely because this Being is Self-aware, and this means not only that the Whole is aware of all Its parts but also that each part has the capability to be aware of the Whole. Nothing less would be fully Actualized.

Where does this leave us in our present only partially conscious state? This is a question that will have to be addressed later in this work. The pressing issue at this point is Who and What we are in context of Creation and the Consciousness It represents and embodies, both as a Whole and within all of Its parts. It is my contention that in answering this pressing issue the question of our present partially conscious state will be brought into light and become clear and comprehensible.

Throughout all of visible Nature it is made clear that like begets like. Plants and animals of any species reproduce only their own species, generally speaking. Nowadays with the proliferation of so much mutation among species this perhaps could be questioned but only in the context of such mutation, which often involves the transformation of the entire species into something slightly altered or something else almost entirely new. This is called evolution and has its necessary place in the survival and ongoing development of life and Creation as a whole. Yet there is built into the entire structure of life an orderliness that both generates and maintains life at the same time as providing for its continuing evolution. This is a crucial point that must be applied to ourselves also, if we are to come to a greater comprehension of who and what we are both as human and as spiritual beings. The Reality that is recognized here is that just as physical beings are born into the physical structure of their parents, so too are spiritual beings born into the spiritual structure of their parent as well.

The very fact that we are physical/spiritual Beings existing within the context of what is for us an immense Creation, born out of an Existence that we ourselves did not create, suggests to us in no uncertain terms that we are ourselves of one and the same species as that Creation Itself, whatever That may be. We may not know yet what that Is, although I suspect we may all have some ideas or sense of it, if we actually stopped and in deep inner reflection asked our greater knowing and waited there in silence for the reply. Still this brings to mind that as spiritual beings we must consider ourselves as in gestation; that we exist in this universe as babes yet in the womb of our Mother. Flowing from this inherently, come our sense of God as Mother, "The Mother of God" and Divine Mother. Creation is reproducing Itself; It is pregnant with every life form and Being that is a part of Herself if you will.

A Brief Review

This may be a good place to pause before we go too far into the hitherto un-thought of.

Creation is Alive; It is a living, breathing, self-aware entity with a life of Its own. It is in every way imaginable Conscious and Awake. That this Consciousness of Creation envelopes All that Is in this and all Universes that comprise what this Creation Is. That this Supreme Consciousness of Creation in Reality is what we call the Whole or Holy Spirit, and that we are bonded to that Holy Spirit through our own Spirit that exists in connection and as a part of that Whole Spirit of Creation. That this is what Consciousness in Reality Is, and that the evolution of all forms of life as we know it is a process by which their Spirits of Consciousness are growing more and more into the context of the greater Consciousness of Creation, their Divine Parent.

A New Paradigm

"I come to bury Caesar not to praise him." [4]

First of all, how do I know this? Or is this just some sort of speculative philosophy that has no way of empirical proof or disproof and is therefore as some agnostics might say, "meaningless" as a metaphysical statement.

Fair enough, this is a common challenge of our time and one that begs the question of empirical proof. Let me begin by stating clearly that I do not present these ideas as some kind of hypothesis in quest of verification or disproof. I present this information quite differently rather as a Cognition which I can state from my own Knowing born of what I am as Consciousness. The difference is very significant even to the point of representing an alternative or new paradigm as an approach to science and knowledge overall. How so? Let me explain.

The word cognition has a modern usage and an ancient one as well. Merriam-Webster Dictionary states: "the act or process of knowing including both awareness and judgment; also: a product of this act." [5] Psychologically it is often applied to the reasoning process or capability, as applied to awareness and judgment. The ancient Vedic Tradition of India regards the ancient Seers or Rishis as having Cognitions of the various principles of Creation or its processes, which subsequently were recorded as scripture known as the Vedas. This is a very special kind of Cognition, which taking place when the world was more newly created and thus pure of the chaotic and negative influences that arose later on, the Laws of Nature or if you will fundamental principles by which Creation came into being and thus sustained were more audible, visible, touchable, cognizable if you will, than perhaps they were in later days after the world became busier and eventually violent. Activities of a negative or destructive nature tend to cloud the view as it were, confuse the mind and sometimes the heart as well, resulting in a more dysfunctional state of living and affairs.

These two views of cognition are not mutually exclusive, yet the ancient one offers a much greater and more complete appreciation of the full potentiality of the human Consciousness regards Its ability to know Itself and Its surroundings. It is in this fuller view of Cognition that I offer this information of the Consciousness of Creation and all the implications of that herein, as a look into the Knowledge and Truth of Reality. This therefore represents for me, and I here present it as such, a direct Seeing into that genuine Ultimate Nature that identifies who we really are and our relationship to the All of Creation, and therefore to ourselves as well.

Yet is this verifiable? I submit that it is, for I am after all human, and I suspect that all of you reading this are also. And as I have the greatest respect for my Guru's teaching that "anything is possible", and by anything he truly meant anything; I must accept also the likely possibility that perhaps some highly intelligent non-humans, such as insectoids, reptilians, cetaceans or others may be reading this as well. I welcome the broadest possible audience. We all share this One overall over-riding Consciousness of Which we are all a part, kin and united. More of this will be coming up.

How do I know this, and how do I dare stand by the Truth of it? The answer to that rests in the mystery of Cognition itself, from where our thoughts and our minds originate and what this represents in the greater context of Consciousness. This is not simply an Empirical knowing that relies upon research and verification outside of ourselves, but rather this is a much more reliable and profound Spiritual knowing that stands upon a direct awareness of the very core of our Being that is Known through inner research done from within ourselves that reveals a vision of Reality much more intimate than any Empirical only process could provide.

Objectivity and Subjectivity

Western Science prides itself, of course, on its objectivity, yet in reality relies upon personal cognition all the time. As children growing up we have to learn how to think; logical or right thinking does not necessarily come naturally to us, as is evident with the social and family problems we have if we are not taught properly or at all. As children we are easily conditioned into patterns of thinking, feeling and belief by parents, teachers, the media, etc., and it is critically important that these patterns be true and honest and clean and not distorted by untrue or unknown beliefs that likewise will result in distorted thought and emotional patterns that can effect us for life. High Schools and Colleges offer courses in logic and philosophical systems define and stress the importance of right thinking, and even with modern education ethical misconduct still persists. This is to say we require education, and therefore must go through a process by which we learn to process thinking in a logically valid and true way. This we say is one of the key qualities of the state of being educated; that is knowing how to think. Yet before we can practice the art of rational thought, we must first possess the capacity to have a thought, which is totally natural. When we first become aware of a thought we say we are cognizant of it. Still awareness itself even without a thought present is the first form of Cognition, and with that pure Awareness what we are as Consciousness is at least in alignment with the greater Consciousness of Creation of which ours is born and a part.

What then is true objectivity or for that matter true subjectivity? The answer we find for this question is vital, and the more profoundly we can address this issue the more reliable and valid will be the science and knowledge that is based upon it.

The objective paradigm requires that the "object" of study be tangible and material enough that it can be measured and observed as separate and distinct from those doing the observation. This is rational enough, as the observer wants to get a true and valid observation, as if he or she was not present and therefore not interfering with the results or information gathered. I do not have to give a litany of praises for this approach, as it has been the bulwark and foundation for modern western science and technological achievement since the Renaissance. Therefore I will not bore you and myself by heaping more fader on the fire of technological prowess by restating what we already know and are not reading here to learn. I will continue by stating two primary and critical limitations to this empirical approach.

First, objectivity is limited to the material and tangible that can be measured and observed in this manner. The metaphysical or spiritual is purely and simply out of its reach. This limitation alone I intend to show is fatal to human culture and humanity overall.

Second, we know from the "Uncertainty Principle" that anything we observe is somehow mysteriously changed or altered by the very act of our observation. [6] This limitation it turns out is key to opening our insight into the very nature of both the problem with empirical approach and the solution to that problem, for it is an indication of the Reality of the overriding Consciousness that connects all individual awareness.

Now let us have a look at subjectivity.

Subjectivity is more fundamentally related to the Self, the subject doing the observation. It is directly related to the inner mental, emotional, spiritual contexts of who and what we are. Such questions as, Who am I, Who is the Knower, Who is the Doer, Who is the Experiencer, are traditionally regarded as metaphysical in nature, and therefore outside the range and scope of the objective or empirical approach, yet these are the most fundamental and basic requirements of any philosophical or scientific system to know and answer with clarity before any other observation can be made with genuine validity and truth of certitude. Only in the past subjectivity had been regarded as unreliable precisely because these questions could not be answered to the satisfaction of everyone if at all, and also because the objective approach itself has been inadequate to answer them.

Hence the dilemma of our modern and contemporary humanity, the dilemma of our scientific age itself, that the very problem that makes subjectivity unreliable also renders objectivity unreliable; even though modern science has been loath to admit this. One of the greatest philosophers/ metaphysicians of Western recorded history is Nicolas of Cusa. I have personally found him a source of wonderful inspiration and insight over many years and still to this day. He spoke of what he called "the Coincidence of Opposites".[7] This is how he explained Intrinsic Unity, the Oneness and non-dual Nature of Reality. That we live in a world of opposites that for all practical purposes is dualistic, yet if we turn our attention inwards to deeper and finer aspect of manifestation, through the Chain of Being towards the Source of Being Itself, more and more we find as we go deeper into this Awareness, that opposites begin to coincide; that they come closer together until at the Ground of Being Itself they merge together into One and are no longer opposed but are united and indistinguishable as separate. This I submit is a universal realization of all genuine Yogis, Saints, Sages, Masters and Avatars throughout time and traditions universally. All who go to these deepest and highest stages of Oneness realization will attest to this; that at the level of Pure Being where the appearances of opposites coincide and cease to exist, subject and object gently merge into One. Thus, as Sri Nisargadatta Maharaj pointed out so beautifully, pure objectivity and pure subjectivity are one and the same merged together in the Pure Being of Existence. [8]

I submit most clearly and emphatically that the paradigm so urgently needed for our time is one of balanced subject and object into a singularized Awareness of this Oneness underlying and amid the appearance of diversity. This spiritualized awareness if you will applied to science and knowledge, will produce a point of reference at the same time reliable and practical, valid and true, verifiable and integrated, that will empower the spiritual potentiality and foster Its growth and maturation, so as to render humankind more capable of utilizing technologies of both creative and destructive power with moral integrity and responsibility for their genuine use to serve only the Good.

Principles and Practice

For lack of a better name and for purposes of identifying underlying principles I call this the Cognitive Process or Approach to science, knowledge and awareness. Hence the term Cognitive Science, if you will, to distinguish it from a more purely empirical approach. This process is cognitive, because it recognizes the validity of cognition within the overall wholeness of Awareness and also the wholeness of Consciousness Itself from which Awareness has its basis, and that the entire process of the emergence and development of thought, itself an aspect of Creation, is One and inseparable from the process and act of Knowing. The recognition of these principles is of vital importance for several reasons. Firstly, it establishes that the ideal of pure objectivity is an illusion and simply practically unattainable. It is not practical to expect us to separate ourselves from a thought process that is rooted within our own nature and Being. Yet, both in spite and because of this, objectivity cannot be as genuinely reliable as has been believed for so long. Without the fundamental knowledge of what a thought is or even from where or how it emerges into awareness the very concept of objectivity becomes unreliable at best and absurd at worse. Secondly, the Cognitive Approach allows for a balancing of the two primary entities involved in any inquiry, subject and object. Granted there is a certain artistry and skill in attaining this balance, but now we have the foundation and basic framework to move towards that balance and arrive at a knowledge that is truly integrated and spiritually aware. This also is something that before just wasn't happening. Thirdly and moreover, the benefits of this type of balance will prove incalculable and invaluable to humanity's capacity to compassionately address problems and find solutions that honor ourselves in ways never before achieved. This is an area that we can hardly even begin to address here. The implications for upwards progress are so vast it defies imagination even, and simply put the sky is the limit. I suspect the sky has no limit regards our capacity to develop and mature and grow further into our true Being.

Imagine if you will the Consciousness of Creation; that Creation is a Conscious, living, breathing Being, whose Awareness extends to all beings animate and inanimate within That. That our own Consciousness or Spirit if you will, is born of That, and therefore no different from It except in that ours is not yet fully formed and developed. What we are, I believe, is growing into what That Is. The more we recognize this, the more we come into the genuine balance of awareness of subject and object merging into One.

As Nicolas of Cusa put it, the closer we come to that Awareness within our own Core, the more the apparent opposites of subject and object merge or coincide into That One single Reality of Being. The awareness of this Reality, I submit, opens humankind's awareness to the possibility of reaching the highest varieties of Enlightenment attainable in our Earthly lives, that of a non-dual awareness of the Intrinsic Unity of all existence, what Maharishi Mahesh Yogi referred to as Unity Consciousness and earlier schools of Christian saints called the Unitive Way.

A Cognition to Consider

I realize there are multiple trains of thought going on here in parallel. Now may be a time to begin tying some of these together. It is in this context as Cognition that I present the various premises and insights contained herein about Spirit, Consciousness, Awareness and their nature. There is no hypothesis here; rather these insights into the Consciousness of Creation and how our individual Consciousness, that is what we are as Consciousness, fits into That greater Awareness is to be understood here as Cognition put forth for your specific consideration; that is to look deep within your own Core to see if you can find verification for it there in your Essence. In this way we allow our Heart or Core Essence to be natural, in a manner consistent with Its true structure and faculty, that of Knower. This very process we will see later on is consistent with our inner structure as Spirit, Mind and Body. Ultimately this fact will prove the validity of this Cognitive Process of Knowing, and this too is its beauty. It works because it is consistent with our True Nature, thereby enabling us to verify what we come by insight and reason to understand.

In this technological age a great many devices have been made from the simple to extremely complex to test empirically any hypothesis, as it pertains to the physical and tangible world. At this stage of our development to reach a stage of inner and spiritual maturity and balance, it is now necessary for us to learn to recognize a valid Cognition from within and apply that Knowing practically for ourselves and society as a whole. Without this awareness we continue to stumble in the darkness of uncertainty and ignorance. Many great scientists of the West have known this already. Albert Einstein relates his own discoveries to deep intuition and insight, which he states he already knew must be true, and only then after that initial cognition set out to prove his theories empirically for the world.

The difference now is that humankind as a whole is to be reset to this level of cognition universally, so that at the Core of Awareness we will be fine-tuned enough to recognize the Truth or untruth of any Cognition we focus our intention to know. This is not a simple matter of achievement, and in the past would have been so wrought with pitfalls as to not have been possible, yet the revolution of Consciousness that is upon us, and I would like to suggest even this book is a part, is making the heretofore impossible now possible. The sheer recognition of the True Nature of Consciousness and that Creation Itself is a living and Self Aware Consciousness, brings our own Awareness into recognition of the ultimate and present Oneness and Unity of all life, being and Creation.

Have I stated this already? I intend to say it at least several more times from different angles throughout this work. To do so is part of that Cognitive verification, as well as part of the Cognition itself. For a Cognition is not necessarily a single individual thought, but rather is more often a host and bundle of insights wrapped together as one. It is a bit like Indra's Web. In the great Vedic mythology of the Ancient East, the god Indra is shown to have an immense mansion high up on a great mountain. Floating over the mansion and extending out forever in all directions is a most intricate and complex web interwoven and connecting all of Creation. At each intersecting point on this Web, where strands from all directions merge together and intersect is held fast there by a jewel of great brilliance and beauty, multi-faceted, each unique and awesome.

Yet each jewel reflects the beauty and contains within it the Essence of every other jewel and of the Web as a whole. [9]

So it is with us! What each human being is as Consciousness is like one and each of these jewels in Indra's Web. The Holy Spirit, the Consciousness of Creation is like the entire Web to which we are all connected by virtue of our very Being. Indra's Mansion standing beneath the Web is the structure of the physical Universes, and the fibers of the Web, which holds all the jewels in place, connecting them all with each other and with the Universes as well, is like the All Knowing Cosmic Mind of Creation. These Three taken together form what Christians know as the Sacred Trinity, as depicted in Vedic mythology, and also the Ancient Vedic vision of Trinity, I believe.

Not bad for literature that predates the coming of Christ by several thousands of years. Not bad for any age and how precious for us today in this age to finally be coming into a clear and unambiguous recognition of these Realities in a way that is to transform our very definition of Knowledge and what it means to Know. For the first time in recorded history, our civilization is to come to know the true Knower, and It is our own Essence.

And so It Is!

But I digress. The beauty of Cognition is in the solidity of its insight. There is according to Vedic Wisdom a level of awareness known as Ritambhara prajna. (Yoga Sutra 1.48.) It is a very fine level of Heart Awareness that allows only Truth to enter. In that very fine Awareness the Truth about anything can be known. It is a process of asking from Heart and waiting for a silent response from the vast Empty Awareness that opens just where this Heart Awareness meets or touches the Ocean of Being at the Core of our Essence. This is a level which transcends ordinary thought and any concept of time we can hold in the mind. It is a level of timeless Knowingness, from where all existent being emerges but exists there only as a kind of lively potentiality. The blueprint of Creation is there in a pure un-manifest state full of brilliant Divine Intelligence, yet needing to do nothing to be anything other than just be as it is. This is the Source of genuine Cognition, and this is also the level of its authentic verification. The Awareness that This Is, is inherent to all forms of Consciousness, and this is one aspect of what is referred to as Divine Source. It is our direct conscious connection to God, or as I have preferred to call it here, the Consciousness of Creation. In order to be cognizant of This, a person has to expand the conscious capacity of their own Consciousness to Its fullest extent. This is most commonly done by bringing the conscious awareness deep within to become acquainted with Its own Source at the ground of Being through a regular practice of meditation over the course of some time. Yet this alone is not enough. In addition to this expansion of Conscious Awareness a person has also to end or break the habitual addiction that we all are commonly brought up with of dwelling in our minds. From here it is necessary to learn to dwell within the Heart.

Heart and Mind Revisited

What does it mean to dwell in the mind or to dwell within the Heart? Even more basic than these, what is the mind, and what is the Heart? Here begins the genuinely fascinating inquiry and observation into what we truly are as Consciousness, which must be distinguished from whatever it is we may think or have ever thought we are.

To dwell in the mind simply means to use the mind to determine what is real. This is commonly experienced as believing ones' own thoughts and feelings to be True, without questioning them, simply on account of them being your own. As it turns out our belief in what is real is central to our concept of self of who we are. Hence, the reliance upon the mind to determine reality also focuses responsibility of self-identity upon mind. The mind now becomes the observer, the knower, the judge and jury, the executioner of reality. This is a tall order, and one fraught with pitfalls and problems. To see into this condition, we must answer the more basic question of what is the mind.

The mind is a faculty that contains certain abilities; these are to think and have thoughts, also to feel, as in feeling mind, to intuit as in subtle thinking and also to understand such as with reason and intellect. The mind is a tool for all these abilities and has the capacity to be sharpened and fine-tuned, as many complex and highly evolved tools may be. This is to be respected and honored and befriended, and known thus to be treated with care and compassion for the masterpiece of evolution that it is.

The Heart can also be described as a faculty but in a different sense. Heart is much closer to the Core of our Being, and as such far closer to our true individuation in that It emerges from the Universal Being as the first indication of a new creation that is to become unique. Heart is the faculty of Knowingness and of True Knowing. It is the seat of Knowledge in the most Real sense, and It in fact houses our very capacity to genuinely know anything. Knowing, therefore is to be distinguished from understanding, which is the function of the mind. As it is possible to understand without knowing, and also it is possible to know something without understanding it. There are reasons for both of these conditions, but the greatest integration of Heart and mind is to have knowing with understanding. That is the most complete and balanced state.

So whereas, Being is the seat of Consciousness and Source of Creation, Heart is the very first stirring of Consciousness as a specific Creation. This is the most delicate and sublime process that the Vedas expound upon in great detail and at length. It is not possible to go into that in great detail here or even necessary really, what is necessary here is to understand the nature of this movement and how that appears within our human awareness.

On Its own, the Being does not move; It remains silent and stationary, content and complete within Itself in need of nothing, pure Emptiness. When Being is then gently stirred by Consciousness, in the most subtle ways it begins to move as pure Love, Tenderness, and this gentle flow is the first subtle impulse of Being just beginning to become lively and active. It is Celestial in nature, the first fruit of Being becoming manifest as a new Creation. This is a timeless moment, as it takes place before time even begins, outside of time if you will. Yet this moment is occurring continuously over and over from the very birth of our Universe and constantly ongoing

23

without end. Every new thought that anyone has ever had, every new impulse of creative energy, every new breathe and movement in nature in every nanosecond of time is another such arising of this new stirring of the Being by the subtlest most Tender motion of Consciousness, the True Creator. The discovery of this Reality and how It occurs is the journey of the human Heart. The recognition of this process and appreciation of it is the fulfillment of Consciousness Itself, become fully Self Aware and Realized. That coming together of Being and Consciousness, that connection between them is rightly called Heart. This touch of Divinity of the Creator's Will that stirs the Being into the finest motion and gives rise to Tenderness is the Grace of the Heart that is the True Core of each human persons Essence and the true home of our individuality and everything that makes us Real. There is no ego in this Core, only the genuine Grace of divinity that rises as Creation. The Consciousness that is moving is not new; It was never created, as That exists beyond time, only the expression of That is new and represents a new creation that gives context to the Consciousness that always Is. And yet that expression too is rooted in That which is beyond time, and is therefore timeless and eternal as well. Like begets like; as above so below. The eternal Being is our Being; the timeless Consciousness is our Consciousness; It is just our birthright, as ancestors are the essence of posterity in the sense that we are all bound together by a common Nature, and above that in the sense that we are all of One Essence without beginning and without end. Life is Life and Being plus Consciousness which equals Tenderness Is Its Essence.

This reveals the importance of residing within the Heart exclusively and not getting caught up into the mind where this direct Cognition of Essential Reality is not known. The mind has no direct access to this kind of Essential Cognition that at once recognizes Truth and validates Its Essence. In this balanced relationship of mind and Heart, the mind serves more as a reference library offering facts, figures, information that can be helpful to the Heart for verification of accuracy and validation, but is not the primary source of ideas or interpretation of the information. The Heart's cognitive Knowing is both source and interpreter of the Cognition Itself, as in a direct transmission from Consciousness. This is the pure stirring of the Being by Consciousness to produce the softest, most subtle expression of Being becoming manifest. Hence the balancing of subject and object is needed to produce the pure and reliable Cognition; mind offers reference points without interpretation or meaning, and Heart ascribes meaning and interpretations based upon Its innate Knowing that is directly connected to the greater Consciousness of the Whole. In this way the Truth, validity and goodness of the Cognition are confirmed and ascribed to without doubt or need for further Transmission for the Knower. All that remains now is to transmit this Cognition to others by any of a variety of means.

Transmission of Validation for Others

This work is itself an attempt at offering an example of this process. It is my intention here to offer both such a Cognition and the methods of its verification for oneself and others. Though I will accept that the methods I hereby present by no means have to be exhaustive. It is my hope to provide at minimum a few.

The first and I submit most basic method of verification is one that I will call Consideration, which I am also using in the presentation of this volume. Here the Cognition is offered by way of explanation in the most clear, exhaustive and also simple terms that do not compromise its fullness, for the consideration of another who will then accept and admit that vision, if you will, to his or her own Heart for verification by the greater Consciousness as is assessable to that person. One of several possible outcomes of this process may result. One, the Cognition may be verified by the Knowing of the second person doing the consideration that the Cognition is True. Two, the Cognition may be verified as True only in part, with the other parts remaining either unknown or verified as untrue. Three, the Cognition cannot be seen clearly as true and thus is accepted for the time being as unknown. Four, the Cognition may be declared as untrue on the face of it. It is not possible that a Cognition would be completely devoid of Truth and totally untrue, as like all creative impulse it emerges from the Source of Truth, and thereby must maintain something of That no matter how greatly distorted it could become. Some inclining of Truth is always necessary to hold the Cognition together. Without that the whole concept would simply disintegrate into non-existence.

This process may be used most often for Cognitions that are spiritual or philosophical in nature, but aught not be limited to such. It can be a very valid approach to the efficacy of all sorts of projects in the physical realm involving nature and environmental issues. Any project with moral implications is best considered within this process in addition to all other methods that can be applied. The primary consideration for this to be most effective is the clarity and purity of the Consciousness of all those considering the Cognition, as well as that of the person first offering the Cognition for consideration. In all aspects of this Cognitive Process, those engaging in this type of Knowing and validation must be present within their Hearts and be of pure and clear Awareness. This can now be verified empirically through brain wave function and Cognitively through actual experience of Consciousness. The later must support the former however.

A second approach that is far superior to Consideration I would call Transmission. This approach like the first is nothing new, Transmission has been used by spiritual teachers to communicate and present Truth to their students and even I would say to humanity as a whole since time and life began. On this level, Transmission can be defined simply as the direct transfer of thoughts, concepts, images or any mental or emotional content from one individual to another by Consciousness alone. It may be accompanied by words, music, drawings or art of any kind but not necessarily so. It may be considered to be mental telepathy, but Transmission is much more than telepathy; although telepathy can be one form of Transmission. Transmission is superior to Consideration, as it is so much more complete as a method of communication between beings of all kinds. It can also be very quick, instantaneous in fact, or may take place in stages over some time, but regardless of the duration Transmission can convey an entire Cognition whole and complete with complex ideas, visual images and understanding of intentions, functions and all applications that the original Cognition may itself contain.

There are some very important advantages to Transmission over more conventional forms of communication that involve spoken language or even art and music that must be appreciated and widely understood. All beings which have or are Consciousness, which is everything in Creation, have always communicated in this way within their own level of being and awareness. This is the most primal yet also most effective and the original form of communication. It is most intuitive and natural and above all most Heart centered form of expression of Self to Self, from Core to Core, Heart to Heart and mind to mind between all beings. Transmission is the direct manner in which Holy Spirit communicates to us and to all kinds and varieties of Being throughout Creation. It is this touch of Supreme Awareness at our very Core that is the Consciousness of Creation sharing Itself in the form of wisdom, insight, understanding and direction in ways that are often instantly known and grasped as coming from the Divine Source without reservation or doubt, but rather inform the being of what is happening, what is to be done and sometimes even how to do it right then as may be needed to allow the good to manifest in its divinely right intention. This is a special kind of the stirring of the Being by Consciousness that begins Creation and all creative processes.

Until now it has been a little known Reality, but is destined to soon become widely known and commonplace that Transmission as a form of communication is well within the potential of all Human Consciousness and is to become a common and preferred form of communication for most interactions between humans and non-humans alike. Additional advantages of Transmission as communication are that it eliminates all doubt, as it touches Consciousness at deeper levels prior to the formation of doubt; it also prevents miscommunications and misunderstandings by virtue of its completeness and the profound Yoga or Union of Awareness it fosters between the Consciousness of individuals thus communing. There may be no more powerful form of communication than Transmission to be found anywhere, only the depth and degree of skill applied can be developed to greater extents, but the basic method is there for all.

How this applies to the verification of Cognitions is revolutionary and mind boggling. We now have an effective direct means of communicating that does not allow for misunderstanding or omissions of forgetfulness. We now finally have the means to truly understand one another and to verify the Truth of the Cognitive Process with certitude.

A third verification for Cognition can be called Recreation. This is a process whereby a second person can, after receiving the original Cognition either by Consideration or Transmission, take that into his or her own Heart and review the Cognitive Process within himself, so as to see if it can be recreated there. This is a finer aspect of Consideration as it was described earlier, and would be effective and reliable for those of sufficient clarity to warrant it. And this process of Recreation leads us into our next topic of consideration.

Heart and Verification

One final method of verification that I would present here is also a prerequisite in some sense of the Cognitive Process itself. This is a state of Self Awareness that is best simply called Being in the Heart. We have touched upon this earlier, but now we can go into this state and process in more depth. As stated earlier the Heart is a faculty of Knowing; now we can also look at Heart as a state of Yoga and Unified Awareness or non-dual awareness. Because of the Heart's position at the Core of one's Being, it is uniquely situated in a place of direct Communion with Divine Being, such that It Knows first-hand, so to say, the Being Itself. Whether the whole Consciousness of a person is pure or impure rests upon the relative state or purity of the Heart. Any alteration of the Will at the level of Heart will distort what a person is being within their Consciousness somewhere at grosser levels of that persons being and awareness. Hence the slightest dishonesty of Will at the level of Heart will manifest itself as greater tendencies for deception through intuition, emotion, thought and intellect, and may even manifest further into the physical body in the form of health issues or illness.

This is how central Heart is to the entire Human Being. Purity of Heart is both the birthright and responsibility of everyone. The state of one's Heart is critical to the Cognitive Process in two vital respects. First purity of Heart enables the fullest and cleanest access to the direct Cognition of Being; second it then provides the surest access to verification both through Transmission and also through the Recreation of that or similar Cognition within the Self of another.

The deepest recesses of Heart provide us with our window of Awareness to see into that which is Transcendent of all relative existence. However we want to call this, this is the vast and eternal and for the mind incomprehensible Ocean of Being that pre-exists all Universes and Creations. The clarity of our individual Cognitive Process is dependent upon the depth and clarity of our inner Awareness of That. The Vedic Literature contains the very famous quotation "Tat Tvam Asi", "I am That, Thou art That, All this is That". (Chandogya Upanishad 6.8.7) That unbounded infinite un-manifest Ocean of Being, pure Blissful Existence Itself, is the Stuff out of which all relative existence is born and made. That is also the Consciousness of the Whole. Hence, our inner Awareness into That is also our window or vision into what Maharishi Mahesh Yogi called Unity Consciousness on the human level, so we can begin to access a genuine state of Yoga and non-dual Awareness as everyday conscious Reality.

Now we have a vision into a Real and livable state of being that is unified and all connected with Creation; where subject and object are truly One, observer and observed are Aware of each other as a single Being, not physically but rather in Consciousness. This is what is known as Unity Consciousness, and it is the entryway into the highest levels of Enlightenment available to Human Consciousness that we are now aware of.

Consciousness and Holy Spirit

We began this examination of Consciousness with a look into the nature of Spirit and the realization that Creation is a living and conscious Being. It is the first Cognition of this book that the Holy Spirit or Whole Spirit in Reality is the very Consciousness of Creation, and that this Whole Consciousness includes within Itself every being animate and inanimate throughout all the many Universes of Creation, however vast and varied they may be, with all their many galaxies, worlds, and relative realities within each of them. That the Consciousness of this vast and incomprehensibly diverse Creation taken in total is what is rightly known as Holy Spirit. Spirit and Consciousness is in this vein One and the same. This is an important realization that we need to acknowledge and become familiar with, for the implications for our understanding and appreciation for the multiple Universes to which we are all so connected depends upon this.

Once we can come to grips with the vital meaning of this, the Reality of a Unified Awareness such as Unity Consciousness becomes available to us on an experiential level as well, and this realization itself allows the Cognitive Approach to knowing and awareness to become practical. What is happening for us in this regard is that our own individual Consciousness is awakening and thus beginning to grow into the fullness and wholeness of the Creation Itself, and in this Way we are maturing spiritually into the divine Beings we are meant to Be as spiritually mature and developed Consciousness.

If this appears to be revolutionary it is. It represents the true revolution of Consciousness, that is the next great step of humanity on Earth and this Solar System as we know it. It is dependent upon no specific human institution or endeavor save that of each of us applying our best abilities and intentions in an everyday awakened way to this outcome. We participate in this effort consciously by engaging in disciplined spiritual practice such as deep conscious meditation daily, preferably twice per day, that enables us to become increasingly familiar with deeper and broader levels of inner Awareness and opening up our thought processes and comprehension to these newly awakened levels. Also gentle breathing practices and physical stretching postures practiced with proper guidance are helpful in cleansing the body-mind system, but primarily meditation is essential to facilitating the opening and deepening of Awareness, and this enables all other practices to be more effective than could be otherwise. These tools of Yoga have been given to Humanity by the Divine Grace precisely for these purposes, and humanity must very soon grow into a mature enough condition to utilize them well. Increasingly qualified teachers of various persuasions are appearing to assist people of all cultural and racial backgrounds in ways most suitable for each. This manifestation is correctly recognized as Divine Intervention into human affairs, for at the same time as It uplifts human Awareness, it also encourages social and political action that uplifts as well, in the contexts of increasing closeness and cooperation among peoples. Our ultimate unity with ourselves is made evident by this kind of Awareness, and thus the destructive conditions our recorded history and personal experiences are so full of become less and less until soon they are to be a thing of our dark and distant past. Wars, famine, disease and all manner of suffering due to our ignorance of our own Nature and inability to access the enormous inner spiritual resources can be forgotten forever; while at the same time survival and progress and enlightenment will be assured.

This is just a glimpse of the glorious future that is upon us as humanity matures so naturally into this higher spiritual state together with the vital paradigm shift that this book is attempting to present in terms more clear and specific than have heretofore been offered. There is much more material to cover to present this fully, but thus far a glimpse worth looking into more deeply has been offered.

Consciousness Based Education

One of the great proponents of social paradigm is the system of education. This is where primary change is needed in order to promote from the root of our social soil the more True and life supporting wisdom that will make the fruits of this new spiritual paradigm available and practical for our world. For most of us, when we think of Pneumatology, if at all, it is not directly associated with our scientific paradigm. Indeed, the study of Spirit is not thought of as an empirical science, which it cannot be due to limitations of empiricism previously noted. Until now the study of Spirit has come under the realm of the intangible and non-material, and thus non-verifiable by empirical means. But now as we move towards a Science of Consciousness based in a Cognitive Paradigm, we can begin to see how this kind of a science interweaves the depths of our inner Awareness with the appearances of our physical/material world. The very Spirit/Consciousness that is our own Essence is the Essence of the visible, so called empirical world as well. As material things possess and contain Consciousness by nature of their biological and material structure, all objects animate and not have a place within the Consciousness of the whole Creation. Although there are many types of consciousness, owing to the great variety of species and nature of objects and their purposes; there remains only One Consciousness of Creation that is whole and entirely contains within It all

35

kinds of limited Consciousness that the innumerable parts and aspects of Creation may contain, express and embody.

What has been missing in our educational systems throughout most of the modern era has been this underlying foundation and understanding of the role that Consciousness fills within the Nature of life, spirit, matter and all manner of being as a whole. No one can be truly or fully educated without this wisdom as working knowledge in their everyday life and affairs. The time has arrived for the renewal of this knowledge, the return of Spiritual Science to the forefront of education and culturing to promote this unified Awareness into our families, social circles, nations and world civilization. With this we will see massive reductions in the social diseases of ignorance such as the violence of addictions, rage, poverty and desperation and above all the horrors of domestic violence and violent crime of all sorts. The more sophisticated crimes of corporate and governmental corruption will lose their allure and glamour, as we begin to realize the true cost of these atrocities can never really be compensated, and that the criminal is the ultimate victim of his own corruption and decay.

The basis of this problem has always been the simple yet glaring reality that education as we have known it fails to teach and convey to students the meaning and value of their own Essence. In other words, while information is being directed to children, young adults and mature learners, never is the nature of the learner himself addressed in a real and genuine way if even at all. So called knowledge is imparted without the Source of knowledge ever being known. Just as a building cannot stand without its foundation, so education that does not include a clear experiential underpinning of the Source of all thinking, feeling, knowing is lacking the very foundation for the knowledge it is seeking to impart. Such education cannot truly educate and does not serve well or satisfy the greater spiritual and emotional goals of life, family and society. The individual is left lacking the means for self-fulfillment and actualization.

Never has global humanity needed more desperately than now this foundational aspect of education and human fulfillment, and yet never before in the memory of human history have we been better equipped and Graced than now to recapture this spiritual basis not only for survival but for the ultimate achievements of advancements and progress in all fields of endeavor and aspects of living. Human Awareness is set to expand beyond our wildest imaginations, and with that the Human Heart will burst forth with compassion and creative energies across the vast extent of all Universes known and unknown.

It is not Empiricism that will take us there but rather Cognition and the new paradigm of Cognitive Process that will serve humanity well; once the initial vision of pure Awareness is recognized by a critical mass of our total population. On a daily basis people everywhere across the globe are awakening in greater numbers and with ever sharpening clarity to this unbounded awareness and the Reality it reveals. This fact together with the divine assistance that the entirety of Creation is providing our present Earth bound humanity makes our success in this regard a divine destiny.

The Intelligent Creation

As the Cognition of the Consciousness of Creation suggests, Creation Itself is highly intelligent. This Reality is made self-evident by Its Self-Awareness and Its magnificent and orderly functioning. Also the abundance of life on Earth alone gives profound proof of this brilliant intelligence. As humanity's awareness of the universes around us expands the discoveries that await us of an even greater abundance of life throughout Creation will prove this Reality to the last remaining holdout skeptic.

Looking at the Earth Itself, it has become apparent to even our empirical scientists that the planet is really a living being that expresses its aliveness as biological functions that can be identified and even measured to some extent. This is evident as respiration, circulation and excretion. I would suggest that the absorption of energy from the sun and perhaps other cosmic sources represents ingestion of food which must also be assimilated by the equivalent of digestion. The Earth is indeed alive, and the native flora and fauna are Her children, which She provides a home for and cares for. These Realities must be Cognized and Known by all human Beings who live here for our world to fully transition into the peaceful and glorious place it is destined to be. Our new Reality is upon us! And we of this Earth's Humanity are the heirs to this special and beautiful Kingdom.

The aliveness of our beautiful Earth also expresses itself as Consciousness, and this means simply and profoundly that the Earth is Conscious, as are all beings in Creation animate and inanimate. It follows then that the Earth's motherhood is conscious and deliberate through Will and Yoga and also full of compassion for Her children. As no mother is without Her nurturing aspects, neither is the Earth Mother and this too is self-evident everywhere we look into the ecosystems that She provides for the life She sustains upon and within Herself.

To this writer the self-evidence of these Truths is so highly obvious that stating them here seems almost ridiculously redundant, yet evidence suggests that saying so is most necessary, as thousands of years of our recorded history and the behavior of modern mankind clearly indicate that Western civilization and often the East as well does not appreciate or acknowledge this Reality. No individual or society can behave in the sorts of destructive ways that these records and our experience bear witness to and still be aware and cognizant of our True relationship to Earth and Cosmos. To be sensitive and sensitized to this overbearing compassion and connection through our common parentage and Being simply does not permit these destructive behaviors. To love our neighbors as ourselves is a Reality of Unity Consciousness, and not merely a nice ideal to be strived for in some other better existence. It is our birthright for the here and now, and any lesser level of realization is selling ourselves and our posterity far short of what the Conscious Creation Wills for us and for Itself as well. I say this last point, because of the inherent quality of Compassion and Loving Understanding that is the nature of Providence, the Divine Plan as It unfolds throughout the multiple universes that comprise Creation. My teacher, Maharishi, was fond of saying, "the Almighty Father is so merciful that He made Bliss omnipresent." [10] As we grow as Spirit/Consciousness into the wholeness of Spirit/Consciousness the Oneness of All that Is becomes increasingly self-evident and Real both in an ultimate sense and as our present Reality. There is no escaping or avoiding this inevitability, as it is built into our very spiritual blueprint; it is the nature of the Being of our Spiritual Parent, who we are growing to be as members of a common species. In short it is just who we are, and that simple.

Does this mean that we are destined to become Creators of new Creations ourselves? That remains to be seen, as it is also subject to free will and how we choose to express divinity in our own Hearts. Yet this is a possibility that cannot be denied except by the ignorant and those who would control others for their own reasons of power or dishonesty. The Reality of whom and what we are is no longer to be messed with by beings of deception and control for their own private agendas and comfort. These sorts of distractions from Reality no longer serve any imaginably useful purpose and cannot be allowed to continue except at the cost to Creation Itself of Its own purpose, and such a thing would be self-destructive for the very Essence of Consciousness. Such a condition is anti-intelligence, and anti-spirit, and interestingly enough encapsulates what is called diabolical. That is the definition of evil that runs absurd and contrary to Consciousness Itself. It is this dark element that has been used to run our world for the past several millennia only for a specific purpose of experiencing life within a delusion of separation from Self. It has run its course and served its ultimately divine purpose and is hereby at its final end. Time will attest to this and humanity's Awakening bears out this Truth for all eternities to come.

In short we must come to grips with the reality that even evil exists relatively only to the pleasure and Will of divine Consciousness Itself. It is not that evil is by some divine decree destined to occur, but rather that the effects of atrocity is somehow assimilated into what Consciousness is re-Creating Itself into. Hence, evil serves some high purpose in that context and then again dissolves or is transferred back into the Being from which all emerges. This time has come for the Earth and our entire solar system. Humanity is now being liberated from this Cosmic illusion and being set free.

The Mystery of Existence

If we begin with the premise that pure Existence, as pure Being is the Essence of all that Is, then we are still presented with the question of what is Existence and how can it have come into Being? There have been many philosophical approaches to this question, some more satisfying than others, some deeper in essence and others based more in thought and mind. Many see this as a flow of energy through various frequencies, as explained in part by ancient Indian Seers as the process Prakriti in the Three Gunas. There are numerous versions of similar views in other spiritual philosophies East and West. Other less metaphysically minded thinkers have put it simply, "I think, therefore I am." Yet we know that Consciousness must precede thought, just as pure Being must precede being something. The orderly structure of the Universe, even as we know it empirically, has a well-defined hierarchy, and in all ways the finer comes before the grosser in this creative process, and without the finer for the grosser to rest upon like a foundation for its own existence, the grosser would simply cease to be as in loose its existence.

This concept in the West is referred to as the Chain of Being. Everyone who practices a form of deep meditation as a regular spiritual discipline experiences this Reality and becomes increasingly familiar with it in a deep personal way over time. It is thereby possible for a person to expand Awareness so as to become Conscious of multiple realities or universes simultaneously even while living fully in what we call the physical world. This would be approaching a state of one who might be called a Fully Conscious Being. That is to say aware of all levels of his/her existence and able to interact positively as may be necessary on each of them. It is a very high state of evolution and development of Consciousness, and as we may soon see our galaxy is inhabited by a great many such Beings. This in no way conflicts with the experience of Unity Consciousness, as it is Consciousness Itself which unites all levels of Being and all Universes as well. A single Creation encapsulates them all, and this Reality pervades all, unifying all existence into One.

I ask the question where does Existence come from initially; largely because it would be in error, I feel, to omit it or gloss over it with a mental assumption or belief, as many may hold that Existence always was, and therefore needn't be questioned. Rather I find it far more honest and within integrity to question all such notions until we can for ourselves, each one of us, confirm the Truth of such assertion by direct personal Cognition. In this way alone can anything be truly known and in all honesty and integrity be asserted as True as Known to oneself. Even as such it is still necessary for each person to verify for themselves the Truth or untruth of any assertion or teaching for any of us to remain in Real integrity and honesty within our own Consciousness. Hence it is essential to not simply accept as true any teaching or statement whatever, regardless of its origin or traditional context without setting it first to this test of questioning within one's own Heart at the Core of one's own Being. The one possible exception to this rule is in the case of when the teaching is being clearly stated by a genuine Master whose words, gestures and expressions are Known by you in that same Cognitive Way to be always and without exception True. In that case the statements of that Master can be held as Truth, on the basis of its source, yet even here the full benefit of that Truth can never be fully known until it can also be verified by direct Cognition within the person who hears it.

A cautionary note must be stressed here in that the clarity of the source is vital in this case. Either the Master involved is personally known to you and you have heard Him or Her actually speak the words, or they are written in a form the Master has actually approved and authenticated, or lastly you can genuinely verify the clarity of the statement by virtue of your own Cognition. It is all too common for people to use the Bible as a source of teaching, taking the words therein literally, without recognizing the facts that the words they read there are translated, often several times over, by sources that can not be verified, and that in some cases the originals themselves have been subject to manipulation by others whose motives are unknown to us. So even here sources must be verified and statements accepted as Truth only to such an extent as direct Cognition can attest to. Integrity requires that anything else which can not be so verified be held in the neutrality of Awareness until such time in future as it can be known for certain as True or untrue.

It is vital that even Existence Itself be held to this standard. In this Way the fullest power of Knowing can be garnered through Its Realization when it is finally thus Recognized. So that the extension of Awareness and expansion of enlightenment can be most fully realized, we must learn to so question everything. This is not a process of doubting; I must add, but rather one of vital enthusiasm and rigorous honesty. It is simply good science as applied to Consciousness.

In this precious Way, the mystery of Existence can be grappled with and Known in a satisfying manner from the depths of Heart the faculty of Knowing, rather than from mind where understanding would fall short of the capacity to gain direct Cognitive Knowing and lead to frustration and a debilitating sense of failure, as has been the experience of mankind for the duration of these recent dark millennia.

A Place for Understanding

If the mind is not the place for direct Cognition but rather for understanding, wherein lays the mind's glory in its relationship to Heart? Mind as we have seen earlier is the faculty of understanding first and foremost as well as for all levels of thinking, subtle as in intuition, and more concrete, as with intellect and reason. Also feeling and emotion can be included in this conception of Mind, involving various areas of brain and nervous system functioning in different degrees of coordination with many other aspects of the physical body and the flow of energies throughout the more subtle energetic system.

These processes all become extremely complex, as is noted so well by the many biological sciences of East and West and medical systems that have evolved from them. The astoundingly complex understandings developed by Chinese Medicine, Indian Ayurvedic Medicine and Western Medical traditions, not to mention the great variety of indigenous medical and shamanic systems, all pay homage to the profound complexity of relating to and treating the various vehicles of Human expression and how they are envisioned to work. The network of energy vortexes such as meridians interacting and chakra systems each with their respective areas of influence in relation to all the others is itself some of the greatest testament to the supreme intelligence of the Creative Consciousness that has given rise to these truly awesome systems of Being expressing

Itself as life and living beings. The Human Mind is a creation of this Consciousness of Creation, and as it is also our faculty of understanding, it follows in a sort of mysterious way that this Mind is a way for Consciousness to understand and thus more fully appreciate Itself. Yet our Mind is also supported in both its function and existence by the structure and functioning of the physical system with all its energetic as well as chemical components. These seemingly two aspects of ourselves do not and cannot exist independently or separately from one another. In reality it is only for the sake of understanding that we can even look at them separately, for they are not separate at all but are integrated components of one single being. Just as in the physical body, hard and soft tissue do not exist or function independently of each other; at the same time that our skeletal structure gives shape and form to the body, the soft tissue that envelopes it holds the skeleton together; each gives the other the means to fulfill its purpose. So it is with our minds and bodies, and in fact all of our vehicles of expression, however we care to name and delineate them must thus be so interdependent, so as to be in expression and in reality simply one complex whole created by and supporting at the same time what we are as Human Consciousness.

The function of understanding in this context is one that shines light upon the glory of the Reality Itself. The capacity of the Mind as faculty of understanding is not only to shine this light upon what the Human Being is Itself, but also to shine this same light upon all of this Creation. By fulfilling its purpose Mind provides humanity individually and collectively with the capacity to fulfill a greater function within Creation, thereby satisfying a divine purpose as intended by That Supreme Consciousness in Its own activity of Creation.

This gives an insight into the true glory of the human Mind and its function and capacity within the greater context of Consciousness, not as the Knower but simply as that capacity to understand something that may be Known already within

Consciousness. The significance of this cannot be overstated or overemphasized. We shall see more of this later on. But first it is important to recognize that the tendency of some traditions of wisdom to put down the mind as a 'monkey' or some other kind of enemy that needs to be restrained in order for us to reach a higher realization can be problematic in that these ideas tend to cause their followers to denigrate and misinterpret mind and its powerful purposes in the divine contexts. Mind must not be seen as an enemy, but really it is our friend. Only we must adjust our attitude and understanding of its part and role to play as an instrument of Consciousness within the whole of Creation. Mind as faculty of understanding is different from Heart as power of Knowing, and thus must not be confused with genuine Knowing, nor can it be expected to answer the kinds of questions of Existence that can only be Known directly through the Heart by Cognition. Mind can offer Its understanding to be sure, and it must to fulfill that function, but it is Heart that has to be entrusted with the Real Knowing for that is what the Heart Is.

Part II

CONSCIOUSNESS
AND WHOLENESS

Thus far we have established that the Consciousness of Creation provides the basic foundation and Essence for all Consciousness wherever present in this Creation throughout the multiple Universes that It may contain. The place that Human Consciousness holds in this context must be looked at carefully and appreciated to the fullest extent. To accomplish this there is no substitute for each person who has Human Consciousness to personally research this aspect through the depth and breathe of their own Consciousness by going deep within by the regular practice of a meditation process that allows for conscious awareness to transcend the thought process entirely, thereby going beyond Mind itself, and realizing the direct experience and therefore Reality of Transcendent Being. This Transcendental Experience will liberate Awareness from the confines of the mental thought and feeling processes only, and thereby expand Awareness to the Reality of Existence itself beyond this perceptible Universe to the existence of other possible Universes and what we call higher states of Consciousness.

The importance of this direct experience for every human being is paramount. This provides the practical proof, the scientific cognitive evidence that sustains and supports the real premise of the Cognitive Process and any genuine Science of Consciousness or Spiritual Science, as I am here presenting it. Furthermore, the practical implications of the Realization of a Whole Consciousness that pervades all of Creation, which we are about to begin examining here, cannot and have not ever been realized without this direct experience to verify and support it directly as well. It is this experience that shines the light of Truth upon the Reality of what we are as Consciousness, in addition to what Creation is as Consciousness and how all things are interrelated as One grand and glorious Whole expression of pure Creative Will and Genius. This experience and wisdom is essential, indispensable for Humanity to stand within and recognize its True place in the Universe where we find ourselves and live and within the Creation as a Whole. Human Beings do not exist by accident or some flight of fancy. Indeed we have a purpose and function to maintain and be a part of the whole within the All of what Is that we call Creation and Its Consciousness. Until this is realized by us all, and it can and will be; we will continue as we have been through our brief recorded history, essentially lost, unfulfilled and spiritually and otherwise pathological. How amazingly practical is this Cognitive Process, as it uncovers our genuine purpose it also reveals the cure and solution to all Human ailments and the other problems we cause by our ignorance of who and what we are and why we exist.

These pages cannot provide the meditative experience needed to gain this deep Cognitive inner balance and insight we are discussing here. I do maintain, however, to offer insight to inspire and motivate each and every one of us to seek this inner Awakening through Core Honesty and practice of going into the Deep by regular meditation as part of our new and life supporting lifestyle fitting the dignity and grace of a truly civilized society of free and awakened sovereign Human Beings with reverence for all Life, Consciousness as Divinity incarnate throughout Its grand Creation and design.

Furthermore, by providing a clear and right view of proper understanding, as I am endeavoring to do here, the Way to this inner experience can be thus shortened and made more assessable and straightforward for all who embark upon It with reverence and high regard for Truth and the fullness of Life. Many pitfalls and distractions of untrue assumptions and mistaken understandings can be avoided, as they are no longer necessary with our greater openness and clearer insights into our own True Nature and Real Self. It is Truth alone that sets us free; not any tradition or institution of education, religion or social collusion can substitute for the efficacious and genuine Reality of Divine Consciousness acting directly on behalf of Itself to nurture and nourish Its own Self in the context of Its own Creative Act of fulfilling the handiwork we call Creation. And so we embark upon this action of painting a picture of Wholeness as Reality.

The Meaning of Oneness

It is rarely inappropriate to define terms, even when they appear obvious. In this quest to understand Consciousness there is literally no end to the benefit of refining and fine tuning our insight into the subtlety of Reality and the terms we use to aid in our understanding. Oneness is one such insight that can always increase in its power for us to cognize Reality through refinement of vision.

First off we must realize we are not looking at an intellectual construct of Oneness. The philosophical construct that we can somehow attain to real Oneness by intellectually refusing the use of opposing terms as applied to ourselves and the world we find ourselves in is a serious misconception and trap of the mind we are best setting aside from the outset. There is no problem whatever with the recognition of the practicality of concepts of Good and evil, up and down, this and that, light and dark and so on. The Earth plane as we have known it is a world of opposites that must be managed carefully and properly to enable our own survival in this world. There is something dishonest in using them as such for the sake of survival but then to deny them intellectually in an effort to make a philosophical point, as some would profess to do, as if that somehow qualifies their views as a system of non-duality or Oneness. Genuine Oneness is not mere intellectual non-dualism. Real Oneness is a realization in Consciousness of an Ultimate Reality that is Immanent here and now as well as

Transcendent. This realization shows to the mind what is True; it is not a mental attempt to believe and behave as if it has seen what it has not or knows without truly Knowing. While it is acceptable to take the word of someone who has seen on faith that such Intrinsic Unity is Real; it is not acceptable to substitute such faith for direct Knowing of this Reality. That is like letting someone else do your homework for you or cheating on a test in class. Merely checking off the correct answer does not teach the meaning of the lesson. There is simply no substitute or getting around the deep inner research of regular spiritual practice that effectively allows Awareness to Transcend the mind altogether and get this firsthand look into Reality.

Now we can begin to glimpse the genuine significance and powerful implications of Real Oneness. Imagine if you can a world where in spite of all appearances of separation and difference all things are One: Where I and You, this and that and all apparent opposites are merged together somehow without conflict or stress or divisiveness of any kind. Does the thought seem too unfamiliar to even make sense? Does it sound absurd on the surface of it? Generally speaking to the mental faculty it will. The mind is a discerning faculty of understanding, and to understand it is necessary to draw boundaries between things, to separate and delineate for the purpose of making these distinctions. Without that quality the mind would not be able to make sense of things or even distinguish up from down let alone navigate the complexities of the physical world in any effective way.

Yet when understood properly this is what makes the mind so good and effective at doing what it is really designed to do. The mind is a faculty that is made to see outwardly into the physical world around us; it sees by light and not in the dark. The very structure of mind is set up for our survival in the world; it is meant only to understand and function in this way, as a tool of outer perception and guide to action that is thought out and efficacious for a healthy outcome. The mind can understand how to build houses and engines and plant gardens and hunt and fish. The mind understands to come in out of the cold or to flee a burning building. These types of things it can excel at and is necessary for. All understanding is in the light, and the mind requires light to understand and function.

When we are asleep where is the mind? In deep sleep when no dreams are occurring there is no functioning of mind. There may be measurable brain activity, but this is of a restful nature of the physical organ of the brain that indicates mind is not working. Where then is the mind if there is no thought activity and no mental awareness of itself or surroundings? I submit to you that mind at that time does not exist. Mind, according to Sri Nisargadatta Maharaj, is a bundle of thoughts, so without thoughts there is no mind.[11] When conscious awareness returns in a way that gives rise to thoughts, then mind returns and begins functioning again, as when we begin to dream or wake up. Likewise in deep meditation when we enter a state known as Transcendental Consciousness, or become as Awareness simply Self Aware with no thought present, mind in that moment as well is not present; it does not exist in that state.

So what does exist in that state of Transcendental Awareness with no thought? Consciousness exists in that state, the underlying Awareness of Being or Essential Isness, the Essence of All that Is remains as Pure Awareness. That is an Absolute Knowingness of what Truly Is in its entirety; that is totally beyond the mind or any thoughts we might have about it. Mind is not required to Know this; mind is however necessary to understand it; that is something else, and that is the mind's job and its glory to understand the meaning of what it is to genuinely Know.

As stated before the real Knower is the Heart. As Human Beings we habitually run into trouble by asking the mind to do the Heart's job. The mind is not capable of knowing, as the Heart is not capable of understanding. Understanding occurs in the light, as this is how the mind sees. Genuine Knowing happens in the dark, as this is how the Heart sees. In perfect stillness without even the movement of light, the Heart Knows the True Essence of All that Is, including Itself. In that stillness Heart Knows Itself to be that Wholeness of the All and nothing other than That, as in "Be still and Know that I Am God." (Psalms 46:10) In that absolute stillness there can be only One I. The Knower and the Known, the Seer and the Seen are One and the same. Nothing can be separate from That, that has any Existence at all. Therefore there is only One Consciousness in that Reality, and That Consciousness is the Whole, the Consciousness of Creation Itself with nothing excluded or left out. Consciousness is the Whole and the Whole is Consciousness. We are One.

The Appearance of Separation

From where does separation appear? How does it arise, and what makes it so convincing to us as real? These are necessary questions to ask and understand in terms of Consciousness in order to proceed in this understanding of ourselves as Consciousness.

Obviously, the physical world as we experience it is full of things. Objects in their seeming individuality demand recognition for their practicality and implications for our safety, convenience and creativity. Tools are just that and have their applications on every level of human activity. It is the duty of the mind to recognize these and apply this discernment for the greatest good individually and collectively.

It is important to understand that there is no conflict within Consciousness Itself between the Reality of Its Oneness as All and Its expression as All things as well. This is key. That which Is All is manifesting Itself as All. Simply stated that is the Reality of Universe and Creation. If there is a problem it arises in the mind only, and this leads to a misunderstanding about the True Nature of what is actually arising as the world and our place in that world. A misidentification takes place as to who we really are that leads to a loss of sight of Consciousness Itself as the true backdrop of the manifest world. What is this misidentification? It is the subtle thought of "I".

As has been stated above, there is Really only One I, that of Consciousness. The Heart resting in stillness Knows this to be

True. As the mind becomes active, for reasons which will have to be gotten into in a subsequent section, it is possible for mind to dissociate its thought of I with that I of Consciousness. This begins the process of an appearance of separateness that if not recognized early on can lead to a state of ever increasing belief in the appearance of things to the mind away from the more quiet and settled Knowings of the Heart.

This may seem abstract, yet as it takes place in mind it is not; it is only subtle or clever but actually very concrete. The mind, remember is a faculty of understanding. If it is in a state of understanding without knowing, it can be easily mislead. Once the thought of "I" is accepted as real, the mind begins to loss conscious connection with the True I of Consciousness. When this happens then "I" becomes a thought instead of a Reality. Mind now is identifying with itself as separate from its source and foundation. Hence the sense of I becomes uprooted from Its Ground of Being and is now susceptible to become lost in a world of things. This has no bearing upon the Reality that still maintains Creation and our own lives, but it does represent a drop in conscious awareness and our ability to participate and interact with our world and our ability to appreciate and love ourselves. Once this drop in consciousness occurs we begin to loose pieces of ourselves and become only partially conscious beings fighting with our environment and other partially conscious beings in that environment for survival, security and all manner of limited resources that seem never enough to go around for everyone. In short we get stuck in a paradigm of not knowing who and what we are, a paradigm of ignorance.

In this Science of Consciousness we might liken this situation to that of Heart failure. It is also a form of mental disease. In a fuller sense it is a kind of virus in Consciousness that produces this Self ignorance and non-knowing state of being. The Heart stops functioning as Knower, and the mind becomes caught in a maze of misunderstanding of all that it thinks and feels without any inner grounding in something Real it recognizes as genuinely True. This appearance of separation taken to be reality is the definition of ignorance of mind and spirit. It causes us to believe that we are separate from the world and universe as we perceive it and even separate from our fellow humans. It fosters our misidentification with our body, thoughts and feelings. It leads to misidentifications with our lives and experiences, as if we are the things that happen to us or that we do, when in fact these are more like the classrooms we attend at school. A child might say, "I am in the first grade", but never do we hear the child say, "I am the first grade." Such a statement would clearly be seen as absurd, yet as adults we all tend to identify with the things we do as job, occupation, parent and so on.

It is a clever and fatal disguise, for as the mind and spirit become so diseased so does the body. Without the nourishment of True Spirit by direct conscious connection to sustain it the body loses energy, vitality and resilience. Our ability to heal and simply recover from daily stress dissipates, and we begin to age. The aging process, till now taken for granted as normal and a fact of life, suddenly happens, and then we die. Death is a fact of partially conscious existence only; it does not occur to fully conscious beings, who by their nature are Cognizant of their eternal Nature simply as an aspect of Life. The body is sustained by the Consciousness flowing and expressing through it, hence the quality of Consciousness is critical to all aspects of life. The body is the physical expression of that Consciousness and can only be as viable in health, longevity, strength, stamina and all manner of capability as the relative or absolute fullness of that Consciousness allows. The good news in this is that death is destined to pass away in the fullness of this Realization of who and what we are as Consciousness.

The Restoration to Fullness

The process of restoration to fullness of Consciousness for each individual and humanity as a whole is a process of returning to our True Spiritual Home. It is our return to genuine wholeness as Being and represents a vitally important aspect of the fulfillment and glorification of Creation Itself. We are not separate parts of the whole, but rather fine details within a hologram, like the jewels in Indra's Web, that contain within themselves all that this Creation is in Its fullness with nothing either missing nor in any way imperfect. In this regard we are the Creator's prodigal children coming back to our senses and returning naked but Self Aware to the Way of our One and only Parent, the Source that sustains existence and vitality of all forms and expressions of Life.

So what is the method of this process, and how to proceed? What we shall each learn with regards to Consciousness is that Nature is Itself its own healer: that this process is so natural to us, because it is inscribed within our own True Nature. The question is then, how to be natural; the answer of course is by being natural, by being your own True Self without intention or effort to be anything other than that. It is so exceedingly obvious that, as teachers immemorial have stated, it has been overlooked. It is time now to revisit this process and see again just what about it needs to be relearned and revisited.

In our present only partially conscious state, human beings are in large part conditioned and controlled by ideas, concepts, thoughts, misidentifications and the like that go mainly unquestioned and unexamined. This statement may be shocking to some or self evident to others, but with any degree of self examination in honesty the presence of hidden agendas and unquestioned assumptions that are held beneath the conscious thinking process becomes clear and apparent. To modern psychology the mere presence of the so called subconscious mind indicates a suppressed awareness that is acting upon not only the conscious mind but also the physical body and the spiritual state as well, as it must be recognized that all of our cherished beliefs whether conscious or suppressed have their impact upon each and every of the forms of expression of what we are as Human Consciousness. In this regard the total may be said to be the sum of its parts; even as we realize the Infinity that is Consciousness in Reality is greater than the sum of all possible parts no matter how large. Infinity is an irrational number in mathematics, and It is an irrational concept to the mind's capacity for understanding. Yet Infinity is a perfectly Knowable Reality to the Heart, which finds It within its own nature.

A good example of the influence of subconscious mind upon awareness can be seen in the difficulty or inability to trust that many people experience in their lives. While often there may be a rational explanation on a conscious thinking level for this such as past experience that appears to support it, there must also be a suppressed or subconscious belief much deeper in the mental process that states, "what I've experienced before I will experience again," that resides there as a kind of prophet of doom that bad or painful events cannot be avoided or prevented from happening again. Typically this kind of dynamic remains as reoccurring patterns as an indication of unexamined and suppressed beliefs implanted there. This is one form of conditioning that would be self-evident in this kind of situation.

Without getting hung up on these concepts, as this is not a book of psychology, but rather of pneumatology, it is helpful to appreciate in this the great power of Consciousness over the fullness of the expression that we are. When we speak of Consciousness in the way it is addressed here; we are speaking of a creative force that is either all powerful or potentially so. The Consciousness of Creation is the Awareness of the Creator or Creator Itself. The Human Consciousness is a mirror of That; in as we experience It as a developing stage or only partially aware state this partial awareness of Self leaves the human being in a very vulnerable condition that is thus susceptible to the negative effects of conditioning and misidentification and mistaken beliefs. Whatever the nature of these negative effects they grab hold of the tremendous powerhouse of Consciousness and distort its creative process to result in the manifestation of illness, disease, old age and death. This powerful capacity to distort the Creative power to produce a non-existent illusion as if real is itself an amazing demonstration of this supreme creative power of Consciousness, even as expressed as the human form. It is one thing for Consciousness, the supreme creative force to create according to Its own Nature; one may argue that this requires no effort at all, yet it's quite another for That to create in some way in opposition to Its Nature; that demands great effort and comes at great cost to the Self. Certainly the dark illusory force called evil might agree so, yet to no other end can this strive but to that of self destruction.

This may be the fate of we Earthbound humans, to suffer from this subconscious disease, pay its extreme price, and in this time of our world be cured and resuscitated and after having witnessed the process of this machination be restored to the Light of honesty and Truth so as to bring this knowledge and insight with us to the Consciousness of Creation as a new insight and offering to the True Creative process.

The restoration of wholeness is both process and a Way of Being within. As a process it requires time and patience, as a

Way of Being it takes place in an instant and remains as it is in the present moment without change. The process is one of gradual deepening and integration that takes a lifetime and continues on without end. Let us have here a preliminary look at first the Way and then the process.

The Way

There is nothing new to this Way, nor is it unique to Human Consciousness in that it is the Way of all Consciousness according to the Nature of Spirit. Only each spectrum of Consciousness as relegated to kingdom and species upholds a particular brand of experience of Consciousness that is unique to it. Such as in the animal kingdom, elephants may possess what we could call Elephant Consciousness and mice might possess Mouse Consciousness and so forth. In the plant kingdom there are Rose Consciousness and Pine Tree Consciousness, each fully consciousness, yet each unique both for its own particular expression of That and for its own experience of That. In addition the spectrum of Consciousness that each type represents is unique and limited accordingly to its kingdom and species. A rock possesses a unique quality of Consciousness that is fully Consciousness yet a limited spectrum specific to itself and fully meaningful for itself and what it represents within the greater context of the fullness of Consciousness and Creation. Human Consciousness is exceedingly profound in that It represents a full spectrum of Consciousness whether any individual human is fully awake as Consciousness or not. A full spectrum of Consciousness means that such Consciousness contains within It everything that is in Creation. [12] It is a reproduction of the very Consciousness of Creation. This Reality is of utmost importance and defines the Humans' place in the Cosmos, and hence must be known and understood or we become spiritually crippled and essentially non-functioning as spiritual beings.

Our Way of Being within accordingly as this Consciousness determines if we are being Real or unreal, True of untrue, Honest or dishonest, clean and straight within or bent, crooked and distorted. What we are being within, that is our Way of Being, determines what we are to become and evolve into ourselves. Whether we become something clean and True or something distorted will be according to our inner Way of Being. This is how vitally important this process is and how high the stakes involved.

This True Way of Being is defined by what we are being in the Core of our Being. It is defined by our True Nature. This being the case, the Way of Being that is True is characterized as Tenderness, Honesty, Straightness and Steadfastness of Consciousness, Gentleness, Humility, Goodness and Truth. There can be many other words of this ilk that can also be used, but in essence the meaning of this profound inner cleanness is conveyed in these terms. There is contained in this deep inner honesty a willingness to be transformed by Truth, so that every aspect of one's Consciousness is inherently awakened from within and cleansed of the effects of conditioning and misidentification and thereby realigned with Truth from the inside. There is the quality of always listening to that soft, still voice of Being or Spirit within, the softest, faintest whisper from the Core of ones Being that can be sensed or heard at any time and always following That without agenda or attachment to the outcome but solely for love and devotion to something within the Heart that one knows to be True. This kind of fearless devotion to follow Truth no matter where and no matter what is the primary hallmark of this Way. It is loving and valuing that simplest softest little bit that is recognized within as Truth more than one can value anything other than That. This represents our conscious and deliberate connection to the highest value of Consciousness we are able to directly be Cognizant of at any moment, and following that essentially is our Way Home.

The Way of Being that is True is properly referred to as God in much of the world and also from the East as Tao and as Dharma. The commonality of these terms as they relate to the Way is a liberating realization in itself, and I believe significant and helpful for humanity to regain its tender sense of universal love. This simple realization has a major contribution to make for the cause of world peace, as we come to know ourselves truly as One more and more by virtue of our common Essence amid the beautiful diversity of the various aspects of culture, language, color, food and costume.

The Process

As process the restoration of wholeness comes alive over the span of lifetimes and of history. As process the Way is lived in real time so to say, that is from moment to moment in the world and wherever we may happen to find ourselves. It is as process that the Way leads us to ever deepening Cognition and fuller knowing and understanding of the Real. The living of the Way in this instant and in each instant ongoing becomes this process of restoration to wholeness that can be rightly called Yoga or return to Oneness and Unity from the inside out. This Oneness and common Essence is more than an abstraction or theory, but rather It extends outward to the gross worlds of thought and action and physical nature as well. We are driven in this process to recognize both inwardly and outwardly our true relationship with all others including humans, animals, plants and minerals, the planet herself and our place in the cosmos, which means the higher kingdoms as well, angelic and so forth. There is no end to the merging into Oneness that takes place, and this merging occurs throughout Creation on all Universes and dimensions. If we were to look at Reality from a perspective of pure Being, we would find the various frequency ranges of energetic vibration coexisting layered over one another all embraced by a singular Consciousness of Creation. Within that One greater Wholeness is a Cosmic Intelligence that guides all these universes simultaneously and arranges their harmonious and integrated evolution all together and toward a common goal that might be called the Divine Plan or God's Will. This is the nature of Providence.

Now that we have looked at this Process on a grander cosmic scale; we need also to have a closer examination of it in context of individual life, and although the individual being can never exist for a moment outside of the context of the Cosmic, it has been our common experience that we are not often so aware of that connection. This lack of conscious and aware connection remains at the root of our common difficulties, and what is often referred to as the human condition upon this Earth. It is indeed the primary symptom and indication of our partially conscious state.

The Process, therefore, of restoring wholeness on an individual level is one of also reestablishing this conscious awareness of such direct connection to the Cosmic Whole. In this way both the individual and the Universe in which he or she resides become simultaneously Self Aware. From moment to moment, as a person practices this inner Way of Being that is genuine and True a growing sense of inner Self Awareness naturally extends through the deepest points of his or her conscious awareness, and in a most natural and increasingly effortless way expands to include more and more of what that person is as Consciousness. As this takes place a process of purification happens that at times may be more or less intense, but that is mainly continuous and completely necessary, such that without it the entire process would stop dead in its tracks. On a conscious level that purification will take the form of inner realizations or outer challenges to our heretofore unaware and unconscious beliefs that are one by one revealed to us as untrue and/or problematic. Once this occurs we are faced with a recognition that something we had believed to be true or acted unconsciously upon as if it were true is in fact not true, and at that point if we remain grounded in Being within our inner Awareness and hold to our value of That in all honesty, we are faced with the option to let go of that untrue belief and allow something else that we do in fact know to be true to move in and take its place. In this highly significant action a healing within Consciousness happens, and a piece of us that Consciousness knows as Itself that was before twisted by our untrue belief now begins to relax and untwists and straightens, so that this strand of Consciousness is restored to a natural and straight context and condition.

Consciousness Twisted and Torn Apart

The unnatural state that humanity has found itself in for so much of recorded history and perhaps prior to that for some millennia is in itself a fascinating study in the understanding of Consciousness and Its Nature. Imagine if you will, Consciousness to be a fertile field vast as an ocean of tall flowering grasses. Animals large and small roam and make their homes amid these grasses; honey bees and all sorts of pollinating creatures enjoy the sweet nectars of these flowers creating food for themselves and ensuring the propagation of these grasses into future generations. Yet the grasses to be healthy are to grow straight and tall, free of any kind of blight or disease that distorts their stems, leaves and flowers or keeps the roots from deepening and finding moisture and nutrients as need be. Now imagine also that the fertile soil of this vast field is unbounded field of pure Being out of which the endless number of individual strands of Consciousness are growing as this boundless sea of grass. Almost like the vast prairie lands of central North America or the great ancient savannas of Africa and Asia and the Tibetan Plateau, if these were a vast unbounded field of Consciousness as they arise out of the pure innermost Being so we might imagine for a moment the Consciousness of a Human Being to be.

Amid this vast infinitude of grasses each separate blade of grass, if we could for a moment think of each as separate, has somehow to grow by its nature straight and clean into its highest and finest Self. It must be fed and nourished with sunlight and moisture, elements of all sorts to enjoy the fullness of its own Being in its finest expression.

Yet imagine, if it were possible, for something to somehow interfere or alter that natural process causing a distortion in the growth of a single blade of grass somewhere, anywhere in that vast oceanic field. A single blade of grass grows turned in some way, twisted, brown or grey in color instead of green. There is the beginning there of a disease, some kind of illness in Consciousness that is effecting a single blade of grass to grow in a way that is less than its full and perfect Nature. What might cause this in that field; what might cause this in Consciousness?

In a similar way, Human Consciousness grows in strands like blades of grass, and these are structured to grow straight and tall and reach their flowering height where they can produce the fullness of their highest expression of the Being that they grow out of and that nourishes them. For this kind of growth to happen properly requires that the Consciousness maintain a state of cleanness of remaining true to its Being-ness, that is its own Real Nature. In this way the entire growth process can proceed accordingly to its divine encoding. In Consciousness there is a profound state of Honesty that is implied by this condition. This Core Honesty extends from the soil of Being through the roots and strands all the way to the flowering essence that gives fullness of expression to its Being and purpose. In physical form we call this health and vitality; in Consciousness we can call this Honesty of Consciousness or cleanness and straightness.

A later teacher of mine, John de Ruiter, explains this entire process most masterfully. [12] I am giving here a more basic explanation first to provide a foundation for understanding these aspects of the nature of Consciousness and what allows It to express Truly or causes Its distortion. By Core Honesty we are not talking about intellectual or emotional honesty or honesty to an ideal or feeling. What is of concern here is Truth and how That is recognized and either followed or listened to or disregarded and ignored. There is for all being animate and not an inner Knowing of itself and its nature. In the lower kingdoms the following and Knowing of the True nature of Being-ness is accepted and followed without question. For Human Consciousness there is the capacity to make a deliberate choice as to how to respond to That. The essential element of free will in Human Consciousness is just this capacity to say yes or no to anything we, in this core sort of way, do in fact Know to be True and Real. For Human Consciousness to develop in the True Way it is essential that this kind of Core Honesty be present and active throughout Awareness and Consciousness so that the entire growth process can be continually guided by the innermost Being, by Truth and essential Knowingness. This is how human beings grow into their full potential spiritually and on all levels, and this is what allows us to give our fullest and finest expression to the Being-ness that is our Essence and to our very life purpose.

The Effects of Dishonesty on Consciousness

Dishonesty is a trickster. In some spiritual traditions the mind is called the trickster, but in Truth, I find it is not the mind really that tricks but rather an inner distortion that takes place, that is allowed to take root in Consciousness that can distort the cognitive process so cleverly that the conscious mind can even be made to loose touch with it. These kinds of distortions in Consciousness are the effects of dishonesty taken root at deeper levels of consciousness in ways we may and may not be aware of at various times and levels of the cognitive process.

What is this dishonesty of Consciousness, and how does it occur and take root to change and distort the strands of Consciousness that it touches and at what cost? The answers to these questions can read like the stories of our lives and the rise and fall of civilizations. I am not about to write the great American novel here, nor am I to write a volume of epic proportions; what we are about here is to gain a deep understanding of what Consciousness is as well as the how and why of what It and therefore We are. There is contained in this Knowing a realization of what can be called the indications of Consciousness; these relate to the ways which Consciousness communicates with the conscious mind, and these also must be understood for a person to be fully educated in what he or she is as Consciousness.

As stated earlier on, our educational systems with very rare exception do not teach anything about the nature of

Consciousness or much else about who and what we are even as living beings. We are filled with information about things other than ourselves and even there much of this information is inaccurate and sketchy at best. Empirical science and historical research are constantly revised and revisited bringing out newer more enlightened theories about how things work and what really happened way back when. Such information about the ever changing world is made even more ephemeral by our almost universal lack of knowledge and understanding of our own nature and the Consciousness that makes us what we are. As a result the information we are taught is without basis in anything Real. As shocking as this may sound at first glance, it is the simple Truth of the matter, and recognition of this fact is necessary in order to restore the essential Core Honesty needed to awaken to the Real Nature of who and what we are as Consciousness.

There is a fundamental distortion that takes place in Consciousness whenever we accept something as true without a genuine knowing that it is in fact true. This comes about from the basic dishonesty that this act implies. It is a dishonesty to Self; when we allow ourselves to believe without a Real inner verification according to the Cognitive Process discussed earlier. Anytime a statement or perception is accepted as truth without first having been recognized as True from within our Core we are allowing for a subtle dishonesty within that puts an effort or strain in our Awareness that first weakens our conscious connection to Being and then begins to invite further untested assumptions and ideals to build upon the first, starting an ever growing tendency of distortion through the effected strands of Consciousness. Over time, over years and lifetimes these distortions can become quite vast and pervasive. Over the course of thousands of years of human interactions and dishonest dealings to our present day, these distortions have become virtually all pervasive in today's world. Our contemporary societies have become riddled with lies, fabrications, distortions of all sorts to a nearly universal extent. Throughout the last century and into the 21st we have many times found ourselves as a civilization on the verge of self-annihilation to the extent of destruction of our world and potentially all life within Her. This kind of overwhelming, unconscionable self-destructive tendency would shake to the very Core any human beings with even the slightest degree of inner wakefulness. If so many of us find ourselves numb to such feeling when confronted by such facts, it only attests to the degree of unconscious stupor so many have sunk to in these later times. Never before has mankind possessed so much destructive technological power with so little spiritual wisdom to manage it responsibly or with a creative will to do good with it. And while many in our time have been inspired to realize plans of what is possible to achieve with the resources of the present age, the financial resources needed are so often denied them by those who serve their own distorted beliefs in greed and selfishness.

The conditions of our age are self-evident. The universal lies that form the cultural base of our global dealings are devastating on a daily basis. Wars and ongoing threats of wars; war for profit, war for conquest, war for sheer hate and bloodlust, the addiction to killing because it is all that is known to some who crave power with closed hearts. Epidemics of global hunger in a world that produces enough food for everyone, nearly universal poverty in a world of teaming abundance horded by the few and powerful who believe only in personal profit for themselves, are all the distorted flowering of dishonest and corrupted consciousness that fails to recognize the True Divine Nature of Life itself and so fails to value it beyond what they see it doing for themselves. This is the effect and the cost of dishonesty of Consciousness upon our world, our lives and our very destinies. In addition domestic violence and the tearing apart of families on account of financial stress and the seemingly endless propagation of patterns of abuse from generation to generation together with the almost universal financial tyranny typify the political and economic structure that has been building over centuries to our present day world. The spiritual state of organized orthodox religions have been corrupted by the same disease such that they serve well the hidden interests of this rotten state of affairs.

The list can go on and on, so I will shorten this diatribe of the immediate and ultimate consequences of dishonesty as it infests who and what we are as Consciousness like a deadly virus. Still the point must be made and clearly so; a little bit of rot in time destroys the whole bin of grain; there is no getting away or around it. We owe it to ourselves, our communities and families, our nations and our world, and also we owe it to Consciousness Itself and the Whole of Creation to be Honest to the very Core of our Being. It is not difficult; it is loving and compassionate however. And this is also a matter of Will. Do we have the clarity of Will or the purity of intention to make these changes effectively? What does this even mean?

The Opening Within

In this discussion I am using the terms opening and awakening as equals and synonymous. I intend to show clearly that there is a great deal of overlap in their respective applications, but in addition their differences provide an enriching meaning and insight into the fullness of the Reality of what it means to be Awakened that I believe has been missing from traditional understandings, to our great detriment and spiritual confusion.

Deferring once again to my teacher John de Ruiter, [12] who expounds this wisdom so masterfully; although it originates with the birth of Creation Itself from the very outset of time, and no one can put his or her name to it, as It belongs to That Consciousness; I will offer a brief explanation of the three areas of inner opening and awakening. These three areas are the Mind, the Heart and the Will. We shall look at the respective awakenings of these three areas in this order with the recognition that each is unique in its own right and that the actual perception of ones Self and world, as well as the experience of Being also, is totally different and upheld differently by each. What we know and believe and the person we aspire to be is totally relative to the degree of Awakening of these three factors, and we shall see in this the profound distinctions to be made regards various levels of what we call "enlightenment" in them.

First, let us look at the opening and awakening of the Mind or that of the mental level. The Mind is the most superficial of these aspects. The Mind remember is a faculty of understanding, built and designed to perceive the outer world with its boundaries and distinctions necessary for our survival. The mind therefore must recognize and observe opposites. The mind perceives things as large and small, hot and cold, good and bad and so forth. By the very nature of its style of functioning the Mind exists in a world of duality, because without such distinctions of contrast the world in which it exists could not be understood. Even the concept of time is created out of these constructs, and so it is divided up into past present future. For Mind the present moment can only be understood in terms of the contrast of what is remembered to have appeared before and what may be anticipated to happen in future. Imagine for a moment that if the present now were to be removed from those contexts of past and future, the world we live in, in this present moment would suddenly be radically changed from anything we've experienced before.

When the mind opens and expands in depth and breadth of Awareness there is an increased appreciation for infinity and an expanded vision of the possible. A deeper inner Intelligence becomes assessable, along with an increase in inner resourcefulness. You might say that the container for understanding has expanded, and so greater understanding becomes evident.

The Mind in this context remains the faculty of understanding as such, and so all such insight continues in a context also of duality. That is all is understood by contrast to either its opposite or other different but similar shades of grey, so to speak. Mind may continue to expound its understanding in terms of likes and dislikes or preferences even. Ego and the sense of "I" as in the person I think and believe myself to be are still present and become more deeply suppressed into the area of the Heart, where it can still be effectively hidden, because there remains the blind spots not yet awakened for it to hide.

Nonetheless, this is a process which can happen if the Mind awakens first while the Heart remains largely closed unconscious and asleep. Compassion has not yet occurred to this mind, as it still sees itself as separate from its surroundings in spite of its expanding awareness.

There are difficulties and problems that can arise with this style of awakening. If for reasons that are common to the conditions of our world, such as brutality and trauma of all various kinds, the Heart does not follow along with Mind in this expansion but remains closed and tight, there is a great tendency of Mind to abuse and misuse the insights of expanded awareness for its own perceived gain, and in that likelihood becomes distorted and capable of all manner of atrocity. Human history has no shortage of stories of those who have gone off onto the left handed path of power in distain of the Way of Truth and greater Awakening of Spirit. The Holocaust and genocides too numerous to count have left their scars upon the Earth for those of us awakening to Truth in this new millennium to seek to heal and somehow make offerings to the Divine Will.

Such horrific acts carried out by the cleverly insightful criminals who have amassed great inner resourcefulness and power to command sufficient resources of nations have often been people of this kind of awakening of mind that denies the meaning of Heart and keeps That within themselves tightly closed.

The Opening and Awakening of Heart

The Heart as we have stated earlier is the faculty of Knowing. It is the inner Knower the True Knower. In its pure state and at its Core, It is beyond ego or the "I" thought. In cases where the mind awakens first without the Heart's deeper awakening these aspects of ego and hidden personal agendas retreat deeper from mind to areas within the Heart, where they can remain hidden in the unawakened areas remaining there.

The True Way of Being that we have been discussing here is a Way of awakening the Heart first; some spiritual traditions have called this the "Path of the Heart," but frankly, I find the term "Path" as problematic for a number of reasons, the first of which is that Truth is not a path at all. The term "Way", I find, is far more accurate and clear for reasons I hope to make totally clear through the course of this work. As the True Way of Being naturally sets the Heart upon the right course for Its honest and complete Opening.

Let us look now at what this means and how it works.

The Way of Heart may also be called Tenderness and Tender Honesty. These are the qualities that first and foremost qualify the Human Heart for this natural unfoldment. The first step that is required of all who would embark upon this Way of Heart Opening is to look within deeply and honestly to one's Core, the very essence of Being within. This isn't so much a soul searching as a Self searching or even a Truth searching, as we shall see. All we are looking for in this inner search is the smallest, littlest bit of something that we can genuinely know to be True. As the Heart is the Knower, this can only be done through and by the Heart. Mind can not conduct such a search; it can not know, but Heart can and must if as Consciousness It is to awaken. And so you must choose to conduct this search and look with clean inner Honesty for that simplest smallest bit you can possibly identify as genuine, Real and True.

A hint here, it will probably speak to something about your essential Self, your existence and therefore Existence Itself, and It will also be characterized as tender, compassionate and Real. Whereas the Mind sees with the outer bodily senses and recognizes Being as the vastness of the apparently outer Universes, the Heart sees with the inner senses into the Being as infinitesimal and supremely small. The Mind sees Creation as expansive moving outward into infinitude; the Heart sees Creation as the big bang, if you will, first emerging from a single point and then contained within that one infinitesimal point, irrationally tiny, yet somehow holding everything in perfect grace, tenderly within Itself. So it becomes clear to you as Consciousness, that the vastness and the tiniest, the infinitude and infinitesimal are One in the same Reality, as perceived through the different faculties of Human Consciousness. The Knower, the Heart, knows the source as seed atom, the tiniest little bit; while the Mind, the Understander, sees the resultant flowering of Creation and acknowledges Its vastness.

This is a fundamental advantage of the Heart's awakening, as it provides for this fuller and more diversified vision of Reality. It is possible for Mind to awaken and leave the Heart behind, even then to choose to keep Heart closed in order to pursue ego driven dreams and delusions, and hence runs a risk to become something evil and destructive. On the other hand for the Heart to awaken it will always bring the Mind with it into Its greater and fuller vision, leaving no room in Heart or Mind for ego to hide. The Heart then, in accepting a Core deep Honesty in turn makes the Mind honest as well.

This is the glory of the Heart, to be the doorway for the Awakening of all of Consciousness. As has been said by the Great Master, "I am the gate and the gatekeeper, all who would come to the Father must come by this Way (by what I Am Being); anyone who approaches by some other way is a thief and a marauder." (John 10:1-9)

By contrast the mind awakened to whatever extent that attempts to use its expanded vision of what it knows to be Real for its own agenda, that is its ego, becomes harmful and destructive in its efforts to force that agenda upon Nature. This is the nature of the demonic or diabolic entity that has become the embodiment of a distortion of Truth, and in that distortion seeks to replace Reality with itself, and hence loses its capacity to create good but only destroys whatever falls within its influence.

Awakened Will

"But not my will but Thine be done." (Luke 22:42)

As John de Ruiter further explains, the deepest and last of these three areas to awaken is the Will. Within the Human Consciousness this may be the final frontier in this regard. In our world at this juncture of the early 21st century to encounter a fully awakened Mind remains relatively rare. To encounter in a Teacher of Truth a fully awakened Heart is still far more rare, yet this phenomenon of the awakened Will is by farther still the most rare degree of enlightenment of all. Such a Teacher of Truth would indeed stand out among Masters as a Master among them of the most high renown. Let us look now into what this means.

When the Heart and Mind are both fully awakened there remains one last vantage area for whatever vestiges of ego and personal agenda to retreat and hide within, so as not to be discovered by an honest probing of Awareness. That last area to be thus explored is known as the Will. The volitional body, as it may be referred to, is a subtle energy vortex within the greater energy field which remains largely subconscious to mental and emotional awareness, and so it offers the deepest hiding places for the ego even after the Heart Itself has fully Awakened. Hence, even the enlightened Saints have often found to their surprise the profound discovery of a deeper personal agenda that they may never before realized, which can still emerge as a subtle yet powerful preference or craving triggered by an event either anticipated or not.

It is important to realize that the entire natural process of Awakening on all levels is one primarily of Grace. For all the things we can do from our side to assist in this deep inner growth, such as a regular practice of deep meditation in a transcendental manner and dedication to the principles of Core splitting Honesty, including total devotion to Truth as a guiding source of inner goodness and Knowingness and the total surrender in patience for however long this process may require of us, generally our whole lifetime as it is the Way of Being of all Consciousness, the movement of Being as Tenderness through us is the very Nature of Grace Itself, and there is simply nothing to substitute for That which alone is capable of doing what for the individual mind is not possible, but for the Divine Consciousness is easy as in Its own Nature.

The prime example of the Awakened Will in our culture is that of the Christ in the Garden of Gethsemane. Here on the evening before He Knows He is about to be delivered into the grasp of those who hate Him and subjected to the extremes of humiliation, torture and an excruciating death by crucifixion, and Knowing that Heaven with all the power at Its disposal will grant Him whatever He asks, He does ask that He be spared somehow this bitter fate and not be made to suffer so horrifically, and yet even in the midst of this Knowing and deeply Heart felt request He also prays that "not My Will but Thine Be Done." That even when He feels something with the full depth of His entire Being, He can still surrender, stand down if you will, to That supreme Will of God, the Consciousness of Creation Itself, and offer this Prayer that for the sake of the Truly Highest Good not even this most bitter pain be spared Him. It was not even for His own sake He had to go through this most terrible suffering, but for the world and beyond that even for the whole of Creation in ways we are not yet aware that this supreme sacrifice had to be made in That Way and at that time.

And so this supreme Divine Master carried out His mission for the redemption of all of Nature and Creation Itself in ways even till now we still can not fully appreciate. Nothing less than a fully Awakened Will could have accomplished this, nor could anything else have satisfied the need of Creation in that crucial moment in our evolutionary process, as Human Consciousness subjected to the darkness of ignorance or as an aspect of Creation under the pressure of an evil distortion seeking to destroy whatever good it did not and could not create.

From this vantage of the fully Awakened Will the ego is finally no more. The last vestige of the small self is fully surrendered into the Divine Cosmic I, and only That One I remains. The "I" thought has been reabsorbed and dissolved into the True Cosmic Self, and yet mysteriously a new fully expanded Consciousness remains as Its True Self, One with All and still individual in Its Self Cognition. A miracle of Divine re-creation has taken place, and Creation can once again witness Itself from a new perspective of One who Knows and Is only That which Truly Is. The purpose of Creation has once again been fulfilled; even in the midst of all appearances to the contrary; even in spite and regardless of all such appearances, the Reality although remaining hidden from the view of those still taken in by a hologram of separate identity is fulfilling Itself and satisfying Its Creator's Purpose and Its Consciousness is fulfilled.

This has been the nature of the unfoldment of spiritual evolution upon the Earth Plane as we have known and understood it during the short course of our limited remembrance of human history upon this world. It has been characterized by a profound misunderstanding by all of us who've ever been misled by a belief in the separate nature of things based upon the perceptions of mind as such, and what we have been taught to believe by our religions and other institutions. As Humanity awakens to greater and greater degrees with the onset of this new millennium, we shall see and experience as ever more commonplace the complete naturalness of this perceived Reality. With That new solutions to apparently old problems will emerge and new means of personal and global prosperity will become available for all to prosper from.

These fullest Awakenings of Heart and Will hold the keys of what Humanity is destined to become in this great time that is upon us. This complete Union of Heart Mind and Will are our True Destiny as our Earth based civilization comes of age as the new global star nation of this bright and precious solar system of our beloved Sun, Solaris.

Higher States of Consciousness

Maharishi Mahesh Yogi offers the most masterful explanations of higher states of Consciousness with his modern scientific interpretation of the ancient Vedic literature that I've seen presented anywhere. It dovetails nicely with a medieval Christian tradition of threefold path, and with some highly insightful details that offer a more profound appreciation of the entire process of the growth of Human Consciousness into the fullness of our Being-ness. All this taken together with the three areas of awakening just discussed can provide important insights necessary for a more inclusive conversation about Consciousness and Wholeness that I find of special value.

Again, what I can offer here is only a brief summary of these explanations, which Maharishi provides at length and great detail in works like *The Science of Being and Art of Living*, and also his translations and commentaries upon *The Bhagavad-Gita*. [13] All are encouraged to make a deeper study of his Vedic commentaries as you may feel drawn to according to your inner sense of Truth. It is, however, the purpose of this volume to establish vital connections in the overall framework of who and what we are as Consciousness in order that we can appreciate clearly what this all means and represents for us as Human Beings. It is in this spirit that I here embark upon such a vital and yet delicate topic as higher states of Consciousness. For there are few subjects of greater import that we all must familiarize ourselves with if we are to have any hope of grasping our own True Nature.

According to Maharishi's outline there are seven basic states of human consciousness. Scientifically, a state of consciousness is defined by a unique mode of perception of the world and self that is accompanied with an also unique style of physiology within the body. The first three states are universally recognized as sleeping, dreaming and waking, and clearly meet these definitions. I will not go into any discussion of these here except to acknowledge them as the starting point from where our common experience of ourselves and world emerge. More may be said about these later on in light of a greater Cognition, but for now we can agree that this is a basic understanding we as humanity all share.

Beyond these first three states, a fourth state of consciousness has been proven to exist within the human experience by research done on people practicing Maharishi's techniques of meditation that is also defined by a unique subjective experience of self and the world and recognized objectively by a unique style of physiology in the body. This fourth state has been called by the names of Transcendental Consciousness and also Inner Wakefulness. It is a state of consciousness that is often measurable when a person is meditating quietly and undisturbed by outer stimulus. The inner experience of this state is known to provide a person with an appreciation of Consciousness as Existence Itself; that is that Consciousness exists independently of any objects or things that one may be aware or conscious of. It is a unique experience of a kind of nothingness, that offers a perspective of Awareness as different and new to anything before recognized in the first three states of consciousness. In Vedic literature this is referred to as Samadhi; in Buddhism as Satori, and I submit in early Christianity it was known as the Kingdom of Heaven Within or simply as The Kingdom; at least that is how this state is effectively referenced in early Christian literature.

It is worth noting here, before going farther, that within each state of consciousness there is perhaps an infinite range of possible experience or energy level that will further define a person's specific level or quality within that relative state. So for example, within waking consciousness there may be as many levels of awareness as individual people in our world, that at any given time may indicate mood, attitude, sentiment, feelings, mental and physical states of all sorts, yet subjective and objective parameters may all indicate waking consciousness in all of us. Likewise is true for dream state, and we can also say a great deal for the quality of deep sleep, as it too can vary so much between individuals. Even Transcendental Consciousness has a wide range of potential experience regards relative clarity, depth, intensity of insight and duration and so forth. The possibilities here too especially are endless. The same is true for the 5th, 6th and 7th states, as Maharishi defines them. [14]

These last three states have yet to be discovered or defined empirically, and it seems uncertain if they can ever be; given the limitations of Empiricism, but they most certainly can be so proven and verified Cognitively, as would be the case determined by each humans' experience who realizes them.

The 5th state as Maharishi and other Vedic sources define it is called Cosmic Consciousness. This indicates a condition of the 4th state Inner Wakefulness or Transcendental Consciousness so fully and deeply established that It remains throughout the ordinary experience of Waking Consciousness and also even during sleep, so that there is a quiet witness, if you will, within of all outer experienced events and of inner thoughts and emotions as well. This corresponds in many ways with the awakening of Mind, as discussed earlier, and with only limited expansion of the Heart. This is a relative state with a huge variety of potential experience and levels within it, as it is characterized by endless degrees of Heart awakening, and it is also subject to changing attitudes of what that

Heart Consciousness is, a dualistic state, as the silent infinite Transcendental inner value is experienced as separate from the active and ever changing outer value of daily life. In other words, what the inner value may mean to it according to ones' relative understanding or lack thereof. Cosmic and outer are held apart as separate experiences. This distinguishes Self from non-self, subject from object, oneness from diversity. There is a constant and increasing identification with the Silence within as separate and different from other experiences of activity and motion. The Mind experiences this Silence as vastness, as huge and as infinite, and by itself can not bridge this gap to the activities of life which it recognizes as finite, having boundaries and limitations of space and time.

It is the Awakening of Heart that in time bridges and connects these which the Mind experiences as two. As Heart expands these apparently separate values gradually come together and eventually merge into One, but for now the relative Awakening of Cosmic Consciousness is, if we are so graced, slowly moving forward in a positive way towards the 6th state of consciousness, God Consciousness.

Now Cosmic Consciousness is not a bad place to be; there is a cosmic element an infinite awareness to it that transcends the ego self; it is just not the ultimate merger into a Divine Union that is the higher meaning of Yoga. Maharishi has called Cosmic Consciousness, "Enlightened Ignorance." It corresponds in the ancient Christian tradition of Threefold Path to what is known as The Illuminative Way.

It must be made clear here that in both traditions this state of consciousness is seen as a stepping stone on the greater Way to a much fuller Union with God or Divine Essence. That also there is no reason for the Heart value to not expand and grow in Its awakening and opening even before the Mind arrives at such a cosmic awareness. In fact there is great value in this happening as such, since it is the awakening of Heart that draws the opposing poles of duality, silence and activity, stillness and motion, into the Oneness that is called Yoga. So that the greater the Heart's levels of expansion before the Mind gains a level of Cosmic Awareness the higher and more full the relative realization within the range of the 5th state of consciousness will be. In Cosmic Consciousness there is a relative aspect where action can be said to be spontaneously right as in life supporting or infused with a quality of goodness. More of this in the next section.

The 6th state of consciousness as Maharishi describes it is called God Consciousness. It may not be a separate state onto itself at all, but as he defines it is the very highest level of Cosmic Consciousness when the Heart has reached Its fullest level of expansiveness and devotion to the Supreme Consciousness of Creation. Here, in this state, Heart can be said to be overflowing. This experience has sometimes been noted as the Beatific Vision, as witnessed by so many of the saints. At this point Mind and Heart stand together as equals in terms of Awakening, and yet something still is missing or remains to be seen. There is still an ever so fine distinction separating Self from Other, stillness and motion, if you will. It is nonetheless a level of great saintliness of which few of us have ever been so fortunate as to be so Graced.

What is still to occur is for the Heart to assume Its rightful and supreme place as Knower of Reality and Master in relation to the Understanding Mind, which now must accept Its own role as Friend and Servant to Heart. This subtle and oh so powerful shift from God Consciousness to the 7th state Unity Consciousness corresponds to this final surrender of Will to give over in pure devotion to What It Knows to be True the last vestige of ego that has been so secretly remaining hidden there throughout all of this growth process and inner awakening.

Now with Heart fully Awakened and expanded the volitional body is finally prepared to offer the last remaining secret it has been holding onto for so long. The Will can finally give up its need to be in control, call the shots as it were, and the Heart in Its Knowing can effectively bind together the apparent duality of silence and action, stillness and motion within Its ultimate field of Being and Knowingness.

Beyond this there may be nothing further to define from an Earthly or Human perspective, certainly not from one of common waking state awareness. Yet the Ocean of Being is bottomless and unbounded, and so suffice it to say that the deepening and expansion of Awareness goes on and on; it is simply endless we must assume both in this life and in any to follow.

The Three Fold Path

The ancient and venerable Christian tradition of higher states of Consciousness known widely as the Three Fold Path offers much valuable insightful perspective and wisdom along these lines, that also serves nicely to round our understanding to its fullest and most complete. There is great value in this, I believe, for several reasons, not the least of which is to aid us in bringing together the great religious traditions of our world that have for too long been held in positions of antagonism against one another believing themselves to be opposed, when in Truth beneath the obvious accidental or surface appearances there lies in foundation a common experience and wisdom emerging from the One Being and Consciousness of All.

As with the perspectives already noted, I am here offering what I feel to be merely a brief summary of introduction necessary to open this dialogue into Consciousness and invite readers to pursue these studies farther as they feel so led. My former professor at Fordham University, Benedict Groeschel, provides a fine overview of this teaching in its own traditional context in his work, *Spiritual Passages*. [15] As before, I will intersperse my summary with my own insights, as they integrate nicely in the context of Spirit as Consciousness.

The three aspects or divisions of the Three Fold Path are the Purgative Way, the Illuminative Way and the Unitive Way. These correspond well with Higher States of Consciousness as presented by Maharishi and also the Inner Awakenings of

Mind, Heart and Will as taught by John de Ruiter. Let us have a look at the Three Fold Path.

The Purgative Way, as is implied, indicates a time of purification or purgation, if you will, that represents a profound transition in a person's inner Way of being and relating to self and God. It is a process of going home spiritually, whereby the seeker is confronted with his or her untrue beliefs and assumptions and is presented with the grace of letting go of them in favor of something else that is actually known to be True. It is this voluntary letting go that is purifying and allows the seeker to move ever more inline with Truth and the genuine Reality of his or her own Being. God in this awareness, may still be seen as Other, yet there is an increasing sense of closeness with That and an awareness that we are not alone, even if one often feels alone, and that we are somehow participating in what the Universe is, and that our presence here and what happens with us actually matters to others and the Cosmos.

If a process of deep inner meditation is practiced as a regular daily spiritual exercise, this too will lead to a purification of mental and physical stresses promoting this deep healing modality to proceed in a natural and healthy manner. If both these approaches are taken together, then the purgative process proceeds with greater efficiency and the chances of the seekers' successful navigation through this Way to the next stage are greatly enhanced. Either way, perseverance through this purification process is key to ones ultimate success, and this brings with it the fulfillment of Illumination, which represents a far more settled and harmonious type of experience. Although it is to be noted that with increased Grace also comes greater responsibility. Yet the inner joy and sense of accomplishment also increase with greater achievements.

There is no telling how long this period or process can go on for; it is highly individual and within their contextual framework, but it is a finite process and if the seeker is steadfast and perseveres through what often appears as hardships a point is reached in grace of insight into the Nature of what is Real. This inner insight provides a sense of grounding for the seeker, which may offer a knowing of being found within a context of being that yet remains largely unknown or unfamiliar, almost like a feeling of belonging yet somehow still being lost in space. It is a sort of "I know I belong here, but where is this?" kind of sensation. It follows a series of relative awakenings of mind and heart that lead to the second phase of the Illuminative Way. This is a state of expanded Mind and mental awareness with relative expansion of Heart; that corresponds very well with the insights of Cosmic Consciousness and the Awakening of Mind, as described earlier. It is in its own right a dual state of inner silence and outer activity, of inner wakefulness and relative awareness of the world of action, doing and consequence.

It is worth noting here that the growth through the Purgative Way into the Illuminative Way is such an inherently natural process, that the transition from the first to the next is totally Graceful such that it is often unnoticed as any change at all by the spiritual aspirant. It is a smooth and gradual uplifting and growth through increasing insight and inner purification that the Heart, Mind and Body simply move accordingly in this ever more natural state of affairs, such that these faculties give expression to the innermost Being with increasing ease and grace and the inner silent witness grows increasingly strong and self-evident to direct Awareness. In this way health, creativity, even intelligence and inner clarity naturally increase along with a resilience towards the stress of everyday life and problematic situations. There are of course personal variations to this according to relative psychological states and individual life experiences and such, yet the overall trend in all cases will be one of improvement and increased abilities to accept and achieve in higher levels of functioning.

As with the Vedic traditions' wisdom here, the progress towards the Unitive Way through Illumination as such is one of growing devotion of the Heart expanding and expressing Its highest values through all areas of Awareness and in all aspects of life. As the inner senses of the Heart develop and perceive Reality more deeply the apparent separateness of inner silence and outer activity, inner witness and outer doer merge ever closer towards ultimate Union until "the two become One." This also is a gradual and natural process of Grace and the increasingly Tender movement of Heart in Its quietest and most delicate values. No intellectual description of this can be adequate to the deepening growth of inner subtle perception of Reality even to a celestial level. The Christian tradition knows this celestial perception as the Beatific Vision and direct insight into the Hierarchy of Heaven Itself.

All that remains now is for the Will to offer Its final surrender to Truth so recognized and so profoundly adored. Now the last remnant of ego still hiding out as the final shadow place within can show itself in the Grace of Reality for tender honesty to see and be straightened and healed by this gentle exposure. The final merger of self and Self can now occur in the sweet presence of innermost Being. Heart once again takes Its rightful place of leadership of Human Consciousness, as this Unitive Way becomes the new permanent Way of Being before all humankind and the Consciousness of Creation.

The full experience of the Unitive Way or Unity Consciousness or the Awakening of Will in the fullness of Heart and Mind is not definable, I believe, in any intellectual format. That would be like trying to force the mind to Know what is way to big for it to even understand or using a hammer to do the work of a microscope. For our part it is enough to trust the Truth to unfold Itself as need be for our continued expansion of Consciousness according to the divine order and timing. Understanding, however, who and what we are as Consciousness and how that is designed to unfold for us is crucial to the success of this endeavor of Creation and our own role within that. There is no way to overstate the great importance of this, as it is also vital to our survival in a technological age.

Shiva C. A. D. Shankaran

We simply can not live in the type of world we have created for ourselves with such powerful destructive capabilities without also being spiritually mature and responsible. Freedom and responsibility are essential to our well-being as stewards of a planet, the solar system and being healthy galactic neighbors in the greater cosmic community.

Wholeness Reviewed

All of Consciousness is One complete totality comprising what in Reality is the Consciousness of Creation. This Whole Spirit of Creation, as it were, is what is Religiously known as Holy Spirit, and is the very Life Essence of God and ourselves and all of life as a whole, wherever it may exist throughout the multiple universes of this entire Creation. All Spirit, Consciousness and Life is One divine Essence that is indivisible and Whole. Nothing truly exists separately or independently from anything else, regardless of all accidental and superficial appearances to the contrary.

Humanity upon Earth has suffered from spiritual and mental amnesia for some untold thousands of years, which has led to a profound degradation of the human condition here, as the Earth Plane has been overcome by demonic forces that have manipulated humankind in our amnesia induced ignorance of who and what we truly are. As Consciousness we have been mined for energy of various kinds, and as such have been driven down repeatedly by these diabolical influences in order to prevent us from awakening to this condition or thereby restoring our True Nature, which would have at any time put an end to the mining process.

Throughout the course of recorded human history over these thousands of years all human suffering, pain, misery, violence and warfare have been used to promote this exploitation of this amnesia for the purpose of drawing off free energy from human beings as their life force was literally drawn away from them. Hence humanity in this world grows old and dies in a state of ignorance of their True Nature, no more Awakened and enlivened than they were before.

With rare and precious occasions certain human persons have Awakened spiritually to the Reality of themselves and the Creation we find ourselves in to various extents. Some of these have evolved to an Ascended Master state beyond the levels of Unity Consciousness described already. By Grace and Divine Will these Great Ones have stayed on with the Earth and her humanity to plan and carry out our eventual re-Awakening. By Their Grace and Divine Consciousness and Intention the long standing amnesia of Humanity is coming to an end, as we are in this phase of early 21st century coming back into the fullness of Consciousness that is our True Nature and Divine Birthright. To every Heir of the Kingdom there is a new and unique Kingship. So it is with us; throughout the depth and breathe of this grand Creation we are One amid an infinite variety of forms and appearances, places and unfathomable distance. Like Indra's vast Web, we are One eternal infinite expanse of Being-ness like Its Creator, without end.

Herein lies the Nature of our Wholeness, the Magnificence of our Oneness, the Truth of our Being, the Beauty of our Essence and the Glory of our Creator. Anything less is an absurdity with no claim upon the Real. And So It Is. Blessings to All, and Glory to God.

Communion and Community

Be of One Mind of One Soul, Be of One Heart and Know there is but One Body that is the Whole of Creation in all Its aspects and parts.

Maharishi was fond of saying, "The hardest thing for an enlightened man to do is to keep from laughing!" There is an inherent joy in directly Knowing such a wondrous Truth; that All is One and of an infinitely abundant and Blissful Nature. In this highly integrated Cognitive state of Knowingness the Truth of ultimate Union and Yoga is so apparently obvious that the mystery, if there were any, is how that supremely apparent Reality seems to be kept hidden from so many who do not see it. The Heart which Knows the Real as It Is can see, yet that which is being unreal is evident only in its inability to see and misidentification with what it is not. Hence the dilemma of ignorance arises but from where? Somehow out of the True Knowing arises the inability to see and know clearly, for from where else could it come when nothing else Exists?

The faculty of understanding can seek explanations to this apparent problem, as if there could be some possible intellectual solution to a fundamental quirk of nature that allows for Wakefulness itself to pass into a state of non-wakefulness or a condition of sleeping as Consciousness. Yet terms like distortion, evil, corruption and darkness do little to satisfy the Heart's capacity to Know what Is, as these are descriptors of what is not. Looked at from this viewpoint of Unity, the non-existent simply does not exist. Its absurdity is fundamental and clearly obvious to that Knowing faculty. Yet the impact upon the world and humanity and all life within that world appears to be all too real.

In the final analysis, if we can glean anything from the thousands of years of humanity's dark and cruel experience upon an isolated and quarantined Earth it must be that there can be no practical solution to an absurdity whose very essence can only derive from Truth with an intention to experience unreality in a state of ignorance of Itself. There simply is no practical solution from within that isolated and separated condition that is itself the stated dilemma. That would be like trying to solve a maze without moving outside of it; in this case the maze is set up with no solution, no way in or out, only an internal condition of confusion and dismay.

The Truth of this condition of ignorance is just a matter of energy and frequency. The life force of Consciousness is made to resonate at such a low frequency level that if it could it would barely even resonate at all; it is the condensation of Consciousness into matter, which is energy at its lowest most inert form possible before it would otherwise disintegrate back into its original essence as pure energy without form at all. In this state of extreme density, materialized energy becomes incapable and insufficient to vibrate with Consciousness in any way that can support any degree of Self Awareness. Consciousness becomes lulled into a kind of sleep state, loosing awareness of Its own Essence, and hence is now vulnerable to manipulation and further distortion. Introduce into this state a diabolical element, which is itself Consciousness taking upon Itself the role of demonic entity for this very purpose, and the Earth becomes a laboratory of conflicting energies in revealing how resilient and resourceful life can be while flittering upon the edge of energetic non-existence.

There is no resolution of this internal dilemma, other than the uplift-ment of these resonant frequencies into a range of frequency capable of clarity and genuine insight. This is the resolution that our world is coming into at this time. This is the ascension process that is spoken of in scripture and so often by insightful teachers of all times. It is the rebirthing of Consciousness upon Earth into levels of Self Awareness and re-Awakening that are destined to bring human consciousness here back into an inner Knowing of Itself and what we are. Now is the time of this re-awakening and the spontaneous movement into a glorious and saving rebirth.

Part III

CONSCIOUSNESS AND THE NATURE OF TRUTH

Seek the Truth and the Truth shall set You Free (John 8:32)

Truth and Being are always in alignment. The direct Cognition of Being brings into awareness an increased insight into something that is genuinely True. Likewise the recognition of something as True will bring the whole of the surface bodies into greater alignment with Being; such that in both cases there is a greater vitality, Cognitive Awareness and life force throughout the system that results from the experience.

The famous Buddhist expression, "Work out your own salvation," often interpreted as to be a burden on no one, is largely equivalent to that of Christ, as quoted above. There is a great misunderstanding among religious and spiritual traditions regards this. It is the Truth that liberates and sets us free, not traditions. The increased awareness of what we genuinely Know to be True within increases the whole vibratory rate, aligns the energy system with the innermost Being and raises conscious awareness beyond where it was before.

Traditions do not accomplish this; they do not work this way. To be viable, to be sustaining all traditions must contain something of Truth, but there is an inherent conflict of interest, if you will, between preserving Truth and promoting its own self identity, which is not part of the Truth. In Truth there is no identity but the One. There is nothing else; there is no Buddhist or Christian, Hindu or Jain or Jewish or Taoist or Islam or anything else. Ultimately there is not even Human. There is just Consciousness, whole and eternal, timeless and without boundaries of any kind, an infinite endless Ocean of Being and Bliss containing within It the potential of all Creations. When it comes to Core Honesty and aligning with That One Core Reality, all other identifications tend only to become distractions and obstructions to the letting go of these misidentifications, and thereby get in the way of this ultimate Freedom.

Of course the traditions are beautiful and very useful for the play of devotion and expression of Truth in context of the manifest world, but as pathways to freedom they can not and do not work. In as much as humanity has placed traditions in the position of spiritual liberator we have been frustrated, disappointed and disillusioned. It is Truth alone that sets us free, and we are intended to allow that process to work in whatever Way It so chooses for us. As Buddhists suggest, work out you own salvation; follow what you Know to be True, for only That can set you free.

This is in no way meant to diminish the wonder and beauty of the world's religions, but this simply must be kept in perspective for the sake of peace, freedom and the fulfillment of human potential. The endless Compassion and Mercy of God would have it no other Way, and we must all be spiritually mature enough to recognize this Reality.

Another way to look at this would be from the position of a star. A star positioned as it is within the great vastness of space is quite a large body as compared to other celestial objects. It may be thousands of times greater in size to planets and such other objects in orbit about it, yet seen from a distance it still appears as a single point of light. The radiation emanating off this great body of light flows out in all directions around it, not only to the plane of its own solar system but also out across its galaxy and ultimately the whole of the Universe where its energy and radiance and therefore influence are felt throughout Creation. A star is a great Being acting as a conduit of life force energy from the great Source of Existence emanating essential energy at frequencies appropriate to each of the coexisting parallel Universes upon which it maintains its presence in context of that Creation.

These many frequency spectrums provide for just as many types and forms of energy influencing Creation on so many levels at once. It provides these not only for its own solar system, the life of which it is dearly entrusted with, but in various ways for the greater galaxy and through that to the whole vast family of galaxies ranging out into infinity. What is the Way of this great Cosmic Life? What sort of Self Identity can such a Being have or suggest for Itself that would be sufficient for what It is? We in our own limited awareness tend to identify a concept of God or Truth or Dharma with a particular tradition to which we also identify ourselves, yet how Real can this be if we are extending a belief that we have either chosen or been conditioned by, without a direct Cognitive Knowing of that belief as genuinely True? These kinds of beliefs into things that we do not actually Know as True have a limiting effect upon us as Consciousness and do not serve any process of expansion or growth or Self discovery. To the contrary they keep us complacent in those limitations and serve to block any real inquiry into the Real and greater Existence that we are all a part of.

So it is with our misidentification with tradition. As much as traditions serve to preserve wisdom, cultural heritage, truth and historical integrity they also create a blockage to the higher liberation of Spirit by these very same limiting constraints. This is not to say we must do away with traditions, by no means, but to paraphrase St. Paul, when I was a child I thought and behaved as a child; now that I am a man (spiritually mature) I put away childish things and beliefs and put on the Ways of a mature human being. (1 Corinthians 13:11) Spiritual maturity means putting away all limiting beliefs no matter how traditional and moving into a Knowing of a Reality far greater than any individualistic tradition can hold. Put simply, the Transcendence of relativity contains within it the Transcendence of traditions. Traditions are relative with a relative purpose however important and may always exist in their relative contexts, but our self discovery of ourselves from partially conscious to fully conscious Beings takes us to a level outside and above the relative context of tradition to a point of fulfillment of that purpose and no longer submissive or subject to it.

If you are a lover of tradition that is good, but love the Truth more; love what is Real and ultimately liberating more and learn to distinguish between them, so you can fulfill the highest meaning and beauty of the tradition you so love. Therein lies one of the essential keys of the Way of Truth.

Truth is a Pathless Land

The Way is not a path. Ingram Smith's biography of the late Krishnamurti entitled *Truth is a Pathless Land* is a lovely explanation of this in the life of one such dedicated teacher of Truth, whose whole life was so devoted to this Reality. [16] Truth is not a path that leads from here to there, as there is simply nowhere to go. Truth is a Way of Being within that is simply Real; that is a Real Way of Being. In this simple regard Being Real is all that matters; what we are Being within at the Core of our Being, whether Real or unreal determines our whole state of Being. The degree to which we are being Real within is the degree to which we are True and aligned with Truth; that is also the degree to which we are genuinely alive. Likewise the degree to which we are being unreal within is the extent to which we are being dishonest as Consciousness and distorting that which we are for whatever cause or reason. Those inner distortions are limitations of life and energy. These are the dark places within that we seek to keep hidden from the view of ourselves and others as secret shames or agendas that may be used subconsciously for different reasons and in various ways. It all represents dishonesty of consciousness, and fills the subconscious mind with everything that makes it a scary or uncomfortable place to visit or look into.

Over the last several thousand years or so, humanity has become expert in stuffing and suppressing that which we would rather not look at into this receptacle as our personal chamber of horrors, where anything we do not care to examine can be dumped and forgotten. This is a prime indication of our unreality, and it has served to propagate suffering and misery, mayhem and violence beyond measure such as few if any of us can fathom or comprehend. Need I recount all the atrocities of our world to make this point; I see no reason for this here. Only it is essential for us to connect the dots with this, and see what is going on with ourselves and our world, and that we are not victims nor helpless and without hope in correcting these horrific errors but rather are fully capable as the Consciousness that we are to remedy ourselves from the inside out and thereby recreate a world for ourselves that truly enlightened Beings can be proud to live in.

It is not the path we choose to walk in life that defines us for there are really no superior or inferior paths overall. Rather the Way of Being we cling to within our very Core is what defines us as honest and Real or dishonest and unreal, and it is from this that whatever path of action or vocation or livelihood we take as individuals takes on the meaning of that Reality or unreality that we are being from inside. It is for us to seek those choices that embody for us individually the highest and greatest good in terms of the Truth we Realize at our Core; such that It can find Its fullest expression in context of that choice. For each person that would be his or her highest good. Seek you first the Kingdom of God; that is Be Truth within your own Core, so that you are Being according to the True Way, and then the paths of this life will be laid out before you.

There are no techniques per se in this; it is simply your Way of Being within that matters, and that is you mirroring at your Core the Way Being Itself is within your Essence. This enables you to Be just as the Being is that is Source of all that Is. Honesty to the Core allows for Truth, aligned as It is with the Being to gain Its fullest expression through who and what you are being through your entire existence. Truth in your Core flowing from the inside out through every layer of your existence right out to the outermost expression of yourself in the world. Hence this True Way of Being within leads you to your highest and greatest path without. In this way life truly is good.

Techniques and Truth

It is vital to realize that the True Way of Being within is not a technique that we do from time to time or even make a regular practice of; quite contrary to this it is a mode of being in each moment as it is now that keeps us ever present in our Core and Heart in Tenderness and absolute acceptance of what simply Is in that moment. It is openness and goodness embodied from the inside allowed to express in kind all the way outside through thought word and action, so touching others and the world as that One gentle touch of Truth from the Being Itself. There is no technique for this; it is a matter of Knowing the softest whisper of Truth within and listening for that always, then allowing that little bit that is Known to be True to have us for Itself, because simply That is True to be and do, and is therefore more valuable and Real than anything else, which is not being so real or so genuine.

Now there are techniques of spiritual practice and mental discipline that are effective and of real value in all sorts of ways. This is not to be denied, yet we must be clear as to the difference, so as not to confuse another type of outcome with being genuinely Real and honest to the Core and pure of Heart, and all that means. I have already acknowledged and continue to the importance of a regular practice of a deep meditation that can lead us to a transcendental or Samadhi experience. This is deep Yogic practice; there are other types of Yoga involving the breathe and physical stretching and postures that have great value for health as well as the deepening and broadening of our inner and outer Awareness. These are of great value and are to be encouraged by all who feel so inclined to practice them.

The distinction to be made here is more one of inner quality and intention, that speaks ever so directly to who and what we are Being as Consciousness in the midst of any other surface doing we are engaged with either as practice or lifestyle or cultural identity or any such thing. As Christ was so frequently fond of saying in effect, what comes out of the mouth is more important than what goes into it. In this sense, what we put into our mouths relates to our doing and what we identify with, not merely as food but the entire manor in which we take in our surroundings; what comes out of our mouth speaks much more to who we are being and our way of being at the Source of speech, which likewise is the Source of thought and action and our Being. It is what we project upon our surroundings, and thus determines the very world we live in; that is how we re-create our world. Maharishi would say, "the world is as you are." Meaning simply that the quality of your inner Consciousness reflects back to you exactly as the way you perceive your world. If someone is filled with hate, they will perceive the world as a hateful place full of 'other people' who hate. When we are filled with love, likewise, we see love in the world everywhere and appreciate that in others too. It is the Way you are being within your innermost Self that creates the world you live in and also influences our collective appreciation and experience of that world accordingly.

Collectively we each have a say in the totality of our human experience of what this world we share in is. What's more is that as an individual Human Consciousness the contribution to that which we each make is extremely powerful; although we have all been conditioned and miseducated to believe ourselves to be almost powerless in these regards; it is so very far from the Truth. This Reality speaks directly to our enormous gifts and potentials as creators ourselves; our returning to the fullest realization of this Truth is in large part what our reawakening to Truth and Self Actualization is all about. More about this later as well.

The Way of Being within that is True is about assuming a state of total naturalness within to the very Core essence of your Being that then is free to moderate and gently control in that manner of perfect Tenderness every strand and fiber of Consciousness that you are. It is not that Truth belongs to you, but rather that you belong to Truth, as in we all belong to God or this Way that can be called God or Tao or Dharma.

Knowing Truth

How is Truth Known? This question brings us back to the Cognitive Process and Way of recognition and validation of thought and awareness. From a pure Heart, Truth can be known directly; this is to say that when Consciousness is clean and without dishonesty or distortion then It Knows by its very nature. Remember, Heart is the faculty of Knowing, and as such comes naturally to It when it too is in a natural state. That natural state for Consciousness is clean, straight, relaxed and effortless and fully alert. Everything that Consciousness is in this genuine state is livened to its fullest potential and thus alert and ready to be and do whatever is called for from that state of supreme activation. As my teacher Nisargadatta Maharaj liked to say, "Existence is Its own proof." [17] So it is with Consciousness. As with Being so it is with all that has Being; life is its own proof; Is-ness is that which Is in its very essence; Truth likewise is that which Is Real, and Knowing is as well supported by the Truth so Known.

This may sound circular in reasoning to some, but it is not. There is nothing hypothetical in this; just as the presence of light is self evident in the seeing, so is the reality of a thought made self evident in its cognition. Awareness speaks both to itself and to any object that comes into its recognition. Without Consciousness nothing exists, because there is no cognition to recognize it. Without Self awareness all knowing of the self is lost as well as all recognition of Self. As has often been said by the great Masters, Reality is so simple and yet profound that It is so often and easily overlooked. We must once again get used to seeing simply, cleanly without seeking to do anything to the vision or make it into what we want or believe we need it to be and thereby distort the very nature of what it is we are looking at and in the process ourselves as well. When we use Consciousness improperly in ways that are dishonest, we end up distorting the very Consciousness that we are, and as a result what we are being becomes twisted, unclean, distorted and all sorts of problems arise. In Truth all problems do arise from this very condition of self distorting what it is being in order to gain something that it is not. Once we embark upon this road all manner of problems develop, and herein begins our story.

How Distortion Begins or Who Done It

In the beginning was the Word. The Logos or divine intention is set out on multiple levels and with many specific missions on various levels of Creation. It is a timeless Reality that refers not only to the so called Big Bang of a Universe but really to the Essential beginning of each impulse of Creation at every moment of the eternal Present. There is an inherent Purity of Heart that gives birth to this new impulse of what Being is in process to become; a manifestation of Divine Artistry emerges out of the nothingness and begins to take shape and form in energetic levels first and gradually into physical planes, if it is finally to find a fuller expression in the tangible world. This Honesty within Consciousness is critical for the divine intention to remain simply as it is throughout this birthing process, that is the Word becoming flesh. This is True whether what is being built is a painting a house or a universe. Even the creation of a nanosecond of time out of an appearance of a sequence of events, so that the mind can formulate its next cognition or thought must follow an essential pattern of Creation that enables this first intention to flower into its internal design.

Throughout Nature this pattern flows unimpeded, as is observable in so many ways in the natural world. The various species of plants and animals and forms of minerals in the Earth and atmosphere display the endless variety of beings in patterns where like begets like and order of intelligence flows amid tremendous variety.

The Human Consciousness is unique in Its capacity to make a choice between what It knows is True and honest to this pattern of Being and something else that It would like or want to be true within that context. This capacity is generally referred to as "Free Will", and represents a great gift and responsibility to who and what we are. It gives humanity an ability to modify nature to our own intention and in effect makes each human being a co-creator with the Divine. The Gift is in the freedom; the responsibility is in the Will.

Everywhere in visible nature we see beings simply being what they are. The Rose can be nothing but a rose; the hippo is nothing but a hippo and so forth. As obvious as it may seem, the human being retains the ability to be something he or she is not, yet this capacity also provides the potential to be Self reflective and aware beyond the capacities of other creatures. Hence the Gift.

Likewise, the use of this capacity to be something we are not also allows for us turning into or evolving into something other than our True Nature. This means that at very many levels of the manifesting process the Human Consciousness can choose to make a change in the pattern according to something not in the initial intention. In as much as this may run counter to the first intention this can cause the introduction of an element of stress or effort that that pattern does not support. Those efforts then must be supported by some other means not totally natural to the process, and therefore causing a distortion both to the process and the Consciousness so containing it.

In addition to this capacity to distort ones self, the individual human Consciousness can also seek to and intend to distort the Consciousness of another. The prior is bad; the later may be considered evil. Hence the Responsibility.

Creation without Victims

In the context of what we are as Consciousness there are no victims. There is no victim Heart and no victim Consciousness. The main point to remember is that we have only two choices in this entire process, and they are to remain open or to close, to remain softened within or to harden for the sake of getting something we are wanting even more than being True to our own higher Nature.

This can be seen in contrast to life situations of crime, violence or abuse where clearly someone of distorted Consciousness is acting upon another person or animal with the intent to cause distortion to that Being as well. Yet the individual Human Consciousness always retains its capacity to remain True to what it genuinely Knows so long as it retains a conscious degree of self control or inner awareness. On a physical, social and psychological level there certainly are victims but not on a spiritual level. Here core Honesty requires a degree of accountability that stops at the Self. We are each accountable for what we allow ourselves to believe in context of what we know to be True and what we do not.

This is an aspect of free Will and speaks to a universal element of Knowing within each of us at our Core that always maintains at the Core some seedling at very least of Truth that Honesty of Consciousness can not deny. That Core Knowing, however small it may be, represents our inner connection to the Divine in Consciousness, which maintains our life force in a body, even in the most distorted condition imaginable. The cleaner and more straight that Consciousness is the greater to that degree is that Knowing. No life form could live even a moment in a state of absolute untruth. So however distorted and distressed a person may be, for that person to be alive and breathing there must be some Truth in them; it simply could not be otherwise. Truth supports life; untruth does not. Truth is in alignment with what is truly natural; untruth is not and distorts the natural into something unnatural.

Because there is always some element of Knowing always present within Consciousness at Its Core, there is retained there the ability to choose what one is Being in the Core, whether that be opened and softened or hardened and closed. The True Way of Being within is always opened and softened and never closed and hard. Truth is a state of effortless Being that consumes no energy in that natural state. Being untruth requires some degree of energy and effort first to establish itself in Consciousness and then forever to sustain that illusion in the face of the natural tendency of Awareness to relax and straighten back into Its natural state. Over time mind and heart can develop habits called patterns of distortion that can go unexamined by Awareness, so long as they are tacitly serving some purpose that is wanted for something, yet from moment to moment that wanting has to remain more important to a person than the much deeper Truth that is always Known to Consciousness, and so a choice is made consciously or not to maintain what is known by Consciousness to be untrue for the sake of what it is getting from that inner distortion. This is a state of being that is dishonest within and gives rise to all disease of individuals and society on every level.

In this way, in Consciousness there are simply no victim Hearts here; there is only an appearance of victim hood that can be used for something if one so chooses to do and be that. This is the meaning of becoming accountable for what you are Being within. To be accountable means to seek recognition of these hidden lies within and expose them to the light of Awareness and Tender Honesty that you may let go and allow the strands of Consciousness that contain them to relax and straighten once again to their natural and true state. Each time this happens we become more Real and more Honest as Consciousness, and thereby closer to a state of Truth within as more of Consciousness comes Home to Its True state.

No one can force anyone else to begin this process, nor can anyone be forced to remain upon this Way once it has begun, but we can all be inspired to cognize it as practical and applicable to ourselves and thus begin our Way Home. This is the meaning of Grace, and also the meaning of returning to Truth as a Way of Being.

Dropping into the Heart

Essential to this Way of Being is an inner practice of dropping into the Heart. What this means is simply knowing when it is necessary to let go of whatever the Mind may be grasping onto, because it is now recognized as untrue to continue doing so. The problem here is caused by the tendency of awareness to become entrapped within the mind. Mind tends to be a control freak by habit. Most of us are well aware of what happens to us when the mind senses it is no longer in control, panic or a tendency in that direction. There is a basic ego need to feel as if it is in control of any situation or environment. This is a long standing condition of human beings that arises out of a state of limited awareness of our own Consciousness and our environments, and in real practical terms this limited awareness is responsible for nearly all human problems that develop in this world.

In practical terms there is an indication in Consciousness that tells us as humans when it is necessary for us to let go and drop into the Heart. This becomes evident whenever some issue or problem being considered begins to feel overwhelming to the mind or emotions. This simple sense of overwhelm, which is so important to recognize early on, is what lets us know that the issue has become too big for mind to deal with and can no longer be seen clearly from a mental perspective. That is an indicator to let go of the issue and stop trying to solve it at the level of the mind and to let the Awareness to then drop into the Heart. To do so mind must relax, at least in the sense it is no longer struggling with a problem, and you can now take inner refuge in a place of stillness and gentleness within that simply Knows that it is OK to just be still and do nothing.

This inner repose of Awareness gives access to Consciousness of Its innate connectedness to the Source of Being within and the higher degree of intelligence found therein. At the same time it allows stress, tensions, fears and all negative emotions to release, improving the state of health overall. What's more is that from this plane of higher intelligence it becomes increasingly possible for a real solution to the issue involved to be found. It has become a common saying that the level of awareness that created a problem can not solve it; this is true, and this is the answer to that inspiration. By this process of dropping into the Heart both we are restored to our conscious connectedness to the inner Being, and the solutions we need to provide real answers to our multi-faceted dilemmas can be found.

Simply stated in a condition of genuine Heart Awakening one would live in their Heart Awareness at all times. This dropping into Heart becomes a permanent Way of Being and living. There is no longer any reason to leave this Heart Awareness, as we begin to even think from the Heart and what was before a separate faculty of Mind gradually integrates or merges deeper down or back into what the Heart is being. So at first these practices train Awareness to drop from mind to heart, and later as it becomes more advanced the Awareness draws mind itself increasingly to drop totally into Heart gradually leaving nothing of mind behind.

Shifting Perceptions with
Shifting Consciousness

As we have established already "the world is as you are." Our inner level of Awareness makes for our perception of the world around us, and collectively this accounts for the overall condition of the world in which we all live. It also has a great bearing upon the individual conditions we each experience in our lives, but here this is not the only factor, as there are other cosmic and collective influences that also weigh in to make up our total life experiences. This is much too large a subject to be getting into at this point, yet it is relevant here to the extent that it be recognized that Consciousness has everything to do with the way we perceive Reality and what we are capable of doing and accomplishing in this life. A relatively small shift in the collective Consciousness of humanity would have an enormous impact for the better in the overall state of our world, and with that the level of joy and fulfillment experienced by people everywhere can be greatly increased. Clearly a state of heaven upon earth is very much within our full potential as a human civilization, and as such we are compelled to explore that possibility.

The New Testament scriptures recount details of a great many miracles, as they are commonly referred to, by the Master Jesus, whom I will refer to as the Christ. For example here I'd make mention of a number of occasions where large crowds of people ranging into the thousands were fed with what seemed only a small amount of bread and fish. (Mark 6:30-44; Mark 8:1-10) In each case the leftovers there collected were greater than the original amounts started with. If we can accept at least the premise that these substantial numbers of hungry people were nourished, satisfied and energized to make their long walks home in what may have been a hot sun and do so successfully without fainting or collapsing, then we have to consider how this can be possible; what needs to be to enable such a marvelous event, and can such understanding enrich and energize us in our world again today?

We know from our modern physical sciences that matter is not what it appears to be to our common senses. Matter is in reality just energy toned down to very low frequency ranges. Solid matter is in fact the lowest frequency range even lower than liquids and gases, and the more dense the solidity or heavier the element as it were, the lower the energetic frequency level is. Whatever energy actually is, at its most essential meaning, it is all the same; that is energy is one essential thing as defined by the Unified Field or Quantum Field in physics. It only manifests in different ways such as electricity, light, sound, matter and such when vibrating within those specific frequency ranges that constitute those energetic forms. In other words, form is relative, but the essence of what energy is transcends those forms and can appear as anything and also disappear equally as easily when made to do so.

So the question is what can make it do so? What is it that has such essential power as to command energy to flow as one form or another, one frequency or another? Clearly whatever could do so would have complete command of the force of nature, as we call it, and could easily change the appearance of our environment and world to its choosing. I submit here that the answer to that question must be found in Consciousness.

As what we are as Consciousness is our Essential Being, the key to all manifestation of Being, and therefore to all conditions in our environment, world and lives, lies Truly in what we are Being as Consciousness. Consider again for a moment the Consciousness of Creation, that Whole Spirit, if you will, of All that Is, and this concept becomes clear. Pure Being through this Supreme Consciousness makes all that Is, and nothing that exists was made in any other way or by any other means. As Human Beings we are in our Essence That same Consciousness in process of being birthed. That which we are and have as Consciousness contains all of it as well. All that remains is for us to realize the Truth of our own Existence and Who we are in this Way. This process of inner Awakening to Truth is key to the realization of our full potential as Human Beings; it is also key to the solution of all problems as we encounter them upon Earth or wherever else we happen to find ourselves within the multiple universes of Creation. Nothing could be more fundamentally True and important than this one Supreme endeavor, as our whole function and purpose for going through this human experience is tied into this Awakening process.

In fact it can also be said that the very function of Human Consciousness within the entire framework of Creation has to do with the total fulfillment of this Awakening as Consciousness. A physicist once said that "the physicist is an atom's way of knowing about atoms." This statement inherently recognizes the unified field of Consciousness; that all Consciousness is One and fundamentally inseparable. On a grander spiritual level it follows that the Human Being is Creation's Way of Knowing All that Is, and I would add of sustaining, altering and refining Creation into an ultimate perfection as would be held in the Heart, Mind and Spirit of God and Creator. We are therefore and in this Way co-creators of this very Creation in which we find ourselves living.

When we look at an event such as the miracle of the loaves and fishes we begin to see from this light not only a new Way of Being in this world and a new Way of relating to it, but also we can see our genuine empowerment regards our creative potential and problem solving abilities. I very much like the term Powerful Goodness in this context. It has been called Invincibility also among other terms, yet clearly we are coming into an awakening that Creativity and Creative Power is all the Cosmos really is; everything manifest is the manifestation of a Creative Force that is capable of everything and incapable of nothing. Once this is realized there is nothing left to do but raise our Hearts and hand to Heaven in gratitude and awe, and to join in Union with That One Reality which alone Is. It is all about Cognition, and once this Reality is Cognized we too become capable of anything and everything for the Good manifestation of Being wherever and however It chooses to become remade.

This is itself the most fundamental Cognition, following which all Cognitions can be tested against for verification. More about this as we go on.

So were these people actually fed, yes absolutely! Did anyone see with their ordinary vision loaves and fishes multiplying, probably not, because the mind will only allow us to see what it can make sense of; that which is too incomprehensible generally goes unnoticed. Yet Consciousness that is so powerfully connected to Its unlimited Source will still transmit what it Knows into the manifest world, and mind will accept what it can see as real. It is no different with the sunrise and sunset that happens everyday. Or with the flowers that bloom every spring, how does any of this happen really? The mind is accustomed to what it sees on a daily basis and has come to understand out of habit, yet the basis for this understanding is nothing more than familiarity. The habitual mind has nothing else to go on. Still the Reality that underlies all appearance must do Its thing to create and sustain whatever Is. Unseen and unheard we as sleeping consciousness go on about our days oblivious to the utmost Power that guides and sustains all life and that is our very Essence.

Nothing Is Impossible

"Nothing is impossible; by nothing I mean nothing." [18]

When Maharishi was pressed about his statement that nothing is impossible by someone certain that he would have to admit something as an exception to this rule; Maharishi gently and firmly confirmed his point by adding to it "by nothing I mean nothing."

Truth does not make exceptions to allow for our relative levels of comprehension; what is Real exists independently of our understanding or belief or knowledge of It. In other words Truth is not dependent upon our recognition of it to be True. It does not require our agreement with It or acknowledgement even of Its existence to be Real and what It Is. The Truth does not exist for us, but rather it is we who as Truth in form exist and belong to That which is Real and True. Nothing is either Real or unreal, possible or not possible simply because of our say so or our belief accordingly. There is a fundamental acknowledgement in this; that Truth does not belong to us, but rather it is we who belong to the Truth; again this is the case whether you accept it as True or not; you do not change Reality by refusing acceptance of It. This is True even though or because of the fact that as Consciousness we are of the same Essence as That which is True, the innermost Being in all the Ways It remains still and also moves.

There is nothing dictatorial or unkind in this, and really the opposite is true, because no one can change Truth by refusing to accept It, we can never be separated from It. If we were somehow able to change Truth according to our own likes and preferences we would turn ourselves into a lie and even corrupt our nature to the very Core. It is testament to the supreme Tenderness and Compassion of Reality that we are not permitted to do this, and thus no matter how dishonest in Consciousness a person may become there will always be something of a True nature remaining in the Core of that person. This is what makes it possible for each of us to return Home at any time regardless of how distorted we may have become and for how long we may have been giving energy into the patterns we have wanted to be true but were not. Dishonesties of Consciousness can never make true what is not really True. We can turn ourselves into a lie, but we do not make a lie Truth no matter how hard and long we try.

The ultimate Compassion of Reality is that no matter how long we have lived asleep as Consciousness and pursued distortions of truth instead of Truth itself, we are capable of returning Home, simply by accepting the Reality and letting go of what we have stolen, so that Consciousness can by Its own Nature relax and return back to Its natural state as clean, straight and honest as It was ever meant to be.

In Its natural state aligned with Truth there is nothing Consciousness can not do; truly nothing is impossible to It, and since that is our Essential Self nothing is impossible to us as well. Fully Cognizant of this, we can say to the mountain be lifted up and moved and it will be done so; we can bless the Earth that the soil will be fertile and healthy for our growing crops and all life that so depends upon it, and it will be; we can bless the waters, and it will be pure and good to drink and on and on. And just as Truly we can say to the wind and the storm and seas to be quiet and still and calm, and it will be done so as we command it. It is Truth responding to

Truth, Being responding to Being, Consciousness responding to Consciousness, all one in the same without separateness or division. This is how it Is and how it is So.

To rephrase this in the positive, Everything is Possible, and with that certain affirmation it becomes clear that in the fullness of Consciousness and with adequate understanding it follows that everything can become practical as well. Creation must be found to be not merely mysterious and far more strange than ever imagined by science and religion until now, but Creation as Unified Field is to be recognized as a cohesive whole in which every part fits together in harmony and balance, so as to create or manifest whatever an individual mind can conceive of. Creation is by no means limited by our limited levels of awareness, yet if we can even think it, it must have been done somewhere in this Creation.

St. Thomas Aquinas, famous for his philosophical thought and a great luminary of the Christian world, spoke in terms of Act and Potency. These refer to Being as both Actualized and Potential. That which is made manifest is actualized; that which is not remains as potential. Humankind maintains within Itself both in that we are partly realized as Being and partly not. We are a work in progress, as we say. God or Creator in this view is Pure Act; that is to say fully actualized in all Ways. God is fulfilled to the Core while man apparently is not, and so yet remains to be fully expressed as Being.

The fulfillment of the destiny of Humankind is in the completion of this Actualization process that is an inherent part of the Creation process itself. All life in context of Creation is evolving into its most full and completely manifested Self according to the Creator's plan for it; whatever that may be. It is of vital importance that we appreciate this, for it reveals Creation as an unfinished work in progress as well. Creation as a living breathing Being is Itself growing and maturing into whatever It is destined to Be, as are we too evolving into our fullest and most True Selves.

It is indeed a mysterious thing to look at from our human level that Creation and therefore Creator may Itself be in process and evolving into a more full version of Itself, yet regardless of the philosophical implications of this, whatever these may be, we can only Honestly remain open to this as possible and also probable. God in this sense is very much like us, only perhaps fully Itself, whereas we tend to be partially unaware or un-self actualized. Hence, the process of inner Awakening on all levels can be seen to Truly lead us into a state of Oneness with the All, Divine Union and a genuine state of Yoga.

When we speak of Everything is Possible, we not only state a possibility but rather an inevitability, and taking that to its rational conclusion a necessity for the Real fulfillment of Consciousness Itself. To look at Creation in these terms of Act and Potency is to recognize that evolution itself is the flowering out of all potency into actualized Being for the complete and ultimate fulfillment of the very purpose of Creation. That the Consciousness of Creation has had this as an Intention in Its own Heart, Mind and Will from the very inception of this complex of Universes that we are calling Creation.

Truly, everything Is possible, and everything that is not already manifest is in process of becoming so for the fulfillment of All life and creative purpose. It is my assertion here that without such an Intention this Creation as we know it could not even exist, as it would lack the necessary creative force to manifest on into a state of fulfillment, as in that it would have reached its maximum level of exertion already and have begun to collapse in upon itself into disintegration.

Creation Equals Unboundedness

Since the great Nicola Tesla, first in our modern times to discover a Unified Field of energy, existing as it were as a background beneath all appearances of forms in space and time, physicists have come to refer to this energy more often as "zero point" energy. It presents as a field of inexhaustible and limitless energy that seems to support all universes as we are coming to know them. A Source of unbounded energy that drives this Creation through Its enormous and complex stages of existence, growth, evolution and fulfillment of purpose simply and fully sustains Creation and ourselves within It as well as Life Itself. Or perhaps is this energy Life Itself? That may be a question for a more fully evolved Humanity to delve into.

What is clear from the outset with this perspective is that for Creation to occur an infinite Source of Energy, unending and always renewable, clean and free flowing throughout Existence on all dimensions and universes and in all places and times is absolutely necessary, or no such Creation could take place in a sustainable way such as to allow It to evolve to Its level of maturity and fulfillment of purpose in any way shape or form. Our own existence in this world also makes this Truth self evident by the Ways in which life is supported on all levels through multiple systems of environmental and cosmic natures. The circulation of water and air, the delineation of soil and their makeup, the divisions of land and sea, the flow of sunlight across the Earth from an energy source largely unknown to us, the movement of that energy across 93 million miles of space, approximately, to reach the Earth at just the right levels of intensity for us and so much more all indicate all to clearly the immensity of resources and intelligence at the disposal of this Consciousness of Creation, this creative force that conceives and sustains the very handiwork of Itself, of which we are part and parcel.

And more so we are the jewels in Indra's Web, each unique cuts of precious stone yet fabric of a holographic Cosmos, such that we each reflect and contain the entirety of all that Creation Is. For Creation to exist and even beyond that for It to multiply Itself so many innumerable times over and each uniquely can be accomplished and sustained by nothing less than a Source of energy so infinite and limitless as to be completely outside any individual human mind's capacity for comprehension. There is simply no way to overstate the significance of this Reality; it in every way defines our Essence and Nature without ever becoming old or worn out to our Awareness. The Knowledge and Awareness of this Truth is forever fresh within our Hearts and Minds and in our Unified state of Awareness It also illuminates and motivates our Wills, so as to keep us ever evolving onto clearer and finer expressions of That intelligence in our lives and societies. It motivates us to be genuine stewards of the ocean of life that presents itself all around us, so that our caring becomes the Caring of God and Creative Force. As our Will becomes One with the Will of Creation, we find ourselves coming online with that infinite energy Source, so that we accomplish greater things for the Good than ever before dreamt of; we live longer and far more healthily, and increasingly as we all deepen into this experience of Oneness together as a global society, we will begin to find the way we experience death will morph into a joyful passage of ascension into even higher Universes or dimensions of this Creation.

So clearly we must agree that Creation equates with Unboundedness in energy and Awareness, and therefore the two co-exist within and upon themselves. Unbounded resources Create by Its own Nature, and Creativity requires unlimited resources to fulfill Its maximum potential into actualization. It may be a chicken and egg question as to which comes first, yet the "two" are so intertwined and in a good way co-dependent that perhaps they are really not two at all but rather sides of the same coin so to say. Creativity equals Unboundedness, and Unboundedness equals Creativity.

Truth and Comfort

When looking at how conscious Awareness grows into the fullness of Consciousness it becomes necessary to consider the interaction of the Reality of Truth and our feelings on a mental and physical level of comfort. Comfort is something we seem naturally to gravitate to in most any circumstance. What is this interactive relationship between our relative levels of comfort as we might experience it day to day with this process of awakening as Consciousness into the genuine nature of Truth and that which is Real? The first thing we can say about growth of any kind is that its nature is change. Change is a fact of life when it comes to growth and the process by which life transitions through all the various stages and phases of maturation and expansion. Awakening into Truth is likewise a process of change of the most positive and regenerative sort, so much so that to genuinely love Truth is also to love the change that leads to this ever increasing Realization. Yet it is also a common human experience that change and the concern about the unknown is almost universally a cause of stress, anxiety and such no matter what the reason or perceived goal of the change. Change brings about a degree of discomfort in virtually all circumstances in one way or aspect or another in all phases of life and life situations.

Still in general the mind tends toward entropy, in that if given the choice it will choose comfort rather than change for this very reason. Mind and body as well value their comfort to such a degree they will stay put and not move into an area of greater awareness of Truth unless a particular condition is first met. It is also important to recognize that for Mind and Heart this condition is slightly but significantly different.

First and foremost the love of Truth must be greater than the love of comfort. In the Mind this is often recognized as a greater good or a preferred goal that is desired, and so some degree of discomfort will be seen as worthwhile to endure for the sake of that achievement. In the mind there is always a mix of love for a good and a self seeking urge to gain something for itself.

In Heart this movement is always more pure in that the love of Truth can be more clearly Known as leading towards the greatest good of a much deeper Union with the Divine, and as such comfort can be seen more as a distraction and a temporal respite only. Now what is this all leading to?

When we speak of our "comfort zone" we are referring to a level or area of awareness that we are so familiar with as to feel at home in that space of conscious awareness and understanding. Yet this growth process of awakening to Truth requires us to move outside and beyond that area of familiarity, as we increasingly Awaken as Consciousness. This process of growth change will always have us pushing the envelope of our familiar zone to keep moving and expanding it outwards. Hence in this process there is always a degree of discomfort, however slight or great, that is inherent to the expansion of Awakening Consciousness. With that our "comfort zone" area will also be expanding to take in ever greater expanse and values of Consciousness, yet still we will be pushing it ever so gently outwards and over time and practice be becoming ever more accustomed to this pushing outward just a bit beyond that zone and the feeling of discomfort this brings. It is not a bad thing or to be made a concern out of; only it is a positive symptom that we are indeed growing along the Way of Truth.

Love of change born of a love of Truth is the key here to knowing we are on the right Way in this. It is not a disregard for safety or in any sense a recklessness born of a daredevil risk taker; rather it is a love for what is genuinely Known to be True that draws one on through the discomfort of yet darkened place into a deeper Awareness of what may already be known to be True but is becoming even more well Known and more fully Realized and bonded with.

This fundamental dichotomy between Truth and personal comfort forms both a basic stumbling block for those who would be Servants of Truth as well as a basic guideline for them. It is a classic indicator of what we are being as Consciousness, and thus is a point we will be revisiting time and again in our quest and search for Reality within.

Finally here, a point to recognize is encapsulated in the phrase: "Seek first the Kingdom of God, then all else can be added onto you." (Matthew 6:33) This represents the ultimate reconciliation of the heretofore conflict between the pursuit of Truth and comfort. The real conflict here is in the putting of personal comfort first before Truth; this is what in fact creates and sets up the conflict in the first place. When Truth is recognized as your first love, then that love of Truth comes first and personal comfort is never a primary consideration. But when comfort is put in that place of first love, then we set ourselves up as deeply dishonest, and this becomes the core of what we are being. In that condition we can never awaken to Truth, because we are not even seeking It; rather we are seeking comfort, which we may or may not find, but whether we do or not is really irrelevant to the fact that Truth can not be uncovered in this way. Truth reveals Itself in Grace only to the Heart that is most devoted to It, if we are loving or wanting or needing something else more, than that Grace will stand by and wait; It will never push or force Its way into a Heart that is not desiring It more than anything else. Truth, Grace, the Being will stand and wait just outside of that Heart for as long as it takes until the Heart asks for It to come in, and only then will the Being move in and find Its new home within that Heart.

The Movement of Tenderness
Within Heart Mind and Will

In Its pure and essential state Being is motionless and silent. It is still and has often been described as flat. Flat Being is an endless motionless Ocean of pure Existence without qualities or boundaries of any kind. There are no distant shores that define a limit however great to this Ocean; there is no bottom that defines Its depths or prescribes a lower boundary beneath; Its depths and breathes are Infinite without rationale or motive other than to Be, pure and essentially as Is. This can be experienced and described as both the Nothingness and Emptiness and also as the Fullness and the All or Field of All Possibilities. It is only the condition or prejudice of the mind that sees into It that determines whether It is perceived as one or the other. In general it can be said that Mind will perceive this vast Ocean as Empty and Nothing, while Heart will recognize It as Fullness and All, the Understander and the Knower each Cognized according to their distinct Natures.

Then something mysterious happens and the Ocean of Being moves. Ever so slightly, ever so subtly this Emptiness, this Fullness rises in a wave the faintest tiniest ripple of motion and energy across the Infinite vastness of a boundless Ocean of Being, Existence and Bliss. Ever so Tenderly there is a movement that by Its very essence implies that something new has been created. The Infinite, Boundless, Expressionless Ocean of pure Being and Bliss is beginning to express and create a form a new boundary of a something that has not been expressed before. This first creative movement of the Being is Love, Tenderness; It is the Being in action; It is also Grace.

When the innermost Being moves; it is Grace, and this movement is Tenderness. It is the finest and first Expression of the Being and mirrors exactly what the Being Is. As such there is a free flow of energy, intelligence and perfect communication between this flat Ocean of Being and this first impulse of liveliness. Tenderness is being just what the Being Is, and the Being as it Is is just as Tenderness Is. The distinction if at all is in the condition that one is perfect stillness and the other is fully and ever so tenderly lively. This finest impulse of Tenderness also contains within itself the tiniest patterns of feeling, thinking and behavior that are genuine, True and most Real, as they also emerge from the Being into manifest existence. Reality as it exists in this first tender moment contains within Itself the very blueprint of all Creation that is to follow and develop further from it. This is the foundation, the celestial expression that maintains in Essence all patterns of evolution, Truth and Ways of being that can cleanly and honestly find their expression in and throughout all the layers of Creation that are to emerge further as this Being continues to move into new and more complex forms of expression and manifestation.

At this level these patterns are very tiny and totally straight and clean, a perfect image of the Ways of the Being Itself, and they remain there to inform all subsequent layers of Creation as to how they are to behave and function as Tenderness moving through them on all levels and in all ways.

Tenderness, therefore, represents for us a major indicator of Consciousness, as to what and how we are being within at any moment. Genuine Tenderness is always honest and never placing an agenda before what it knows to be True. In our Core we always Know this and gravitate back to Tenderness by nature whenever we may drift away. Somehow we always just know that Tenderness within is our Way home, and no matter how far or long we have strayed we know how to return when exhausted and all else seems to have failed. Such is the struggling nature of ego; that it seeks through its own efforts to replace what Tenderness has already achieved by Truth, as if somehow it could do all this better and then get to take credit for itself in doing so. This is the essential key in understanding dishonesty, meanness and cruelty and all manner of lack of Tenderness and hardness within. When we get the fundamental ego motivation we can begin to see into the farce of all this striving and efforting to reproduce by ourselves what Nature has already gifted for us for the simple honesty of Knowing and Being.

As Tenderness moves through the Heart, It is purity and love, as It moves through the Mind It is honesty, intelligence and sweetness, and as It moves through the Will, Tenderness is Powerful Goodness that moves mountains by the effortless touch of God.

There is nothing that can not be done by Tenderness; for all patterns of Cosmic Creation are written in the language of Tenderness, and there is no injury or disease that tender straightness can not heal and cure for this is the pattern by which life itself comes into being and flourishes.

Heart and Mind Revisited

Honesty of Mind looking at the Being sees an Unbounded Ocean of Flat and silent motionless Pure Existence. The understanding Mind sees this as Vastness and an endless Sea on so many levels; It can be Water, Glass, Fire, Light and even Blackness that extends on and on without end. Purity and cleanness of Heart, the True Knower, sees this same Reality with the touch of Love, that Is the Breathe of Life, and in that touch the Ocean comes Alive. Hence that which first appeared flat to the Mind is now lively to the Heart. This motion or excitement of Liveliness in no way disturbs the Silence of the Being that is still the same Reality, only perceived differently to these differing faculties of understanding and knowing.

Another factor here to be cognizant of also relates to differences of Heart and Mind both as to their respective functions and manners of being within Consciousness. The understanding Mind perceives Reality in terms of Vastness, Greatness and Infinity. The Being is seen as infinitely large and incomprehensibly enormous. For the Knowing Heart this perception of Reality is quite different, as the Knower of Reality recognizes This from a truly Knowing perspective, as such this Ocean of Being is also Known as infinitesimal, as the infinite smallness of a single Point, which likewise contains All Reality, and out of which this enormity came. These two perspectives taken together and recognized simultaneously are crucial to the Realization of a Unified Awareness and Unity

Consciousness, for they merge together the perceived Reality of the Infinite and the Infinitesimal. The vast and the tiny, the incomprehensibly large and irrationally small are merged in Awareness as One Reality that alone Is.

Thus we begin to appreciate the magnificent flexibility and intelligence of Human Consciousness that can be so Cognizant of what to the senses may appear as opposite and contradictory, that with effortless Nature It can merge all things into One perfect, complete and harmonious Reality of Being, and do so with Itself both included within That Reality and yet still Cognizant of Itself as Awareness incarnate. Individual without ego, such a Consciousness is indeed a reproduction of the Consciousness of Creation. Holy Spirit has once again birthed Itself as a new born Creation of multiple dimensions and universes, and That is Us. Finally, in that new birth, Creation has yet another new way to Know Itself as this new Creation. Thus the purpose and glory of Creation is yet again fulfilled.

Truth and Tenderness

All genuine Existence is born of Pure Being. To be genuine Existence must be clean, honest, straight and completely in alignment with Truth. Any deviation from that is a distortion of Being and lacks genuineness and honesty. Tenderness is the key to genuineness. Tenderness is the inherent and inseparable quality of Being, and as such is an undeniable quality always present within all Existence that is genuine. Without Tenderness some aspect of Truth is missing, and therefore a lie must also be present mixed together with whatever Truth may be remaining. This indicates the presence of distortion, dishonesty, uncleanness and a departure from Truth.

As the Christ has stated, "I Am the gate and the gatekeeper; no one comes to the Father, but through Me; anyone who attempts to enter by some other way is a thief and a marauder." (John 10:1-9) Here the Lord is speaking as perfect Tenderness. He has identified Himself with this Way of Being that is Tenderness incarnate. The Way to enter the Kingdom; that is the Pure Being is to mirror back to the Being exactly what That Is; that reflection is Tenderness. Tenderness is the supreme quality of the fully Awakened Heart. It allows the fullness of Heart to merge into the innermost Being and brings the fully humbled Mind along with It. "Unless you be like a little child, you will not enter the kingdom." (Matthew 18:3)

Only Tenderness can enter this gate; anything that is not Being That is trying to enter by force in some other way, and is hence attempting to steal and destroy what it is not willing to be in Truth. There are many other dimensions to this aspect as well, as the great degree of warfare and violence of our world plainly attests to. But far more subtle forms of dishonesty abound everywhere in human societies, and all are attempts to get without being true; these efforts are theft and destructive of not only the physical world but also of the very essence of Consciousness as well. All inner distortions of True Self for the sake of getting something we are wanting by hook and crook come at a great price to our essential Nature that is never worthwhile. Both in the short and long term the cost to Consciousness is devastating, and no amount of short term gain can ever compensate for the long term effects both to one's self and to others. To a clean and honorable civilization if honesty is the best policy, honesty must be the only policy.

Tender Honesty defines this Way of Being that reflects truly all that the Being Is and all that It expresses as Creation. There is no other way that opens and enters by this True gate. There is no other truth to compete with It. This is not at all to say that we all are to believe the same way or the same things; it is rather a matter of how and what we are allowing ourselves to be within. Honesty requires from each of us that we believe genuinely only what we Know to be True within our own Core. There is room in this for all to have differing degrees of Knowing, and yet all can be Honest in this True sense of being Real to what they each genuinely Know. Tender Honesty is the Truth of this One and only Way; what we each Know as True within ourselves is a matter of personal degree and discovery which is ongoing and subject ever to the change of growth and inner and outer expansion. Still we all, as Human Consciousness, enter by the same gate; no matter by what name we call It; we still must recognize it for what it Truly is and as Universal to all Humans and what they in Truth are.

As the Veda says: Let us Be One together; let us be of One Mind and One Heart and One Spirit, and let us Know together the One Source out of which we all emerge and to which we all return, and Knowing This recognize All as the One Self. (Rig Ved 10.12.40.) Tender Honesty is the Way and the Truth, and It is also the Essence of Life itself in motion and in stillness.

Life in Unity

Life in Unity is the Reality of living compassion. When there is no separation between the Self and the perception of other; when you look into the eyes of another and see there your own True Self; regardless of who that other appears as, human or not, animate or not, then we become for the first time genuinely life supporting and affirming. A shift then happens throughout the energetic makeup and frequency of what we are manifesting as Being into the Universe, whereby there is no longer any enemy; there is no longer any being less worthy of Creation than any other. All life in whatever form it presents Itself is now seen as the offspring of this Creation and Its Consciousness, and as such is to be encouraged and enhanced along Its unique journey of evolution and Self discovery.

All life whether ensouled or not, weather endowed with Light Body or not and regardless of Its pattern of evolution, such as human, mammal, insect, fish, reptilian or dinosaur or whatever else may someday be encountered are to be nurtured and cared for according to their highest status as divine entities birthed from the Supreme Consciousness of Creation with Its fullest intention and most Loving Will.

What can be the basis of such profound and total acceptance of Life on Its own terms; that nothing can be impossible, nothing unlovable? It is the complete merger in Tenderness and Honesty of all we are as Consciousness with our Divine parent the very Consciousness of Creation; that has Itself given birth to All that Is. As with the prayer of the Christ for His disciples, "That they may be One, as I and the Father are One." (John 17:22) And the saying of the Vedic Masters, "You are absolutely I." [19] In this Consciousness, the perceptions of the senses can no longer overturn the Truth of Consciousness in our Knowing of Reality. We have become so powerful as Consciousness in the relative world that the appearances of the world do not dictate reality, but rather Consciousness holds the world to what It Knows to be True and Real and remakes the world accordingly. And of course this is a process that is ongoing moment to moment, so that in this perfection of Unity the Reality of what It is being continues to grow and evolve with the realization and Cognition of each new possibility. The advancement of spiritual insight becomes the driver of progress in this world; such that not only is our own life enriched by this continual process, but all life we interact with is so enriched and enlivened to the ever increasing fullness of Its True Being and Nature.

Here is the beginning of a vision of our new Earth and new world, as a truly civilized culture of humans in connection consciously with the Divine Source and fully at home within our own bodies and within the Creation in which we find ourselves. A glorious new realization is to emerge upon us, as we are simultaneously re-birthed into the higher dimensional energy frequency of a Universe just above the one we have known for so long. The time has come, and in wisdom it behooves us to trust in the Divine Intention that we are so ready for this new level of Cognition and Existence. A new Cognition of ourselves as Being and Consciousness and a new civilization awaits for our own invention, and we are to move into these by Nature and Grace.

Part IV

Consciousness and Civilization

What begins in the beginning does not end in the end. If we are to discuss the relationship of Consciousness with civilization or society overall in a meaningful and real way, we must recognize of course that whatever we express outwardly into the world is coming from what we are actually being within ourselves first. This is True both as individuals and collectively as societies, nations and the larger world. Whatever we are being within our Core, good, bad, indifferent or ugly is subject to expression into the outer world, and this is the overwhelming fact of our individual and collective existences throughout time immemorial.

Now I would like to be careful here to not oversimplify what has been the human condition on this Earth for some thirteen thousand years as merely or simply a reflection of inner Consciousness, as this is aptly misunderstood by many.

145

We must recognize the great complexities of this Reality first and foremost, and with that recognition remember always the Heart value in looking at ourselves and do so with compassion and the grace of knowing just what it is we have lived through, endured and overcome. The Truth of human existence upon the Earth is one of great heroics and victory over incredible adversity and horrific challenges that appear to continue even to this day.

This said, and with fullness of Heart and divine compassion and in the fuller Awareness of the Unity of all Being and Beingness, I feel it most valuable to embark upon this insightful look into the experiences of societies from small to great as these relate to what Consciousness Is being, doing and realizing. For in Reality, what we are being as Consciousness from within our Core determines also what we are as a civilization. Like it or not there is need for genuine reflection here if we are to do justice to this profound inquiry into Pneumatology and a whole Science of Consciousness. Here a greater spiritual maturity is necessary if we are to genuinely see ourselves as we truly are reflected by our communities, societies, nations and world. Even the state of our global environment is an essential piece of this that must not be overlooked, for its cleanliness or pollution reflect upon how we treat and respect ourselves, one another and the planet.

Do we see ourselves as separate from others, putting a personal agenda first ahead of the best interests of the other, or are we Cognizant of the intrinsic Unity of all of us and as such know that we can not truly advance any good for ourselves by diminishing the good of another? This is not a new question or concept, yet the times as they present themselves are new to us, and the technologies for both spiritual growth and material creation or destruction are now great enough so as to require of us an honest inquiry and response to these questions, or we face self destruction by default. As horrific as that outcome would appear to us, so glorious is the positive alternative.

For as final and absolute a destruction of world could be so even more infinitely incomprehensibly admirably advancing and growing into heretofore unknown achievements will the positive creative choice be for all of us.

We Are What We Are Being

The world is as you are, as Maharishi so eloquently said. He and so many like him such as Drunvalo Melchizedek have so brilliantly merged the ancient wisdom of so many great traditions and peoples from around the world and around the galaxy with the newest and more enlightened insights of our contemporary sciences to come to the transformative recognition that everything is Consciousness. [20] The realization that beneath even matter and energy is Consciousness that Exists outside of time and without conditions of space is also the Cognition that what we are in our Essence is that same Consciousness.

The Truth of Creation Itself and the blueprint of all that emerges out and into it is contained first and foremost in this finest Reality out of which all manifest being arises. In all of Nature everything there is Being just as it is so meant to Be according to that blueprint. Nature is inherently Truthful by Its very nature, and so it must be for Creation to maintain Its balance and energetic equilibrium. There is only a special gifting among the more highly evolved life forms that develop the capacity for intellectual thought that gives them the ability to make choice within the context of that reflective capacity. That gift is commonly referred to as free will. Humankind are one of a great many so gifted beings evolved to the extent of being fully individually ensouled and therefore accountable for what they are being, thinking, doing and intending. This capacity of choice is an enormous gift and grace which confers upon those who possess it great creative powers to the extent that we not only become the creators of our own life but also collectively become co-creators on a grand scale. As we grow and develop further into this we will find the entire Universe in fact the whole of Creation becomes a canvas upon which we can paint.

What is this free will in its essence? I would offer a definition here: the inner capacity to choose at one's Core what to Be and to believe is True and to define ourselves accordingly. This is a huge gift and carries with it implications that go beyond our usual everyday conscious awareness effecting all of what we are being and influencing Creation to Be. This view of free will has three parts.

First, the capacity to choose at one's Core what to Be is in itself mind boggling, especially when we look at it in context of what the Creation is. As stated earlier, throughout nature, especially within the lower kingdoms, everything can simply be what it is and nothing else. Minerals, plants, animals and elementals can be only themselves, what they are made as, and can not choose or direct themselves in any deliberate way to be anything other than that. Beetles are beetles, apple trees apple trees, crystals are crystals, just as they are. Likewise the elementals of earth, air, fire, water perform their natural functions and are just as incapable of doing and being what is outside their being-ness and doing-ness. Unlike this the Human Consciousness in Truth does have this capacity to choose what it will be and manifest Itself as, such that it is capable of being True to Its own genuine and Real Nature or instead to live its Existence pretending to be something It is not; that is to say Human Consciousness has the capability to live Itself as a lie.

We have already touched upon the consequences of this type of decision, and what that does to Consciousness. Without going into that again here, the point to be made is just that this capacity is one aspect of what constitutes free will (to be distinguished from freedom itself).

Second, the capability to believe for oneself what is True then emerges out of the first. Once we have chosen what to Be and in particular if the choice made is to be that which one is not, then a whole story can begin to evolve around that choice in order to support it as being true, even then if in fact it is not.

The main point in this is that in this capacity of free will there must also be an ability to make an argument or case for what we are now being. Nowhere else in nature is this necessary or even imaginable, as it is simply not in the Consciousness to consider. What is, is what is, so to say, and Being really is that simple. But with this capacity to choose at the level of the Core now comes the necessity to argue (if not think rationally) through the story that being what you choose to be entails.

Again, we have discussed already the importance of honesty throughout this process and the consequences of dishonesty to our Being-ness. What remains now is to see more fully and from different angles what all this means. More on this will follow in subsequent sections after free will can be more fully defined.

And third, the capacity to define ourselves accordingly is an integral part of this ability to choose freely. This is where personal identity comes to play, as well as how it even becomes an issue for us overall. Once we have made some Core choice and chosen something to believe in as True, whether in fact true or not, everything we are then being and doing beyond that, that is based upon these previous choices now becomes vested upon our Consciousness as something individual and belonging to us, such that we begin to place an identity of our own self within that belief and being-ness. These identities are of crucial importance, as they are then allowed to define who and what we are in terms of being, doing and feeling, and from that point on we are hooked by whatever choices we've made and thus vested ourselves into.

The greatness of the gift of free will is matched by the enormity of the responsibility that it confers. An animal in the wild is defined simply by its own nature and all its being-ness is expressed outwardly accordingly. There is little question of karma or morality in this. A human being on the other hand is so blessed and so gifted with this capacity for self-identification that he and she becomes totally accountable for the choices made, whether conscious or unconscious, and how these in turn effect the total environment. Questions of morality and karma arise out of this, but as we are seeing even more fundamental to our Essence is what we are being as Consciousness. For as we have seen, depending upon these choices, what we are being as Consciousness is maintained cleanly and straightly as a result of these choices if we are being honest to our genuine inner Knowing, or our Consciousness becomes distorted to whatever degree by them if we are not.

Civilization Is Shaped by Consciousness

Consciousness is everything; if what we are being as Consciousness determines all that we are as individuals, then it certainly follows that society on all its levels is shaped and defined as well by the collective Consciousness of all the individuals comprising it. This aught to be so obvious it goes without saying, yet it is so necessary that it be said and taught everywhere to each new generation and repeated often to ourselves, so that it may never laps even for a moment in our Awareness. This is so important, for without this awareness peoples and nations have committed atrocities in the names of God, country and everything they've held sacred, and were convinced at these times they were justified in such and were actually doing good.

Whatever a nation is doing, the style of governance it sustains, the degree of corruption in political and social life, the ways in which it treats its people and animals also, as well as the life styles of its people and all of their values both publicly and privately, all of this reflect upon the quality of Consciousness that collectively the entire populous hold to, and consequently their combined experience of the world is created and made manifest to them through this. This is not at all to equate higher levels of Consciousness to nations that are more developed or enjoy higher standards of living by modern judgments than to those nations that may be struggling and less developed technologically by any means. As is often the case, more highly developed states are only more materialistic in their values than lesser developed ones and may even be using their technological advances to their own advantage in order to foster themselves at the expense of others. There is no cut and dried standard for looking at this, and we must take care not to oversimplify what are subtle and complex and also deep cultural patterns that deserve respect in their proper contexts.

Ultimately it is the values of the expanded and awakened Heart that reveal the highest and most clean Awareness of Consciousness, and that these can not always be measured in terms of bankers economics or legal and political systems. For there are systems of human interactions and dealing not yet known to us that are only discoverable by a Cognition made available from an even higher degree of Unity Consciousness than we have yet known collectively. When the time comes these systems will be Cognized and seen and come to replace the lesser systems of relationships that had come before. This is what we come to understand as evolution, not as a survival of the fittest, but rather simply an awakening process to greater intelligences and more life affirming and sustaining ways of doing what needs to be done for the highest good of all.

Remember that to a Unified Awareness there is only One Spirit throughout Creation of which we all share and are a part. Hence there is only One Being who is us all as well. This being Known and understood there is no enemy but rather only friend and loved One that shows Itself as so many different forms and beings who are all loved and love Itself. So long as we see others as other, separate and potential enemies or even just problematic we are not there in a Unified wholeness of Being; we are thus still confined to a Consciousness of polarity and opposing forces that must seek to gain and hold the advantage over others who might otherwise make demands of us instead, if positions were reversed.

So long as our Consciousness is defined by polarity and opposites we will continue to foster civilizations that create and maintain conflict everywhere and affirm justification for suppression of those who for whatever reason we choose not to like. We thus engage in dishonest dealings harmful to others and fight wars and the like all in the name of our own interests and greater good at the expense of those we see as separate and of lesser value than ourselves. Such a state of affairs is more barbaric than civilized and barely deserves the name.

When asked what he thought of Western civilization, Mahatma Gandhi said, "I think it's a good idea!" Implying quite clearly that it would in Reality be a good thing if only the West could be civilized. Genuinely civilized peoples do not engage in warfare or enslavement of others in any way shape or form. The pursuit of good for oneself can not be in conflict in any way with the genuine good of another; there is only One Spirit, One Life, One Heart for all of Creation. We are all One Body in that we are all of the same single living entity that is this whole collection of Universes and Realities we here call Creation. The direct Cognition of this as Reality makes the pursuit of happiness a living reality by genuine Nature, and then renders all lesser forms of knowledge or knowing obsolete. Empiricism or knowing only through the observation of the senses becomes the lowest form of information possible. It is the value of the material mind that knows and acknowledges nothing of Spirit. Such nations, tribes and civilizations survive by whatever means they can muster and forever engage in barbaric practices to promote their advantage over others without ever recognizing the harm they do to both others and themselves in the process. They are truly barbaric and not worthy of the term civilization.

One In Being With the Father

Terms like in Being, in Spirit, in Consciousness all indicate one Reality, even as they tend to bring that Reality to light from differing angles. Not splitting hairs here, Spirit and Consciousness are very close, both implying a Being that is lively; while Being can be flat as well as lively; to Be One is to Be One on all levels and in all these Ways. One in Being is also One in Spirit and Consciousness; it simply can not be otherwise. It is the Nature of Creation that there is only One Being One Spirit and One Consciousness no matter how it may appear to mind and the outer mental senses. Mind is the faculty of understanding, and it can understand only through distinctions and the appearance of differences as such. That is the nature of mind the thinker. Thinking, thinking, thinking without end or apparent interruption. When the thoughts stop, mind it no more. Nothing now for the mind to understand; without that even the ego losses its sense of purpose.

Mind is a surface body, and as such it is a superficial outer expression of Spirit and Consciousness. As important as mind is to allow for intelligent functioning in the world of our apparent understanding, what the Heart is, is of an entirely different and more profound nature. Heart is not a surface body; rather Heart emerges directly from the innermost Being as a part of our Core. This is what enables Heart to be the Knower of Being, so that Its subtle senses are directed inwardly towards the Being and knows what it knows directly from that Source.

Heart remains what It is independent of whether the mind is functioning or not, even if mind were to cease to exist, Heart remains. Minds may come, and minds may go, but Heart goes on forever.

In this regard Heart truly is One in Being with the Father, Its Source and also Its Beloved. It is said that the mind is the teacher of the body, and that the Heart is the teacher of the mind. Whatever mind is being, it takes its lead from the Heart; pure or impure the Heart informs the mind accordingly. This is why there is such a huge difference between living in one's mind and living in one's Heart. Unless the Heart is pure it is not even possible for someone to live there, for the unclean Heart will use the mind to cover its dishonesty, so that the ego can believe in what that Heart commands it to believe and suppresses awareness of Truth into a subconscious state. In this way even in ignorance the mind is innocent, for it follows the Hearts lead wherever it goes. Mind reflects the way and values of the Heart and does not stray from that, so that it becomes the innocent victim of the Heart's corruption. It actually can do nothing else, for it can only seek to understand without any real knowing. The Heart, on the other hand, actually does know, and should It act and do honestly or dishonestly the mind follows unknowingly but obediently.

Heart the Knower bares both the glory and the responsibility for what It and mind are being. This Truth brings to Awareness the great importance and auspiciousness that Heart awaken first to then bring Mind along into that fully awakened and profoundly honest state of expanded Awareness. For without this Heart Awakening, it is possible for the Awakened Mind to become just a more powerful tool for the dishonest and unclean Heart to use for Its own agenda, and so instead of becoming the Beloved Servant of Truth, such a person becomes a more clever thief and more dangerous destroyer of the good then he may ever have been before. The primacy of the Awakening of Heart becomes ever more apparent and vitally important by the

Oneness of Heart with the Being. The inseparableness of these in Being gives clear indication of the vitally important role of the Heart in the expression of Being on all levels of Creation and the creative process. For Heart gives closest access to the Core of ones Being where any corruption of Consciousness can possibly come.

These are among the deepest places within that any corruption of ego in Consciousness can possibly hide from view. Cleanse and purify the Heart first and the Mind will by its Nature follow and obey accordingly to step into alignment with its newly purified Master. That is the Mind following the Heart's lead into Awakening to Truth.

Hence the Awakened One is One in Being with the Father. Yet Being is already One, as are Spirit and Consciousness already One, whether anyone is Awakened to the Truth of That or not. What then can this phrase mean on the human level of our relationship to God and to Creation?

In the words of the fully Awakened Master who said it, "That they may be One, as I and the Father are One," it is a prayer for all of Humanity. Yet we are all already One, so clearly this prayer is an insightful recognition for the need for Realization of this Truth. That all of us are to Awaken to the direct Cognition of the Truth of this Oneness of all Spirit and Being, and hence with that Cognition comes the end and solution to all problems of separation and division not only in human affairs but in all relationships of Life Itself. The recognition of Oneness on this most fundamental level of Existence spells the end of all agendas of individual ego and rivalry, and heralds with it a genuine realization of peace, freedom and genuine equality as divine life universal that is simply incomprehensible without it. There is no pie in the sky here; for us as Consciousness this is the Real deal. We Truly are One in Being with the Father, that Divine Being that births Creation before the existence of time even, so there is never a time when we do not exist or will not exist into the future, and thus the process now for us is one of remembering, of returning to our state of True Knowing of Reality, and that Realization, as I have been stating over in many various ways here, is the Realization that is upon us in this very moment and in the midst of the magnificent transition we are now in. Only the moment of Realization remains a mystery soon to be revealed in God's own Way.

We are each co-creators in this Divine Plan, as well as heirs to the Truth of our own Selves. To know this is to see our present collective moment as a time for celebration and exuberance; we are on the verge of the greatest re-birth imaginable, only the labor pains and our lack of understanding seem to be in our way of seeing the Truth of this, yet the Reality is present and once the healthy baby is born all who see it rejoice.

Prayer of the Will

"That they may be One, as I and the Father are One," (John 17:21) and again, "but not My will but Thy Will be done." (Luke 22:42) As we have examined before, the Will is the last aspect of Consciousness to finally Awaken, and when it does the finest and solely remaining elements of ego are released without any further place to hide within. This means there is no more any belief in separateness or delusion of identity with the "I" thought anywhere in Consciousness, and with this last release of untrue identity all of Consciousness is now brought into a state of Oneness with Truth. Consciousness is now fully aligned with the Reality and wholeness of Spirit and Creation, even though there may yet be further integration with higher states or dimensions of Creation. Nonetheless, there is no delusion left to cause any separation of Being or harm to anything throughout Creation by any such influence emerging from that Consciousness. From here on there is only the matter of ever expanding possibility and fullness into all that Creation could ever choose to be and become, and All this is growing Bliss and deepening Realization of Divine Union and True Yoga.

When the Will so Awakened prays it is a holy and sacred act beyond anything Mind can conceive of or grasp without the full passion and Knowing of the Heart as well. Such prayer for Unity coming from the Realized and Awakened Will is a plea of such power that the whole of Creation is compelled to move on to fulfill Its destiny and purpose. Once It occurs it becomes a matter of certainty that in the natural course of evolutionary events the positive fulfillment of that prayer is an absolute mandate and will be brought to fulfillment by the power and supreme intelligence of the Consciousness of Creation Itself. There is no other Way possible, as there is no other Will that is Real. One in Being with Creation leaves no place for doubt, uncertainty or any sort of contrary intention.

Prayer of this Nature, coming from an Awakened Will, as I call It a Prayer of the Will is invincible, unstoppable, inevitable and the very Essence of what I love to call Powerful Goodness. This is the prayer that can not be denied; it is in itself an expression of the very Will of God coming through the mouth of the Master of Truth who now can speak only Truth in the full Knowing of who and what He and She Is. The Beloved Servant has become the Master of Truth, as One who has been Mastered by Truth, such that the Servant's Will and the Will of Creation are now One and the same. It is a state which now allows Truth a voice in the manifest world, and Consciousness a clear channel through which to shine, express and be Divine for all to see and rejoice in according to their own levels of awakening.

Now Creation is cooking, so to say, now Consciousness is truly on the move regards the fulfillment of Its purpose and ultimate destiny, and now Humanity can begin to appreciate Its own divine magnificence and full potential realized and actualized living, breathing and in the flesh. Still It provides just a glimpse of what is possible in a world where the vast majority continue to live in struggle for daily survival, yet a world filled with faith in the ultimate possibility of humankind that Knows this Reality in Its Heart and is ready to become that themselves the moment this world shifts into its new gears, so to say and opens the energy flows of its manifestation to a higher Reality in which Truth is more self evident and not so easily overlaid with density and confusion.

The prayer of the Will for this Realization of Oneness of all of Earth's Humanity is on the verge of fulfillment, and we all of us alive upon the Earth at this moment in precious time are Its joyous recipients. As Consciousness so transforms so does civilization and all aspects of its appearance and functioning. We shall have a look at what the possibilities are.

Awakened Civilization

At this level of Oneness realized, there is no longer any disconnect in Awareness between conscious intention and our Source within. Throughout the whole vast range of Consciousness there is an Aware continuum from innermost to outermost and back again. This Awareness touches all of Creation in Its recognition of the One Being and Spirit of All. Compassion becomes a living Reality because of this divine insight. To love God with your whole strength and Being and to love all life as you love Self becomes as Natural as breathing.

What kind of civilization can emerge from this level of Unified Awareness? Surely, it would look quite differently from what we in the modern world of the early 21st century have become accustomed to. Lacking the common rivalries and traditional feuds that have existed in some cases thousands of years due to the common abilities of peoples to see through these quarrels to what is genuinely important and Real, a new kind of forgiveness and bonding is possible that heretofore the outstanding trauma present within the Hearts of so many would never have been able to allow this kind of depth of Knowing and bonding between peoples. It is difficult to try and envision what such a cooperation of the world's peoples would look like or be capable of producing from our present levels of 3rd dimensional polarized awareness, especially when using the Mind. For the Heart at least it is possible to envision this as a genuine and more full realization of our True Selves and

Reality. Still it may be safe to say that such a civilization will not be characterized by many of our common day problems we now witness. Unbounded Compassion and creativity will solve issues of distributions of food and resources to areas of greatest need, so that no one needs to starve or be hungry or go without healthcare and education. That violence and crime, stealing and corruption of all kinds will not happen at the hands of those so Awakened and committed to the Truth.

Truth is profoundly intelligent, and Its realization makes us far more intelligent, as Itself, than we have ever before imagined possible. The more aligned to Truth we become as Consciousness, the more intelligent we also become accordingly. It is a basic realization and simple yet powerful Truth; that Awakening to Truth increases our fundamental intelligence, and that dishonesty of Consciousness, which is the primary distraction and cause of our misalignment with Truth, diminishes both our intelligence and our Consciousness. In so many ways it is true that we create many of our own problems by our lack of integrity and limited awareness of Reality. These inner Awakenings to Truth, that lead to the expansions of Heart, Mind and Will, eliminate all such issues of dishonesty within the closed and hardened places in Consciousness, such that we gain access to the fullest and brightest potential of the Being.

What could be the limitations of such a Humanity and their civilization? What kinds of problems could such a people find and be challenged by? The practical issues of life and survival that we deal with day by day in our world today will not present the dilemmas that they do for us now. Mainly, I suspect, their achievements will consist more of a developmental nature and the continual evolvement of Consciousness as It becomes evident to us at these levels. These are what my teacher used to call, "happy problems." Choices to be made between various goods, as in which is the highest and such. This is not to say they are of lesser importance, quite the contrary, but rather that such developments are all directed towards the genuine good of all, with only that as a destination and outcome.

Another important aspect of such Awakened civilization is their interaction with the environment they find themselves living within and passing through as part of the daily experience and also as travelers. In our present partially conscious state modern societies generally do not consider their interactions with their environments except in the most superficial ways. The Reality is that we are constantly surrounded by the natural elements of air, earth, water, fire and space or ether. In connection with these all natural objects and life forms interact and share space within the overall ecosystems. Modern humans especially in the West have become completely disconnected from the Earth itself, let alone the Cosmos, so that there is very little meaningful energy exchange with our environments. This is to our great peril on all levels of existence; it adversely affects our health, physical and mental, our Consciousness of Spirit and all aspects of our sustainability regards family, society, nations, economics and even our rightful place in Creation.

Fully Conscious and Awakened civilization can not be so disconnected, but rather must be in continual interaction with the total ecosystem that all of life depends upon to preserve the conditions necessary for life, and more so to give back or return to this Creation its full measure of creative and spiritual support, likewise for the common good of all life, human and otherwise. All life is conscious and intelligent, and this is clearly self evident to fully conscious Humanity. The very fact that life forms of all types have discovered the niche for themselves that works for their survival and the unique expressions of the Being that each represents is proof positive of the Reality of divine Consciousness Being and moving as themselves. This perspective provides yet another look at the Consciousness of Creation as all life and things that exist.

It is a common experience of all Awakened civilizations that active and continual communications exist between themselves and all life around them in ways that are at once creative and intelligent as well as interactive. So that not only do such humans positively influence the evolution of all life around them, and in so doing modify their own environment in the process, but also the very life we as such interface with so in turn influence us and our continuing evolution also. We shall indeed talk with the animals and plants and converse with the Earth and Sky and interact with the Consciousness of water and air and everything else, and all of these will answer and talk back to us in kind and with great insight and brilliant intelligence. All this will be recognized as legitimate aspects of Cognition and Cognitive Process and taken in stride. Whereas the Empirical view can only legitimately take into account evidence apparent to the senses; the Cognitive Approach has at its disposal all of the full range of Consciousness and Its infinite resourcefulness. This being the case, Awakened civilization brings to bare the full measure of its Actualized potential to everything and every situation that comes into its Awareness. The Unbounded nature of Consciousness is uninhibited to come to bear upon the fullness of the life of civilization when this depth of Awakening occurs. As such not even the sky is the limit for the realization of Truth of such an Aware and fully Conscious society and world. The term, life is good, finds its fruition in the Powerful Goodness that is so realized by such a people and their Creation.

Awakening and Peace

As seems almost needless to say, such civilization will be at peace, and war as we have known it will not touch them. How could it be any other way? One might ask, what if some lesser civilization were somehow to attack them, yet from where or how could this be possible? Simply stated, any civilization living and existing on a higher vibratory level and universe knows by its own nature the Oneness of all Life, and that goes also for all forms of ensouled and intelligent life, as well as for animals, plants and the mineral beings. There is simply no way for lower vibratory existences existing as they would in universes of more density, such as 3rd dimensional, to ascend to any higher existence without first being purified of any and all violent tendencies and agendas of distorted Consciousness. Their very narrow awareness and limited Consciousness that might make them prone to warfare disables them from knowing the higher Reality of existence or from approaching it in any way.

This being the case, peace is assured and Reality is safe for all life to flourish and evolve to Its highest and greatest potential actualized. Direct Cognition of supreme Reality opens all avenues for the realization of peace as a living Reality and most natural aspect of life without any down side whatsoever.

One apparent exception to this can to some extent explain the great array of Cosmic visitors to our Earth we now enjoy. There is now present around the world looking on with great interest and curiosity highly evolved beings from all over Creation, not only from this Universe but also the whole array of Universes that comprise the Creation that we are here a part of. This has to do with the use of nuclear power on our world for both a source of energy and as weaponry. This is not a work of physical sciences, and so I will not get into a scientific background behind these facts, but rather suffice it to say some basic principles here that pertain to the present topic of peace and war for higher civilizations on more fully awakened worlds.

Since the discovery of atomic energy in the 1940's, and with the subsequent use of nuclear weapons both in WWII and in testing around the planet, these activities have become cause for concern of many civilized peoples both human and non-human throughout this galaxy and beyond. Of all civilized and technologically aware cultures everywhere nuclear power is used only by 3rd dimensional beings of limited awareness, who do not understand the nature of what they are doing and playing with. Everyone else of higher Awareness knows not to mess with nuclear energy, as it is recognized universally as primitive and very dangerous for many important reasons. Most of all the use of it as weapons is the utmost in irresponsibility and recklessness, and all civilized peoples everywhere bane it as such.

First, nuclear fission is itself a product of instability. Only the very heaviest elements such as plutonium and uranium are useful for this, as they have reached that state of decay that is causing the atomic structure to come apart. This is the end cycle of material energy, whereby mater is collapsing back into an energetic state and disintegrating. It is a process of decay and destruction or annihilation, if you will. Therefore it is unstable by its very nature, and this alone makes it not a good idea to mess with this process, as it is fraught with unpredictability.

Second, and just as important as well as stemming from this nature of the process; nuclear fission, in tearing apart the nucleus of an atom tears an opening in the insulation that separates energetic spectrums or dimensional overtones from one another. This insulation is necessary to keep the various frequency ranges of these dimensions from interfacing and overlapping with others that are incompatible, so as to preserve the integrity of each world, dimension and universe. In short, the nuclear reaction allows a higher dimensional energy into our 3rd dimensional world; this energy is of a much higher frequency that is out of our universe's range of frequency, and as such is extremely destructive when released here. This is the reason that solid objects are vaporized within the range of such explosions, and how they release so much destructive force upon our world.

What is also important to note is that once so released it is unpredictable and impossible to control, and that there is a blowback effect that can and does reappear elsewhere in this galaxy and on other dimensions with devastating power and without warning. Such that the force of the blast can rebound back from this dimension through to others, piercing the insulation into another dimensional world right here or nearby or even at great distance from the original explosion and deliver even greater destructive force there, and that this process is unpredictable from the start and once begun there may be no way to contain or stop it. It is said by Drunvalo Melchizedec that the 2000 or so nuclear explosions that have been set off around our world since the discovery have caused the destruction of as many as 11 to 20 planets within our galaxy. [21] We have no knowledge as yet what else may have occurred in other galaxies and universes to which we are linked. Forces of such destructive power that can not be controlled by us are not to be released at all and certainly not in this irresponsible fashion without having dire consequences for life and our Universe at large. Many if not all of these worlds have been inhabited and their inhabitants have been caused great suffering due to our own ignorance and severely limited awareness.

Another important point we must be aware of is just how dangerous these tests and experimental explosions are, especially those done underground. These blasts open huge caverns and tear at the internal fabric of the Earth in ways we poorly understand. It has been known for many years that the reverberations of these blasts would go on within the Earth for several months, and that if a second or subsequent blasts were to be set off before the effects of the last had completely settled that the new blast would add to those reverberations already occurring and build upon them to dangerously new and higher levels. So if a series of explosions were to be done in too close proximity to one another, such that the reverberations could not completely settle they would accelerate to such an extent and the internal structure of the planet would break apart.

It is now known that each of these blasts individually causes a weakening to the planet's structure and the overall effects accumulate over time even if they seem to be spread enough for the reverberations to fully settle out. It is now known that after all these explosions we are a mere six more underground blasts from destroying ourselves and this precious planet in this way. [22] Hence there is no longer any tolerance among the family of nations finally for any more of these test explosions.

Best now to leave this where it may, and safely eliminate all nuclear weapons and replace all nuclear power stations with new safe zero point technologies and be done with this nuclear threat forever. There is no other Self Aware and responsible course for an Awakened civilization to proceed.

Galactic Neighbors Friends and Family

The official stance of the Catholic Church on this topic is that it is acceptable for Catholics to believe in the existence of intelligent extra terrestrial life in the Universe. I will add, that it is with a sense of great personal satisfaction to be able to report this. As has been reported to Dr. Steven Greer and others, the Church holds that it would not be consistent with an all merciful and infinitely creative God for the vastness of Creation to be devoid of intelligent sentient life also capable of Knowing Divinity and Truth. [23] This being the case, we can assume the presence of conflicting agendas among the leaders of different economic, political and social controlling associations. In particular I'm thinking of the academic and scientific medical communities whose official position in psychological circles is that it is delusional to accept or believe in the existence of intelligent life forms apart from the Earth. The body of good scientific evidence affirming the conclusions that human life can not be unique to planet Earth and that other intelligent life forms of a non-human nature also exist within our own Milky Way galaxy, albeit suppressed by governments and academia, is truly overwhelming beyond the point of reasonable certitude.

These points must be included here, affirmed and discussed for their implications to Earth's humanity and for our whole concept of what constitutes a truly Awakened civilization. For if we are to awaken to Truth and Reality as It genuinely is, what is it about the Reality of the Universes we find ourselves a party to that we are not to acknowledge or Know the Truth of? Our present state of sleeping as Consciousness has led us into this condition of quarantine and of believing ourselves alone in a hostile Universe devoid of intelligence and caring for itself or the life within it.

So what are the implications of this Reality of intelligent life around us that has not originated upon Earth and may even represent very differing patterns of evolution than our own? First of all, let us look at what we do now know of our own evolution as modern eugenics and epigenetic reveal to us. The Darwinian model of evolution is now largely disproved. [24] It is now known that the entire interface of environment and living organisms is a sensitive and intelligent exchange of information and energy on all levels of existence and being. In other words the organism and its environment evolve and generate together with each other in mind from their inception, and that this process is ongoing for the entire duration of the evolutionary process. Evolution is a conscious process that is driven by the Consciousness of Creation Itself and not a haphazard or accidental fluke of nature or chemistry.

In addition, geneticists have found that there is no direct genetic connection between humans on Earth and anything in the animal kingdom, including apes or any other genetic material so studied. It is clear that humans evolved separately from animals and probably this indicates we did not even evolve here on Earth; most likely we arrived here from somewhere else in this galaxy. That suggests that our earliest ancestors who stood upon the Earth arrived here as highly advanced members of a galactic civilization capable of travel throughout the galaxy to come to inhabit this place as a hospitable, friendly environment for themselves and their offspring and to transplant their already existing civilization here along with themselves. When did this happen? Far longer ago than we have any idea, or at least very long before our earliest surviving recorded histories.

Archeological evidence from around the world provides anomalies to our present day accepted theories that must no longer be ignored or suppressed. There exist from around the world many submerged pyramids of enormous size and elaborately decored that could only have been built long ago when these places were above water levels, which often is in excess of 10,000 years, and no one can explain their presence here or by whom they could have been built. [25] Our own records of history on Earth date back earliest only a recent 5,000 or so years; suggesting that humanity today is suffering from a collective amnesia that leads us to only a cloudy and confused sense of our own origins and is inadequate to explain who we are or where we've come from.

The scientific evidence suggests that we have been seriously tampered with psychologically and genetically and perhaps in other ways as well. To get into the how and whys of this kind of thing can lead us way outside the scope of this work on Consciousness and Pneumatology. Suffice it here to say there are good reasons for our current state of confusion and feelings of being lost in our own place we call home. It is time now for us to awaken to the Truth of who we are, where we are and why we are here, to open our Hearts and Minds to this Awareness and Awaken once again to our own Reality. For this to happen we must reconcile all these formerly esoteric facts with our view of ourselves and Creation. There is no longer time or luxury to continue sleeping and pretending such things are simply not real, for they are real and the Truth beckons us to be Honest with It and all of Consciousness.

If Humanity in this galaxy originated from a single source, we are all related; we are all family, and we are all even now still neighbors in the close proximity of this galaxy among so many countless others. I submit here that this hypothesis is already proven, and that the science is presently suppressed by governments and others who will not let the Truth be known for not wanting their profitable applecart upset. A few years prior to this writing Dr. Greer in his Disclosure Project hosted a symposium of retired US military officers with a variety of UFO experiences at the Washington Press Club. [26] The event was covered and filmed by two major networks who promised to air it but never did. Segments were also privately videoed and put out on the internet. At this symposium about 50 eyewitnesses of these many encounters told their stories openly and with full credibility to a discerning and well informed audience.

If anything was made clear at this event it was that we are not alone in this galaxy, that we have lots of intelligent and highly advanced civilized company, and that many of them truly have our own best interests at heart. What's more governments all over the world are aware of this fact and have had more direct communications with such other world civilizations on both a diplomatic and scientific basis. The event hosted by Dr. Greer indicated that over 50 such human races from around the galaxy had been identified and counted by the US government, and it is my understanding that genetic research has been done confirming that we are all related as in one great extended family. At a time when the human condition on Earth appears superficially increasingly tentative and problematic, these facts stand tall not only as profoundly comforting spiritually and emotionally, but also they ring a bell of Truth within the Sacred Space of the Heart. I find a direct Cognitive connection within my own inner Knowing with the affirmation of these ideas and assertions. This is a test of accuracy and Truth that we each must perform for ourselves within our innermost levels of Awareness in regards to all thoughts, feelings and assertions presented; that, we wish to be able to confirm or deny with accuracy and Honesty and confidence of the Truth of our conclusions.

This said, it is time for real spiritual maturity capable of recognizing the potential of all possibilities and willing to look genuinely and deeply into all things that must be considered. Such maturity will never dismiss as out of hand anything that intellectually it is not willing to consider as simply not possible. Intellectual honesty is not Real Honesty; it is Really merely an adherence to a preexisting set of beliefs actually unproven and unknown in the Real sense, that it must adhere to in order to support its chosen view of the world as it needs and wants the world to be. This is Core dishonesty, and this is not consistent with the Way of Truth within and can only be practiced by those asleep as Consciousness for the sake of remaining comfortably asleep no matter what. We have already looked at the cost in Consciousness of this kind of dishonesty and the cost of it in terms of human suffering and misery; at this point it must be clear why spiritual maturity can not allow this sort of reasoning. This present example serves as yet another sampling of how dishonesty in Consciousness can work and how to identify it when seen, so as to honestly root it out and let it go. To be mature means in so many ways to stop being infantile and superficial. Suffice it to say here that we are not alone in this Creation; that we have already been contacted, although most of our governments still do not want us to know this, and that all of it the company, the contact and our becoming knowledgeable about this is good and necessary.

The Collapse of Civilization

Over the brief span of modern recorded history we have witnessed the collapse of several civilizations both of antiquity and the middle-ages. Today we ourselves here alive are witnessing something different and unique to our own experience. Our contemporary world throughout, in every country on each continent and on all institutional levels as well as environmentally across the planet are going through what appear to be unsustainable changes and shifts in their manners of functioning. There is such a strong suggestion of systems breakdown through all of this that we all must sit up and take notice and ponder over the meaning and implications for civilization as we've known it. Can any of this continue and for how long we must ask ourselves for in all likelihood it genuinely is a matter of survival individually and as a species.

It is more than a situation of mass corruption of such systemic nature as to reach every fiber of government and economics throughout the Western world, such that governments can no longer function effectively much less creatively. It is even more than massive economic corruption that has turned the wealth of the peoples of the world into dept owed to bankers who issue dept instruments as currency and claim ownership for themselves of everything built by hard working people on the basis that they own the medium of exchange. We are seeing this more and more in America now, where elected officials, servants of the people openly admit to violating the law with impunity on the grounds that they had no choice, because the bottom line, their local and state budgets were not sufficient to allow them to act according to law. As the Baron Rothschild is so infamous for saying, that if he can control a nation's currency, than that nation's laws or system of governance becomes irrelevant to him. He is then, essentially above their law. Clearly the situation has come to this, where the bankers' rule supersedes the rule of law, and that spells doom for a Republic for a meaningful democracy and any form of government of the people.

Add to this the failing ecological systems and what we are witnessing now is far greater and more complex than an economic political crisis impacting our social fabric; what we are seeing today is a total global crisis of existential proportions that not only impacts our way of life but our whole manner of being. Who and what we are is about to change, and how we see ourselves and the world as well is in a state of transformation. Our response to this crisis is all too critical to our capacity to survive and thrive upon the Earth and to what our world is in process of transforming into.

The nature of this transformation is poorly understood at this time, and so it is important for us to begin to grasp the energetic and vibrational frequency concepts as they pertain to Consciousness as here being discussed. Our safe and clear passage through these transformations will be made far smoother and more successful by a deeper and more insightful familiarity into all facets of who and what we are as Consciousness and the Cognition of Unity and Oneness of all as Consciousness. These transitions are not meant to destroy us, but rather to bring ourselves and Creation to a greater level of fulfillment of divine purpose and further the evolution of Creation as a whole.

Considered first from a scientific point of view, modern Archeology has identified an Earth cycle of approximately 100,000 years that is made up in two parts as relayed by

Drunvalo Melchizedek. [27] These parts are of 90,000 years of ice-age followed by 10,000 years of warm weather as revealed in sedimentary evidence from various parts of the world. These cycles appear to be in constant repeating patterns on the 3rd dimensional Earth. Typically the end of each warm cycle is marked by a short period of global warming. This is highly significant, and it is important to note that these cycles of global warming take place independently of human activity, but in our present case the excessive burning of fossil fuels appears to have triggered the current process into global warming as much as one hundred to three hundred years ahead of what may have been otherwise, yet regardless the present warm weather cycle is very near its end and would be ending anyhow, even without our present human activities, only perhaps it would have taken just a little bit longer.

The critical factor here is in the melting of the polar icecaps, which in turn begin a longer chain of events. As the icecaps begin to melt, they deposit huge volumes of fresh water into the oceans that in turn reduce the salination levels of the seawaters. We now understand that it is the salt in sea water that drives the ocean currents around the world, and that this is not a function of water itself but rather the salt. In order for these currents to continue salination levels must remain above a certain critical level, and that without that sufficient salt content these currents cease to flow.

What functions do the ocean currents serve? Simply put they carry warm water from the equatorial regions both north and south towards the polar icecaps, as they do so they warm the air above them allowing for warmer weather for most of the globe. As these currents reach the polar regions the waters become cold again, sink to the bottom and return flow back to the equator deeper down within the oceans. Again as the warm surface water at the equator moves along the surface towards the poles, the colder water beneath surfaces and is warmed, as it too becomes part of the warm currents moving back towards the poles, and so the cycles continue. Without this flow there is nothing to prevent the icecaps from extending more and more to the equatorial regions bringing the ice-age with them.

Modern civilizations as we've known them can not exist on the surface of our world amid an ice-age. Although this may not seem at first glance directly related to Consciousness; it in fact is, for how we respond to the environmental issues confronting us is every bit an aspect of our development as Consciousness and every bit related to our capacity to survive as a species as well as individually. We will discuss this in greater detail in the next Part, but for now it is important to remember that this cycle of ice-age and warm weather is something which happens upon the 3rd dimensional Earth and not on dimensional plains above this. The collapse of civilization here does not have to mean our own demise, and it certainly does not have to even be a misfortune for us, but rather it may simply be the conclusion of past phases of evolution and the beginning of new and higher ones.

There are other ecological challenges brought about by our own activities that are also directly related to our misuse of science, technology and our capacity to manipulate our environment and the life around us. Massive oil spills at sea and on land and genetically modified crops and animals for food and other reasons have exerted great pressure upon the Earth to maintain her electro-gravitic balances such that her life supporting eco-systems can be preserved. Severe hot weather bringing massive draught continue to destroy huge areas of genetically modified crops; wildfires brought on by similar weather conditions also destroy enormous areas of woodlands and many of the homes there are destroyed with them. Earthquakes and volcanoes occur with ever increasing frequency, and although those who as yet do not want to see deny any connections here; those who do see can not mistake the in plain sight consequences of our actions, and that Mother

Earth is a living conscious Being with an immune system that is rejecting that which is foreign to Her, just as our own bodies might reject a transplanted organ.

History and Archeological records reveal that the loss of civilizations sometimes comes with sudden and dramatic changes to their environments. While there are many complex factors that can be involved in this we must remember that life and its environments evolve together and are not separable. When Consciousness is ready for a shift of major proportions or one that warrants it the environment may change to accommodate that shift, or visa versa. As in our case it may be that the Earth Itself is needing to evolve to a higher Consciousness level, which in turn would also require the life She supports to shift so as to adapt or accommodate the new style of environment that can now be provided.

Suffice it to say here, that civilizations collapse or disappear altogether when either a needed shift in Consciousness fails to be made or when that shift does in fact happen as well leading to a new environmental condition or possibly even a relocation of that civilization to either another time or place or another dimensional existence altogether. We live in a Creation in which anything is possible, and in which the Consciousness of the Creation Itself is in charge here. It behooves us to learn all we can about who and what That Consciousness is, so that we can best live and evolve ourselves in this divine Cosmic system in which we are interconnected and One with the Whole of Reality. Failing to genuinely Know this is at our own peril. As there is only One Consciousness and Spirit, we learn this by learning the Truth of who and what we are as Consciousness; for we are none other than That.

Effects of Dishonesty on Civilization

Another critical realization to understand here is the impact of dishonesty of Consciousness upon civilization as a whole, as well as the effects of dishonesty upon the individual Consciousness and society that have already been discussed. On the greater national, international and global levels the impacts of dishonesty of all types increases with growing destructive effects as we move out from its source. National dishonesty can lead to cultural bigotry from racial prejudice to genocide. Internationally it leads to tensions of various kinds between nations and even to wars; globally it leads to divisive international alliances and from time to time, to world war. Ultimately, dishonesty of Consciousness, that is believing what we do not know to be true, very often leads to the demise and death of that being. On the level of civilization it has been known to bring down entire nations, empires and even global civilizations. Its potential effect upon ours could be just as catastrophic if we do not awaken to the problems we are causing ourselves by our inner blindness to what we are being as Consciousness that are throwing us out of balance and harmony with the environmental systems we depend upon for our survival.

The good news is that the awakening process is easy and natural; we only have to first recognize the problem our modern cultures have created and allow ourselves to feel a genuine desire to correct our ways. From there the meaningful solutions are to be found within our very Core, once we commit to Honesty and purity of Heart and intention. The daily practice of deep meditation, of turning our attention within ourselves to the Source from where all activity emerges, allows for a growing intention to align ourselves in daily action with the Ways and Will of that Source. We must be serious about making the necessary changes to our daily lives and social interactions, business and personal dealings on all levels to reflect this increasing commitment to be and do the Truth, as it is now revealing itself to us from our inner Core, and to cease being the sheep who follow institutions of politics, religion and education simply because they exist and have funding and access to the means of manipulation and intimidation to anyone who does not comply.

There will be guiding this process a growing Cognition of compassion as a living Reality; that will continually increase one's sense of connection and Unity with life Itself through Consciousness, and this will increase the tendency to seek solutions for the greatest common Good, replacing the tendency to strive for a personal good or advantage at the expense of others who we do not identify with or consider an enemy. As the Heart expands and begins to Awaken, one recognizes Tenderness of Being as a Way of Life that is to be admired and followed at all cost. It is the Way by which Consciousness that has become distorted and twisted by dishonesty can release the distortions it has created by its own efforts and return to a state of Being that is just like that of the Being Itself thereby, reconnecting Itself to That which is Its own Source.

Once there is no longer any conflict between the individual self and the Cosmic Self, life and evolution begin to flow without hindrance and effortlessly. There is no longer any tension between organism and eco-system, and the highest degrees of intelligence available to each of us begin to display themselves and express in our daily creative actions and words. We begin to live the Vedic principle of Ahimsa, no-harm or harmlessness.

This is a state whereby we create our own environment without causing harm to anything, not even tension. Such a high degree of intelligence, creativity and harmony is not possible from the Mind alone; it is first and foremost emerging from the Awakened Heart with full access to the resources of Mind and Awakened and surrendered Will.

Adaptation and Ascension

In Truth, Ascension is a natural process. We have been taught by traditions and spiritual teachers for thousands of years that Ascension is miraculous and supernatural. As a culture and scientific community we are now in a better place to understand that the supernatural is really the natural that we do not understand, can not comprehend or is simply outside of our range of explanation. The more ridged we are in the belief that the world is just as we perceive it to be, the more difficult a time we have of seeing anything as scientific or natural that we do not comprehend or imagine to be possible.

In context of this discussion of Consciousness and civilization, as we have been looking at the tendency of environments to change and change dramatically as the result of natural trends and cycles and the greater forces of evolution, we must also consider the possibility of life as we know it to move between dimensions or energetic spectrums, so as to transfer from this 3rd dimensional Universe to another higher, such as the 4th. If modern physical science is correct, as they believe the existence of these parallel Universes to be proven fact, and since in that case we know them to be within our own common Creation, thus existing within the same overarching Consciousness or Holy Spirit, the possibility of such a transfer or movement from one such dimension to another can not be deemed impossible or even improbable. It is just something that to our current conscious minds or limited conscious awareness is simply not familiar to us.

As Humanity upon Earth today is witnessing the stress and strains of socio-political-economic-environmental collapse, it behooves us to give serious consideration to the prospect of global ascension as Nature's choice for our next phase of evolution, spiritual and physical. The very nature of the crisis we find ourselves within at this juncture is an overwhelming spiritual one whose demands will not be met by a mere quick fix or jump start as has been our tendency to consider of late. The current crisis calls for much deeper reflections and adjustments at the Core of our Being that will clearly and most definitely change our whole Way of Being and our relationships with each other and the environment on all levels, global, stellar and cosmic. In short we are to adjust our inner frequency ranges to conform to 4th dimensional Reality, so that we will become able to sustain and thrive in such an energetic frequency and make our new home there. It is not a matter of going somewhere else such as another planet or star elsewhere, but instead we are to remain on Earth but only stepping up our Consciousness to the Awareness of energy that exists at this higher dimensional Universe. Once done we will find ourselves in that Reality by nature without effort or contrivance.

If Ascension is a natural process, we will find ourselves there by nature. What will be required of us is the Willingness to let go of this familiar Reality as we perceive it collapsing all around us and to breathe deeply into a greater energy of Life that will become apparent when the time is right, so as to step into the next higher range of perception and Cognition. We will not have gone anywhere, but we will no longer be present on 3rd dimensional worlds; we will have stepped out, so to say, and stepped up almost as ascending a stair. Higher up but still within the same Creation and in this case even upon the same planet we will have adjusted and adapted to the needs of our mother planet who seeks to preserve and nurture the life she loves as her children.

It is vitally important to realize that this is a conscious process. It is not something we can get to sleep through and one day wake up into; rather there is to be a conscious recognition of something happening that we give our permission to and choose to partake in. That known it is cause for celebration and rejoicing; this is an event that is part of the overall process of Creation, yet it does not happen to and for us every day. It may just be that we are alive upon the Earth today because this is where we want to be and what we want to participate in at this wondrous occasion. As 3rd dimensional Earth cycles into an uninhabitable ice-age, we are not meant to perish with it; rather it is time for all of Earth's Humanity to cycle up to a higher energetic Reality which can support our new level of Knowledge, Being and Energetic Awareness. It is a matter of shifting perceptions with a shifting Consciousness that will create for Humanity a new Heaven and a new Earth. What is more it is a Reality that is very nearly upon us.

Part V

ASCENSION AS A FUNCTION OF CONSCIOUSNESS

The process of Ascension is clearly a function of Consciousness and that alone. We have no empirical data or understanding of this whatever but for the glimmer of theories that can be derived from the very newest physical science in Unified Field, Quantum Field and Super String Theories. Also the ancient mystery schools have much to say on this topic. Yet there is a Cognitive value that if accessed give important and vital insights into a phenomenon that, I believe, we will come to see as inherent and natural to a multi-universe Creation such as this one we find ourselves within. The suggestions of these theories finds that there is a parallel quality to the ten Universes that have thus far been located empirically; again this suggests that any additional dimensions of existence that do in fact exist will also fit into a similar pattern of parallel qualities. In other words, what exists in any dimension such as here for instance, also exists in its relative equivalent in each of the other parallel planes according to the nature and natural law thereof.

This is actually not rocket science nor as difficult to understand or imagine as might seem at first glance; only it is important to pull away from our conventional modes of thinking about our world, because these Realities do not follow standard textbook science or popular thinking about our world and ourselves. Remember first off that we in our present state are partially conscious and limited in our awareness of what and who we are as Consciousness. Second we must remember that Consciousness is unbounded by Its very Nature and Essence. All of Creation is but One Spirit; that traditionally is called Holy. That also gives us indication of Its True Nature both as Divine and unbounded in all respects. Hence that One Spirit is manifesting as Itself simultaneously as all Universes and planes of Existence that comprise Its Creation as Itself. We are ourselves Consciousness, regardless of our limited awareness of that fact, and as we are within that same Creation are ourselves aspects of that One Spirit and in no way apart from That.

Beyond thinking outside the box, we come to the realization that the box does not exist; it truly is an illusion of the limited and un-awakened mind. We here are stepping into the realm of genuine Cognitive Process, for we are following the Heart's Knowing and going wherever It leads. This is not a time for judgmental objections of what simply can not be possible, based upon all our perceptions of this world that have served beliefs in the solidity and definientia of things. This is a time for seeking out Truth as a Cognitive Process into the Heart's inner Knowing of what is True as pertains to our Real Selves.

Understanding Ascension

There are many ways in which Ascension has been understood and misunderstood over the millennia. Religiously it has been seen as a mysterious and miraculous spiritual process of Divine Grace and intervention. It is distinguished in Orthodox Christianity from Assumption, as a way to draw a line between the Divine and the Human, as in Christ Ascended bodily of His own power into Heaven, but His Blessed Mother was Assumed bodily into Heaven by the Grace of the Divine Master. There is an intellectual theological argument made to distinguish between them, but for practical purposes the processes are essentially the same. My intention here is not to discuss the theology but rather to examine the process within the simpler light of the new science and all the implications of what we have been discussing thus far. I hope this does not disappoint any of my readers, but even in this simpler light of scientific and Cognitive insight there is a surprising amount of insight to approach this topic with that needs to be recognized and given its fare consideration as part of our approach to Full Consciousness and Higher States of Awareness of our True Nature and Reality.

First off, Ascension is a Holy Process in that it involves the full participation of the entire Being, Spirit, Consciousness and surface bodies of a living breathing person human or otherwise. In light of the new Physics, I am going to define Ascension as the conscious movement of any being from one dimension or universe of existence to a higher dimension or universe. It is in essence inter-dimensional travel. To the religiously minded this definition might seem a bit odd at first glance, yet I submit it makes perfect sense in both the traditional light and that of what we now know empirically. What makes Ascension greater than mere travel in the ordinary sense is that it contains within it the capacity to remain on the new higher level of existence without any need whatever to return to the previous lower one.

We know already from our previous discussions that what separates these Universes is a range of energetic frequencies that are specific to each one. Therefore the capacity to move to a higher level means the ability to sustain a level of energetic functioning that is consistent and within the range of the new higher dimension. This is more than a temporary shift of energy levels that might then be lost, forcing a return back down to the previous lower level, but it is a genuine shift of Consciousness that is capable of keeping that energetic frequency naturally and effortlessly whereby before it may not have been able to do or be so. This must be done consciously or else this criteria will not be met; the unconscious awareness may vibrate up to the higher level for a time and for a specific purpose, but the overall awareness will have to return back to the lower level, because it is not yet ready to sustain awareness at that level of frequency and energetic being.

In addition, when this movement occurs consciously it then becomes possible for Consciousness to bring the body with it into the higher dimension, which is also an aspect of genuine Ascension. Consciousness which animates the body and fills it with energetic aliveness can now increase the energy levels of the body to make it fit for its existence upon the higher plane; thus the movement is permanent, and the realization sustained.

This is a basic, primary and crucial understanding of what Ascension is. As for the nature of the Process and how it might occur, these are much greater topics that mystery schools and theologians have studied for eons, and we will attempt a superficial look into this subject in these sections that follow. It is an ambitious undertaking, yet I intend to at least demystify and remove much confusion from the subject and establish Ascension as a purely natural and inherent aspect of Life within this Creation; in other words, it is my contention that Ascension is a natural part of the workings of the Consciousness of Creation, and as such it is one aspect of the realization of our own destiny as beings within that Consciousness destined to become what the Creator Is.

The Natural Movement of Consciousness

It is simply natural for Consciousness to move throughout Creation; there is no separation, of course, between Creation and Its Consciousness, for they are One of the same Being and Existence. Creation is conscious, and Consciousness is what animates, sustains, gives rise to and expresses Itself as Creation. It is like a deep and vast ocean where the water flows throughout from upon the surface down through the various depths all the way to the greatest depths; it is all water simultaneously moving on all levels of what the ocean is, yet it serves numerous functions at all the many levels and depths of ocean that make the ocean. On all levels it is all water but water acting and moving in so many different ways depending on the functioning or style of support provided on each level or depth.

In a similar way the Ocean of Consciousness moves throughout all the Universes and various layers of Creation, so that it is all Consciousness looking like so many different manifestations of Being on each dimensional Universe and also on so many differing Universes. It is all Consciousness everywhere, yet with individualized Awareness of Itself and surroundings on each plain and dimension; such that it is possible for Awareness to focus here for example and not be distracted or conscious of Its existence elsewhere that is just as real but being cared for by another aspect or part of conscious Awareness that is focused there. As Awareness expands in its Consciousness of Being, it becomes easier and recognizable to maintain direct awareness of more than one plain simultaneously; this is just a function and aspect of a more Unified Awareness or Unity Consciousness. When that is one's level of functioning this becomes easy and effortless and is totally natural.

Consciousness moving between the many various levels of existence is like ocean water moving between the various depths of functionality within an ocean. Only Consciousness has the additional ability to bring its many forms, as it manifests Itself to be, along with It from one dimension to the next when certain criteria and conditions are right and when the divine Intension is present to do so. When this happens Ascension occurs, and it just may be happening at any given moment or even all the time. In our present state of limited Awareness we lack the necessary unbounded Awareness to appreciate or even perceive when this is happening in front of ourselves or right under our noses. In the watery ocean it may be likened to certain fish and other creatures who live exclusively within specific ranges of depth within the water, yet there are others such as whales for example who can swim to great depths and always return up to the surface to breathe and play in the sunlight. These greater creatures move between the many different layers at will and recognize their functions on each of them, and they even are spoken about as descending and ascending within the greater realm. How much more complex is the greater Cosmos surrounding us, yet as Above so below is a motto that holds True here as well.

So Consciousness moves the Being throughout all levels of Existence as it expresses Itself as them, thereby Creating them as expressed. Consciousness is Creation, and Creation is Consciousness, and Ascension is a vital aspect or function of that entire process. By Its Nature, Consciousness is moving through Creation at each and every creative impulse; although the movement of Consciousness is of a different nature than that of any physical object or body in the physical or 3rd dimensional world. Consciousness is more the lively flow of Being, pulsing in and out, up and down, through the various frequencies of energy and manifesting accordingly in each of them. So it is not a physical movement as we think of it, but rather it is a vibrational shifting and energetic movement along the different frequency ranges in order to Create at each dimensional level throughout Creation. The same Consciousness is repeating this process wherever Creation is manifesting, only at each level It is doing so within the vibrational frequencies of that level; the same Consciousness, the same essential energy is everywhere present, the distinction is in the frequency and intensity of vibration.

These are critically important concepts to understand. Creation is not made up in the ways we think about just from our sensory observation of the physical world and universe around us. To see into the Truth of how Creation is structured and made we must look much deeper into ourselves and our own True Nature, and this by nature is a Cognitive Process; an Empirical approach will always be limited by our technological capacity to measure and observe, and as such can not verify on nearly as deep levels as our ability to directly Know and see into what we are focusing to see into.

Creation as an Evolving Being

Creation is Itself a single whole living entity or being. The ancient motto, "as above so below," is of the utmost relevance in this. As stated much earlier in this work, Creation is a field of all possibilities and is pregnant with its own reproduction, and we humans primarily are it; although it appears in all honesty to also imply that all non-human sentient and ensouled beings are differing evolutionary cycles and within similar patterns of reproduction. Creation is having babies, and we all are it.

Just as all life forms we know of are themselves involved in an evolutionary process that is determining and guiding their development both as species and individuals, so too is this divine Parent of all this life, the entirety of this interwoven complex of dimensional plains and Universes we are here calling Creation. "As above so below", applies here in its most full and true sense. Humanity is very much in the middle of all this, extending outwardly to the infinitely large and also inwardly to the infinitely small; the same patterns of Creation and evolution repeat themselves over and over without end. We truly do exist in the midst of a great hologram expressing itself endlessly beyond comprehension of the intellect or any merely mental intelligence. The sacred geometry as explained by Drunvalo Melchizedek relays this according to the drawings of Leonardo de Vinci. [28] This is also another aspect of the Old Testament Biblical reference whereby Humanity is consistently called the Middle Kingdom. This it appears is both a reference to our relative size mid-way between the size of the sun and the smallest particles in our solar system, and also according to mystery schools that humanity is the fifth in a system of nine kingdoms, with four below us and another four above. (Briefly, these are Mineral, Plant, Animal, Elemental, Human, Angelic, Arch-angelic, Principalities-Dominions-Thrones, Kingdom of the gods-Heavenly Hosts).

So as we know, all life is evolving, and so is the Author of Life Itself as we Know It. Evolution is a Cosmic Reality that somehow serves a purpose for Creation. We could speculate here about what that purpose might be, but I feel it far more advantageous and meaningful to instead actually look into the Nature of this Reality directly. That is to learn what our True purpose and the purpose of all this Creation may be by a genuine Cognitive Process is far more Real and powerful for that purpose, whatever that may be, than to seek some Empirical result by mental analysis.

This is where the direct inquiry into the Nature of Consciousness is imperative, and without that we are left and remain in a pseudo-space of speculation and uncertainty that can neither satisfy our spiritual needs nor allow us to fulfill our life long destinies individually and as communities. For this life to be most meaningful we must be consciously evolving towards the same spiritual goals as the Creator Itself. This does not need to be mysterious, but it must be recognized by us for us to have greatest benefit of the Truth of who and what we are as Consciousness.

What empirical evidence do we have to suggest that Creation is in fact a living and evolving Being, and what further implications can we draw from this Reality? We now know that the Universe is ever expanding and not simply expanding and contracting in alternate cycles. This ever expansion indicates a Universe that is in a continuing state of growth and development and may not have even reached its point of maturation. Also we now know that our Milky Way Galaxy is not yet fully developed and that its spiral arms continue to form and grow, including the formation of new stars and solar systems and the like.

In addition we have the Creation Story of the big bang or as I prefer the fireball theory, whereby the Universe emerges as a burst of infinite energy from a single infinitesimal point growing and expanding outwards towards infinity on all sides. The formation of stars of planets and solar systems and the formation of the infinitude of galaxies all arising out of this one great event speaks of the ongoing evolution of Creation to this point and beyond towards our greatest sense of the Nature of It All. It by all means behooves us to examine this Reality inwardly through our own natural Consciousness and the inner senses of our Hearts as well as through the outer senses of our Minds. There is simply nothing other than our own mental prejudices and bigotries that would suggest we don't or mustn't or ought not to approach Reality through these inner ways, or that to do so is in any way not equally valid if not superior to the outer ways.

Everything is Alive

Perhaps by this point I am preaching to the choir. Nonetheless, these points do speak greatly to the aliveness of all things within Creation, and coming out of such a materialistic Western culture, as we do, these points that seem so simply obvious to the indigenous peoples of the world and to those of us who have already spent a lifetime observing, looking into and studying the inner Reality, it continues to appear that so much of modern culture can not or simply does not see it, and so I can not here take for granted that it is as obvious to others now as it seems to be to me.

Western science is only now waking up to this Reality, that all things are alive with the transcendent energy and Consciousness of the whole of Creation. Historically we know it takes time, 50 years at least for new scientific discoveries to come out into the main stream understanding and popular view. The critical nature of our moment in the evolution of our world along with the vitally important role we appear to be playing in the greater Cosmos do not afford us the luxury of so much time today. So much of our survival as a species in the world now depends upon our reconnecting to our innate capacity to Ascend easily and Knowingly when the divine time for that event occurs, and occur it will, as it must according to the natural progression and order of things.

Typically when we speak of "life as we know it," we are talking about past and conventional definitions of life that include only plant, animal and human kingdoms as we have conscious contact with here upon Earth. The mineral kingdom is not thought to be alive, which it is, and others such as elemental and angelic and beyond have not been empirically explained, and so are just ignored or denied. Clearly the empirical approach has become inadequate to our present needs both individually and collectively, and the time has arrived for a Cognitive approach to replace it as mainstream. If every manifest form and structure is in Truth infused with Consciousness, and all Consciousness is One, then all life is One, regardless of any and all appearances to the contrary. The sooner we begin to operate from this Awareness in our daily lives moment by moment, the sooner we all can enjoy the profound benefits of the Reality of this direct connection to the Divine, the Consciousness of Creation.

When Life is One single living whole, then all life is supported by the massive resources of Creation and no one is left to believe they are alone and isolated. When this Awareness is a living Reality then no one is left in want or poverty or without the Reality of Love in there lives. The implications of this direct Cognition are mind boggling and more than we can ever discuss in this format or ever consider before we as a whole world community begin to share the experience and Knowing of this Reality. In short it will change everything in ways so profoundly good, that we can safely say the persistent problems of this world as we've known it will no longer exist. Our relationships with each other and all things around us will shift as well in ways never before imagined, and we will realize the Truth of the saying "All are Created Equal."

Resurrection or Ascension

Like Ascension, Resurrection involves the movement of Consciousness through various levels of dimensional being. It is distinguished as a different process by which this occurs, however, and the understanding of these differences is important to our appreciation of the various options available to us, as well as the fullness of our Knowing of Consciousness and Its Ways.

When the degree of Yoga or conscious Union with the Divine is great enough a person who is a yogi becomes capable of what is known as conscious dying. That means such a person can go through the death process consciously, rather than have to die unconsciously. There is great advantage and value in passing from our common bodily form while remaining centered and awakened within the Heart consciously and without fear or any sort of anxiety. One moves through the realms of Spirit effortlessly and is able to appreciate more fully the beauty and meaning of these realms. In this movement the departing person has tremendous ability to resolve and remedy any and all negative influences that may still be unresolved from the departing lifetime or previous lifetimes and can appreciate in this fully conscious state all the interactions and effects of events of the past lifetimes upon him/her self and all others. What is so valuable about this form of conscious dying is that the yogi in that state has great resources to resolve and rectify any remaining negative effects that may yet be present; this is unlike the state of those who die unconsciously and can only observe these influences and feel them but are unable to do anything to change them for the good, and so have to return to another earthly birth to continue the process of resolution of these karmic effects and to learn more the Ways of Ahimsa or doing no harm (harmlessness).

Furthermore and even more important is that in remaining fully conscious during the dying process the yogi retains the capacity to restructure his/her human body or return for it, so as to take it to a higher or 4th dimension with himself. This accomplishes the same result as Ascension but only with this one additional step to it in that return for it. In this process as with Ascension there is no need for the yogi to take another human or non-human birth on the Earth plain; although he can for reasons of Compassion or divine mission if he or she were to so choose, such as the case of an Avatar. But that again would take us beyond the scope of this book to go into it here.

A third method of movement into 4th dimension is simply death itself. Yet again it must be done consciously in order to avoid the requirement to return to the 3rd dimension to form a new body, as without the conscious passing over it is not possible to be birthed properly into the higher energetic form. But by simply dying consciously it becomes possible to move through the birth canal on the 4th dimension and be born as a new baby with parents and a family to welcome you there. This is the simplest method available to us, and it is the one most often chosen, as it requires the least sophisticated understanding and insight into other processes such as Resurrection or Ascension. All three of these do require that the dying process be conscious, however, and for that the Heart must be fully awakened and no trace of ego can be still clinging to the Will.

Remaining fully centered within the Awakened Heart is key to going through this process consciously, such that the movement to the higher dimension can be permanent.

The physical heart is linked to the spiritual center within Consciousness, and by this link it becomes possible to allow the heart organ to be our doorway into our True center, as they are not separate and were always divinely intended to provide this passageway for us to return to our spiritual Home. We simply have to remember the proper way to utilize this link. This leads us into our discussion of the inner energetic structures of the Heart, and how we can access these Gifts of Consciousness as fully conscious and Awakened Human Beings in order to activate our True birthright as the offspring of the Consciousness of Creation.

The Inner Spaces of the Heart

Modern biological science has recognized that when the fertilized human egg divides and begins to form the embryo, the heart is the very first organ to emerge. That for a short time the human embryo is just a single heart beating by itself until the tip of the tongue begins to form out of the top of it. It was wondered how the heart could beat on its own like this without a brain to regulate it; until it was also discovered that there is within the heart near its center a very tiny brain of only about 40,000 cells, and that these are in fact brain cells and not heart cells. The human heart appears to have an ability to think on its own and to regulate its own beating. [29]

From an esoteric energetic view of the heart organ we find, according to Drunvalo Melchizedek, two distinct and vitally important energetic fields in and around the heart that are vital to who we are as Consciousness, as well as to who we are becoming by evolution. The terms he uses for them are the "Sacred Space of the Heart" which is the larger more outer area and the "Tiny Space of the Heart" for the smaller more inner area. I also like the term "Secret Space" as well for this smaller area. These are two areas, the smaller within the larger concentric spaces, that are of utmost importance for us to become aware of and once so aware to maintain our perspective from within them. There are several reasons for this that call for special mention here.

First, together these two spaces form the sacred place of Creation out of which the entire greater Creation emerges. Remember for a moment that the Creation with all its included Universes is a hologram, and that being the case time and space or size have little or no bearing and provide no limitations to structure and circumstance of either form or events. There is much more that needs to be said about this as we proceed, but for now hold in awareness this Truth, that the Source of Creation emerges from within the Tiniest Center of the One Universal Heart that is everywhere present within all Sacred Spaces of all Hearts. Each forms a part of the whole. As with all holograms every part contains the image of the Whole, and as in this case the image is that of the entire Creation, so that the same Creation in all its aspects and universes can be accessed through the Core of any Heart within it.

Second, the Tiny or Secret Space of the Heart also contains within it a seed atom of a very special energy field known as the Merkaba. This is a very sacred energetic field that can develop naturally and does so as we evolve into it by degrees. When developed it expands out to surround the person in a kind of cocoon that can become a vehicle to travel at will between the energetic dimensions or universes of Creation. It is extremely important that the only Merkaba so used be the one naturally occurring within the Tiny Space of the Heart, as this is pre-attuned to our Consciousness and the Creation we are a part of. Any variation of this can be either unstable, making it potentially unsafe or simply a fancy of imagination with no substance to it whatever. [30] I do not recommend any attempts at creating a synthetically produced Merkaba, as these do not contain any of the natural safeguards that are inherent to the natural Merkaba, that grows naturally with the diminishment of the ego and expansion of True Self.

The third point about these inner Heart Spaces is regards Its function as a place from which all Creation comes. Referring again to the Hologram of the Center of Creation within the

Heart, we come to realize that in Truth there is only One such Divine Space; that all of Creation emerges from this One point out of which the "Fireball" or "Big Bang" first occurred, and from this same Divine Space expands out all the various Universes of this Creation. Although it may boggle the intellect to comprehend this, it is a Truth that the Heart genuinely Knows once we return Awareness to that place within, that this place of Creation within the Tiny Space of the Heart is the One and the same point within each and every one of us, and it is also the same point out of which Creation first emerges at the inception of this entire Creation.

Creation is structured in Consciousness, and as such all of Creation is Consciousness Itself. There is no exception to anything that exists within this realm and Creation; we are it; It and We are all One. We are all connected at the Core of our Hearts, and we are connected likewise at each and every level of existence accordingly. This is to say that this point of Creation is omnipresent throughout all of absolute and relative Creation and Existence. When we begin to rest with this first as a concept within the Awakened Heart, then gradually it comes to dawn on us as a more direct Cognition and Knowing that this Divine Center of Creation is everywhere and also all that there is. We can not really be separated from it, as we are It as well. Just as Being can not be separated from being; just as Is-ness can not be separated from what Is, so too Creation can never really be separate from Itself, as simply put nothing else is.

These are the simple and Real implications of the Reality of the Consciousness of Creation as Holy Spirit and Life of the All. The Mind that is properly oriented towards the outer experience of the world in which it finds itself is also pre-programmed as a faculty of outer perception and understanding to make and recognize distinctions and oppositions in order to be able to delineate boundaries that are necessary or helpful for the basic needs of survival in the world. As such the Mind is easily distracted from the deeper or inner Realities that are not made visible at the gross 3rd dimensional or surface appearances of things. This is really all right in as much as it is not the proper functioning of the Mind to be so inclined to perceive these deeper inner Realities. The Mind is functioning well when it is attuned to the outer appearance world and engaging well in its survival modes. Human Consciousness has, however, been subjected to a forgetfulness that has resulted from the misuse of the mental faculty due to the ego's attempts to replace the Heart with its own functioning. As such the Mind has attempted to impose itself upon the faculty of Knowing, and this done has left humanity on Earth without its proper Knowing function intact for so very long.

As the Heart reawakens to Its own True functioning as faculty of genuine Knowing, so the Human Consciousness returns into Its own as the Knower of Reality. This again fulfills the definition of True Yoga, and it returns Humanity to its rightful place within the greater Creation. From here we are all in a sacred place to genuinely fulfill our divine destiny as Lights and mirrors, Hearts, Minds, Ears and Eyes of the Creator's own Knowing to Know Itself and All of Reality.

Alchemy and Ascension

In addition to the three basic methods for inter-dimensional travel as stated, death, resurrection and ascension, there is a 4th possible that is a method of Alchemical process that exists outside the traditional Biblical framework, and as such has been looked upon with great criticism by Church organizations and more orthodox institutions, but nonetheless is valid and worthy of mention, as it is likely to become even more important as Humanity proceeds into the new millennium. Within the physical atomic structure of elements there are what are called "pathways" by which particles and elements can pass to move from being a state of one element to another. In ancient traditional Alchemy it has been known for millennia that two such pathways exist by which lead and mercury can transform or move from a state of being lead or mercury into being gold. The purpose of this procedure was not at all merely to make gold; rather it was to find a means by which the lower 3rd dimensional vibrational frequency could be raised to a 4th dimensional frequency and thereby move a person bodily with Consciousness intact from 3rd to 4th dimensional Reality.

This is a process of great value, and as I understand it has been used with a large degree of success over the many centuries of time. Yet because lead and mercury are each highly toxic substances, there has been a great deal of risk with it if all is not carried out with just so precision. More recently it has been learned from some of our galactic star neighbors, perhaps notably the Plieadians, that a pathway also exists from Silicon to Gold, and that this has the added advantage of being safe, as silicon is a non-toxic element found commonly in crystal. [31.] Should this knowledge be made available to us by our Star Cousins, it could very well become an important method for inter-dimensional travel for our future civilization moving forward into the millennium. I would look towards this with great anticipation and excitement.

Basic Review of Ascension and Consciousness

Inter-dimensional movement is a natural and commonly occurring phenomenon of Consciousness. As a single cohesive whole, Consciousness is ever present on all dimensions and universes simultaneously without exception. Consciousness is in fact Existence Itself, and without It, even for an instant, there would be the annihilation of that Existence. There is simply no existence separate from Consciousness, as in "Through That all things that are were made, and apart from That there is no thing that was made." (John 1:2-3)

Yet on an individual or localized level it happens as with our everyday experience that we as Consciousness remain focused on one particular plain where we live our lives and work out the events and situations of the Reality where we find ourselves and our world. This fact and condition does not in any way limit Consciousness Itself or what we are as Consciousness, but rather does provide a focal point for our specific experience as evolving beings exercising our capacity to live life and discover the meaning of Being on a greater variety of levels of Existence. Without this capacity of Consciousness to focus on these localized levels life as we have known it would not exist. Still to lose Awareness of the full gamut of Consciousness to the extent as modern mankind has done so as to feel oneself as separate from all others in a hostile universe is to succumb to a condition of limited Consciousness or limited Awareness that is a kind of spiritual disease.

Furthermore, as an Earthbound Humanity we have come to find ourselves collectively suffering from this disease without any clear understanding of it, and it has come to be regarded as normal, because it is so universal and few if any of us have questioned this state of affairs for so long. It is so problematic that medical science and psychology even to this day will tend to pathologize any such deviation from the accepted norm, so that in many cases truly normal and healthy expansions of Awareness may be misunderstood as mental disorders when in fact a person simply lacks a clear enough understanding either philosophically or scientifically to articulate the experience in ways that are academically or rationally acceptable in our society.

Clearly these are areas that the new Science of Consciousness and Pneumatology can and surely must become integrated with medical and psychological sciences so as to maximize our capacity for healing and understanding to the fullest and happiest unfolding of our human potential. It has been rightly said that no one in a human body knows or understands the full potential of a Human Being. This is largely due to the fact that from within our almost universal spiritual disease it is not possible to see ourselves as we Truly are outside of that distorted pattern of being. Even from a healthy spiritual state it would be necessary to view Humanity from such a high level of Consciousness as to take in the entirety of Creation at a single glance. This would be the kind of Knowing and perception of the Creator Itself, as only from That level of divine Awareness is it possible to appreciate all that we genuinely are as Consciousness and all that this entails.

How many Universal dimensions above ours here are there? So much potential and actualization even beyond our present level and still these very advanced and evolved Beings are continuing on in their states of Self discovery while living out their existences of fulfillment and meaning in an Awareness of the Oneness of All! I find the recognitions of these Truths to be both humbling and gratifying at once. There is no end to our evolutionary movement into fullness and Divine Union, and still we continue to grow even at the Cognition of Creation. The free flow of Consciousness in and as all of Its forms in Existence is the Reality of what Creation Is; it is what makes Life what it is, and it is Life and Truth and the Way of Being that is True.

Being and Existence are One

Taken together there is no difference between Being and Existence. In Western Philosophy over the more recent few centuries it has been given to distinguish by virtue of intellectual prejudice or cultural class distinction that Existence was somehow of lesser value or meaning than Being Itself. The term "meaningless existence" has come to mean a state of affairs which is not seen as particularly valuable or worthwhile to others or society but perhaps just costing resources or money to maintain. Being on the other hand, within circles where It is recognized as valid (i.e. non-agnostic) and therefore meaningful to speak of in Its own right, is more akin to life and living, such as in the term Human Being. Yet in this secular philosophical view there is little or no understanding of Consciousness or Spirit, and these Realities are almost totally lacking in their view of the world. Often Consciousness is mistaken to be simply a state of being conscious, so if a person is in a state of deep sleep or otherwise non-responsive then that person is seen as not having Consciousness. The concept of Being Consciousness is foreign to such philosophic world views, and these philosophic understandings are fundamentally non-spiritual in nature. Put another way, they are lacking in any Real basis in the genuine nature of Reality. In the classical Vedic view such a lack of deeper insight is the very definition of ignorance or the lack of knowledge.

At this point it ought to be clear that without this greater and underlying Cognition of the Reality of Consciousness as everything, the meaningful discussion of Union and Yoga, and of the genuine Nature of Reality would be futile and without purpose. Clearly the discussion of Ascension and the movement of Awareness and form inter-dimensionally is nothing more than a fanciful mystery for dreamers and speculative thinkers until we genuinely See and Know as by direct Cognition. It is my point in this present discussion to establish the imperative need to dismiss these misunderstandings and highly limiting untruths for the conditioned distortions that they are.

Until we transcend the limitations of merely intellectual thinking regards ourselves and Existence, our fear based mentality and reactiveness can not be easily dismissed. Although this goes without saying; it still needs to be said, so long as there remain those who yet do not know or choose to pretend otherwise.

Looking at Reality as One and Consciousness as the All of Existence there is no avoiding the Truth of Oneness, Wholeness, Goodness, Beauty and the Reality of complete integration of Creation as One Spirit Being of which all of us and everything are both the Whole and Its component parts. Yet we live in a world which has reached a point of scientific development where the Reality of Consciousness is Empirically verified as the Ground State or Unified Field and also as Zero Point energy. [32] There is only the lag in popular understanding and education that still remains to question these proven and verified Truths.

Given all the current indications throughout both our natural world, that reveal immanent change to a higher dimensional frequency, and the state of our civilization presently undergoing an overall collapse of institutional functioning, we are clearly on the verge of a collective Ascension. This collective Ascension is at very least on the level of our entire solar system if not far greater. It could easily include this entire galaxy or even the whole of 3rd dimensional Universe. Therefore it is

Shiva C. A. D. Shankaran

with the utmost urgency that the popular mindset come into alignment with the greater Scientific and Pneumatological wisdom of our age and recognize the place of Universal Spirit and Consciousness abounding.

Part VI

CONSCIOUSNESS: THE ONE REALITY

To be Cognitive of Consciousness Itself is the beginning of genuine Wisdom. This is the first transformative insight into the nature of Reality that leads to the door of Cosmic Awareness and Enlightenment. This tender seed of Awakening needs to be nourished and cherished for the gem of Grace and divine Providence that It is. In the spiritual desert that has been the materialistic cultures of our modern world such value has rarely been placed upon these insights, as they had become viewed as useless or dangerous distractions from the ongoing struggle and pursuit of making money and acquiring things for material satisfaction and social status. Needless to say, this must change, as indeed it has been and is continuing to change in our world. But this change over the past five decades or so has met with great resistance and frustration to the point where today the powers that control the actual seats of power in government and finance have brought these

215

important institutions to the edge of collapse in their struggles to hold onto their positions of privilege and power rather than to honestly accept the so desperately needed changes to our social, political and economic structures for the sake of survival as well as for Truth, justice and freedom for Humanity.

The state of lack of Cognitive Awareness of Consciousness as independent and transcendent of any and all object that we might be conscious of is the condition of being asleep as Consciousness, and it is a condition of dire consequence, as we have seen.

Oneness Reviewed

As Holy implies Whole and entire, so too Holy Spirit means the Whole Spirit and Consciousness of Creation including everything and excluding nothing that is. As Biblical Scripture as well as Vedic Scriptures say, God is One, and God is Everything, so too the entirety of Creation Itself is more than solely the Creation of God but Its Essence and Truth and very Body or form in the physical.

It is a pattern in Consciousness that as Awareness becomes more and more narrow and crystallized into matter, the faculties of perception and understanding and knowing gradually loose their abilities to function in higher levels of Awareness, and with this people become more dependent on the outer senses of the mind to gather information and knowledge about the world around them. When Awareness descends fully into matter, becoming so crystallized so as to believe that the physical world is all that can be known with certainty to exist, then the entire process of understanding and knowing becomes so dependent on the senses that even the Mind is ensnared and enslaved by them. In this state of affairs the Empirical process is then alone recognized as the only valid and verifiable means of knowledge or science, and the very Cognitive process by which the original Vedas and Scriptures were made cognizant to humanity of old appears lost to humankind and modern civilization.

This state of affairs is the very present condition in which our contemporary civilization finds itself, so encumbered by the disharmony and distrust of everything and everyone who appears separate and different for any reason; that neighbor rages against neighbor, family members can not see beyond egotistical strivings in their relations to one another, community against community and nations war among themselves and each other to the very edge of extinction of not only our cultures and civilization but life as a whole on this planet as well.

The way out of this dire condition is not more of the same that has lead us to this point. Rather it is through the restoration of the fullness of Consciousness that is our True Natural state from the beginning. As stated earlier, it is not possible to correct a distortion in Consciousness from within the very distorted pattern that is in need of correction. The Way to correct distortions in Consciousness is by Tender Honesty; that is to drop the Awareness out of the distortion and into the Heart where Tender Honesty resides. From this inner quiet place of Truth the distortion can be recognized and seen for what it is, and the Heart can decide to remain True with Its new awareness and the Mind's new understanding. This is the Way out of our present dilemma and the Way back to a True Way of Being in Consciousness and in the world that will be sustainable and harmonious with the frequencies of whatever dimensional Universe we find ourselves in. That will be determined by our collective frequency and by the Will of the Consciousness of Creation Itself, of which we are a dynamic functioning participant. As we are ourselves aspects of the Creation, we obviously can not be separated or distinct from It, and as such the Whole is evolving together as One.

The present almost overwhelming nervousness and anxiety of uncertainty that pervades most of our world is largely due to our uneducated state about the Reality of ourselves as Consciousness and the phase of evolution our planet is presently moving through. I feel that if this were understood broadly by people today there would be great joy and positive anticipation of the coming immanent global changes instead of this prevailing dread of the unknown we now witness in so many places. This is just the sign of our time; that as we return Home collectively we also feel the uncertainty of the sands shifting beneath our feet, and with that the new sensations of living and being on multiple dimensions simultaneously is a bit like standing upon the deck of a small vessel sailing upon rocky seas after being landlocked for a very long time. Yet we are a courageous crew, and our Captain is the All Knowing Cosmic and Whole Consciousness of Creation.

The Experience of Transcendence and Oneness

The experience of Transcendence is first and foremost an experience of Silence and Stillness with a taste of profound and happy Aloneness. This is not to be confused with feelings of loneliness, which is an emotion of a mind that is rebelling against being alone. The Transcendent experience can be either clear or cloudy, completely Silent and distinct from activity of mind and body, or it can be mixed with other mental activity such as thoughts, feelings, emotions and physical activities as well, all going on simultaneously. It is not any activity that makes for Transcendent experience, but rather the direct Awareness of the supreme Silence Itself that is known to stand alone independently of anything manifest at all. This is the direct Cognitive Awareness of the "Unmoved Mover", as it were; it is a direct Cognition into the True Nature of Reality that stands on its own as a valid and vital foundation of all else that can be experienced through the senses, Mind and Heart. It is the direct Cognition into the supreme Self, otherwise known as Atma, in its initial stages, in many aspects of the Veda and expands into Brahman, an 8th state of consciousness, when that Awareness grows to include all of Existence, and is perhaps also the "I Am That I Am" of the Bible.

Up till now this work has been more descriptive and instructive rather than experiential or even descriptive of an experience of the Cognition and Cognitive Process that has been here discussed. Yet the experience that is central to the kind of direct Cognitive Process so vital to this Science of Consciousness must also be discussed and encouraged, so as to enhance the practicality and empowerment of the whole process and insight into the Nature of Consciousness and Spirit. This is what is aimed for in the regular spiritual practice of transcendental deep meditation and what is cultured by the processes of opening of the Heart with the sacred Intention of residing there within as Consciousness.

The importance of this direct experience can not be overstated, for without it the higher Reality of the higher energetic frequencies and dimensions can not be known or lived. Hence there is no substitute or getting around the need for this direct experience of Transcendent Reality or Transcendental Consciousness, as discussed in earlier sections of this book. This experience is simply a necessary part of the process of spiritual Awakening that the new Pneumatology requires for the basic enlivenment of all Humans. This work is here only to help make this Known and available to all peoples of Earth in our time and times to come.

That stated it is time to have a look at how the Human Awareness transcends the relative experience of itself and the world and comes to an unbounded state of Cognition of Its own Being. It is a simple yet vital process that is built into the nature of all of us by the Blessings and divine Mercy of the Creator; that Truth comes to us by Nature and by Goodness.

The Unicorn Story

Ancient spiritual traditions are rich with symbolism regards the Way that Awareness comes into a more whole state or condition of knowing Its True Nature or Being; that is more akin to a remembering or reawakening than what we might think of as learning something for the first time. One such tradition from early Christian mythology that I have always found personally moving is the story of the hunt for the Unicorn. This has been relayed to us by any number of Western researchers, most notably, Carl Jung, who makes specific and powerful references to it in his work, "Psychology and Alchemy". [33] I will make reference to it here more briefly, because of its value as a point of reference in the whole process of knowing and understanding the fullness of this wisdom and how it appears with regularity and great creative diversity throughout many different cultures, times and places in human spiritual teachings and insights.

The Unicorn, the white colored horse like apparition with a single horn emerging from its third eye or center of the forehead has been an allegorical Christ from the earliest memories of this legend. Of all the wild creatures of the natural world the Unicorn is the most illusive and also the greatest prize, for its horn, blood and flesh possess the powers to heal, sanctify and restore to a state of wholeness anyone who can tame it.

Coming out of the ancient and medieval world, the specific symbolism may strike the contemporary reader as hopelessly out of touch with current sentiments, but the Truth of the underlying meanings of the symbols is far too rich and meaningful especially for us today in our present need for this wisdom.

The Unicorn is highly attuned to the states of man and the human condition and is drawn to people who display a state of innocence, sincerity, tenderness within and goodness. In fact, the Unicorn finds these traits irresistible, so much so that It comes out of its forest hiding places to draw near to such a person. We are all maids and virgins in relationship to the Unicorn; that is innocent and pure as conveyed by these symbols. It is innocence and purity that brings the Unicorn out of its hiding to lay down in the lap of the seeker of Truth and Goodness and rest Its head there. This is the captured prize, for the Unicorn brings healing and wholeness to all that It touches and who remain so sweetly with That as to know this as their True Way of Being.

To be sure the medieval stories of the hunt are rife with the blood and slaughter of a real hunt for a wild and illusive beast, yet these elements are all parts of the richness of the symbolism and when looked at properly and in Truth only add to the stories' beauty and power. For purposes of this work here I am only making use of this reference for the point that to capture the Unicorn is to Know God, and that even within this sweet and strange sort of legend the essential principles of how Awareness comes to remember Its own True essence are real and present and can still be powerful for us today.

The Mind as the faculty of understanding rests upon its foundation that is the Heart, which at Its Core always maintains at very least a tiny kernel of Knowing of Truth; that is Its Real essence and Divinity. The Heart is the faculty of Knowing; that once It informs the mind of its sacred Intention to make what it knows to be True its first and highest priority, the greater Heart and Mind begin to follow and align with that which is already Known as True. Hence the tiny kernel of Knowing within the Core of the Heart can now immerge and begin to show Itself to more of the larger areas of Heart and Mind and take up rest or residency within them. This sacred Intention to bring all of what Consciousness is into alignment with whatever little bit is known at the Core to be True is Itself innocence and purity, for it is already in alignment with That. This is the symbolic virgin of the Unicorn story, and in the legend it both serves as bait, as in nourishment, for the Unicorn and also it manifests as the Unicorn Itself, for the Unicorn is the very embodiment of this sacred Innocence and Purity.

The Process of Transcendence

The Vedic interpretations of Maharishi Mahesh Yogi do offer some of the most clear and brilliant understandings of how Awareness moves from gross to subtle along the many strands of Consciousness that constitute our vast network of our Essential Nature, what we are as Consciousness. In it he explains the Mind's own nature to seek out areas of ever greater enjoyment relentlessly. [34] The beauty of this inner Nature is in the Reality that the subtle is always more powerful and of greater joy and energy than the gross or superficial. Now this creates an inner condition that draws Awareness within to ever deeper levels by the Mind's own nature, thereby making the process perfectly natural and effortless when understood and entered into easily and properly. Effort is not a part of this process, only a genuine intention and letting go in a gentle and innocent way is needed, and for the most part only this approach is effective.

This is especially helpful in methods of deep meditation where the effortless and natural are far more efficacious than processes of concentration that require effort to hold the mind steady on a particular focal point, rather than to allow it to gravitate by nature to that which brings greater energy, charm, insight and expanded Awareness of Consciousness Itself. Hence a Truly natural process for the expansion of Awareness is an effortless one in which the greatest joy that is naturally gravitated towards is that inherent Kingdom of Heaven that is within each of us.

It is of vital importance for us to realize here that although the process may be purely natural, it does not follow that anyone will be able to discover it on their own, but rather it must be taught, and this is for two reasons. First, we and our ancestors have been without this knowledge and practice for so many thousands of years that very deep contrary conditioning has set in to our conscious and unconscious minds that actually prejudice us against our own True Nature and even make this process counter-intuitive. And second, relating to the first in fact, we have also lost the knowledge of the true effects of our actions and the influences of everything around us to such an extent that special guidance is necessary to help us navigate through the many levels and experiences of Mind and Heart and Will throughout the process. One example of this is that it is necessary for us to have a sponsor in this process, so that the Awareness can more easily and by Grace transcend the localized awareness and enter into the unbounded Awareness without hindrance. This is where the lineage or tradition of Masters comes in and becomes indispensable. Without these Great Ones as guides who have gone before us and remain within our sphere of Existence to serve and promote our evolutions by their Grace, we would be in dire straights for sure. It is by their Grace and intercession that we return to our Natural state of Being in Truth and goodness of the One. In this we mean and say together as One, "All Glory to the Divine Master", or as it is said in Sanskrit, "Jai Guru Dev."

In addition there are specific manners of transmission by which this precious Grace is passed from Master to disciple over and over again for all generations that are best respected and honored, so that the greatest and most positive results for the student can be obtained and enjoyed. That acknowledged, these are generally aural and not presentable in a book form, but only by direct connection one to the other in the context of teaching, and so are outside the scope of books. It is only necessary to be aware that, all things being equal, when the student is ready the teacher appears. It is the hope of this writer that this book can help to hasten that time in coming.

Inner and Outer Purification

The physical body is totally regulated by Consciousness; although as only partially conscious beings our Consciousness is also influenced by our bodies, what we put into our bodies, eat, drink, levels of exercise, light and dark and also mental and emotional input. What we think, believe and allow ourselves to feel all have profound effects upon our state of Consciousness and degree of Awareness. For fully Conscious Beings the state of Consciousness is not nearly so susceptible to the state of the body, and so such people are far more stable in overall Awareness and purity regards any changeable conditions that the body might be subjected to. This is a far more stable and higher quality of life than is possible for beings in our present state who are not fully Conscious and Aware of themselves as microcosms of the macrocosmic Creation. To be fully Conscious and Aware of True Self is to Know and also experience moment to moment the full meaning and effects of being the offspring of the Holy Spirit, the Consciousness of Creation, and this includes the conscious connection to the full resources and intelligence of that Divine Consciousness. So that the body then, regulated as it is by such a fullness of Consciousness would function to its highest capacity for health, longevity and performance on every level. Such a Heart, Mind and Will would also treat the body and its environment with the utmost respect in order to support that great and highly valued goodness throughout the world and everywhere that Consciousness is known and expressed, which is precisely Everywhere.

In the meantime and on the way to these higher states of Awareness, the body, Heart, Mind and Will all undergo different types and degrees of purification, as this is a necessary aspect of the removal of impediments and blockages to the fullest free flow of Consciousness through its many vehicles of expression and manifestation. In general and for most people when a regular practice of deep meditation allowing for transcendent experience is first begun there is a relatively brief honeymoon period of joyful or blissful experience that serves to ground a person's Awareness in the goodness of what he or she has embarked upon and helps establish a foundation of spiritual intention to persevere through any less comfortable phases of purgation that in time may follow.

When this period of one's highest good karma is used up or completed a new phase of Grace commences that allows for and supports the purification of the inner systems of the outer vehicles of Consciousness and the inner Consciousness Itself; that, depending upon the degree of impurity that a person has begun the process with, can be more or less uncomfortable, painful or lengthy in duration. In the end this is of little significance, and it is important to bear this in mind. What is of supreme value here is the fullness of Consciousness that is realized once the purification process is complete, for this also brings one into a state of timelessness and eternal Awareness that makes any temporary discomfort totally forgettable in the end.

Furthermore, there is a great balancing effect upon the whole of one's outer environment, as this inner clearing and purification takes place, that only increases in effectiveness and power as the inner Awareness grows and fills out to ever higher and fuller degrees. The growing inner purity extends outwards through the surrounding world and Universe and promotes a purifying effect all around, and this cleansing effect only intensifies and strengthens as the inner Consciousness grows. This is by the Nature of Pure Consciousness that this happens and requires no special activity on the part of such a person, only the pure and simple intention to be of positive service and benefit is enough for the Nature to perform its magic and do and be what It is divinely set up for. This effect of purification of the environment is so powerful and effective that it is said by the Masters that just one fully enlightened Human can effortlessly neutralize the negative influences of a million or more non-enlightened people who are still creating negativity and discord by their thoughts and actions. In fact it is nothing other than this purifying effect of the Awakened Beings upon this Earth that has sustained and allowed to progress the human civilizations here through all of the more recent millennia. These can be counted as the last ten to thirteen thousand years of human existence here; prior to that the levels of human Awakening were actually much greater than they have been since, and as such Humankind existed on much higher and more positive platforms of Being, which were self sustaining and spontaneously pure, whole and harmonious.

However this may seem contrary to common wisdom today; it is not contrary to the Truth of our own existence and past development on Earth and elsewhere, and this fact leads us into our next sections here on the origins of Consciousness and our own Human origins at least as regards to the Milky Way Galaxy.

Human Origins in This Galaxy and the Origins of Consciousness

Contemporary genetics has made some amazing and important discoveries that have yet to be made mainstream and public knowledge and which must be brought out into the open for people to fully understand who and what we are as human beings in our Cosmic setting within this Creation. Hence the vital importance of this information both for our universal Awakening and also, unfortunately, for those who might at all cost seek to preserve the status quo of limited Awareness and misery for so many for the sake of the power and privilege that so much ignorance across the world has afforded them for so long. Let us begin with these important discoveries in the fields of genetic research.

It is common knowledge among all the governments of the world today that the Earth and we humans here have been not only visited but also engaged communicatively by intelligent and sentient beings who have traveled here from other parts of this galaxy and also from other galaxies. Virtually all of these beings are from higher dimensional planes or parallel Universes from within this Creation. A few of these I have attempted to identify in earlier segments of this book, but the total number of these beings and their civilizations is far greater, and it is possibly far greater than anyone has been able to count.

It has been reported that of all of the human civilizations that the U.S. government has been able to count there have been in excess of 50 such races they have actually been contacted by. For all we know this number could be increasing even now, yet till now this government has remained incorrigible in its public denial of all of this; still, retired insiders have come forward with their stories and proof to the contrary. [35] In addition other governments around the world have come forward to disclose to their own peoples the Truth of these contacts and some of their implications for us; these governments include but are probably not limited to Brazil, Mexico, India, Russia, New Zealand, and as I've said probably others by now as well.

Among many probable discoveries that may have been recognized from genetic research done on various samples provided by many of these peoples from around the galaxy, it has been discovered that all of these human races including ourselves are related and come from one common and very ancient origin that we all share. It is also clear that we humans here did not evolve into our human state upon this Earth, but actually we came here originally from elsewhere within the galaxy as settlers to colonize this planet and expand the human races to new places where we hadn't been before. These general conclusions can be drawn from at least this much genetic and other information that we have been given by our galactic family and friends.

If all of the diverse human genetics all around this galaxy does Truly come from a single common source, this may serve as an empirical implication too, that all of Consciousness comes from a single Source also. As I have been promoting all along in this book by a Cognitive Process, so too there is here a suggestion that even an empirical proof can be gained by this scientific way of looking at ourselves. Ultimately, only the Cognitive proof essentially matters, but if there can be empirical evidence to offer support for a similar conclusion then this can only help to smooth and hasten our overall shift to the superior paradigm and our new and higher civilization.

As has been established earlier in the field of a Science of Consciousness, the Cognitive proof and experience is always the highest and most reliable verification and ultimately the only acceptable proof of the Truth of any thought, feeling or action. All beliefs or anything that would be believed must be verified Cognitively, as this is the only genuinely honest and sweetly tender approach to our own integrity and genuine Knowing. We are always led back to this Way of Being that Tenderly requires us to verify any new concept, thought or suggestion with That which is already Known as Truth.

In addition, as I've already asserted here, all Consciousness is verified Cognitively by virtue of direct Transcendent experience to originate from a single Divine or Cosmic Source, that heretofore is known as Holy Spirit or the Consciousness of Creation. But by no means take my word for it; take up this practice on a daily basis of deep meditation and cultivate this inner Knowing to greater and greater degrees for yourself. In Truth this is the only Honest and Integrative Way to proceed that will lead each and every One to his and her highest outcome. If I come back to this point repeatedly, it is because it can not be overlooked or avoided and must not be ignored, or to do so would only be to prolong ignorance and misery for all involved, and this is neither what this work is about, nor can any good come of it any longer. The Time for all to Awaken in is Now, and Now is all that is most Real.

One could very well ask, that if all Consciousness limited and Unbounded as we now Know It comes from this One great Source of Creation, that is undoubtedly inseparable from Creation as well, from where does this Holy Spirit in turn come, or what could be Its origins? In deference to Tender Honesty and the need to maintain integrity it is necessary to genuinely keep an open Heart to that question until such a state is arrived at that can genuinely see into that great and powerful Truth. In short the question is simply too big for us to consider or Truly Know from any sort of localized Awareness in our present 3rd dimensional frequency of being. This being the case, an Honest response can only be to continue to ask and seek Truth to greater and greater degrees of Knowing and to move forward in Nature and in Grace towards that Cognition and realization of the greater Reality. We Truly will Know when we are ready to contain such a great degree of Reality within our Awareness and when what we are as Consciousness is expanded enough to embrace It. In the meantime, the Way of Being within the Consciousness that we are remains the same, and the natural process of embracing Truth and letting go of what we come to know as untruth goes on unabated. This is the beauty of the whole process and what makes it so easy in reality and in practice; we get to be just as the Being Is in our relation to It, and that we already Know by pure Nature.

As time and evolution progress, it can only become easier and more joyful for us, and in this there is cause for celebration even now. You have within yourself even now, just as you are right now, the keys to return Home by a simple intention and determination to be genuine, True and Honest to That which is already Known to be True within your very Core and Being. Relative conditions of mind and body can not prevent this, only that trust in the Heart to go Home as is and be perfectly OK in the midst of whatever the relative conditions of the surface bodies presently are in will suffice to turn the attention of the Heart inwards to what It Knows is True and recognize that as Its first Love and highest Good. With this state of being within, nothing relative on the outer world of life can distract or detain you from the Truth you seek. This is how natural and how easy it really is. There is nothing else to do, but to allow the Being and Grace to have you and do what It will with you for the unfolding and restoring of you as Consciousness. Genuine devotion to Truth, to Love, to Goodness and Tenderness will keep you Honest and clean within and without. In This we place our trust, our honor and our fortune.

So Be It, and So Be Us. In gratitude and devotion we accept the Truth as it is revealed to us from within the very Core of our Existence, which is One with All that Is.

The Nature of Distortion and
Evil Within Consciousness

Distortions in Consciousness that seem to take on a life of their own, as they are fed energy that we give them by our mistaken belief in them as real, and what might be called evil, do not constitute a separate being or nature from that Consciousness that is True and clean in its Way and devotion to Tenderness and genuine Reality. Rather these deviations from Reality represent and indicate a condition in 3rd dimensional manifestation that has crystallized itself so deeply into matter and material existence that the energetic frequency needed to sustain this level of manifestation is very low and encumbered. So encumbered is this process at this low end of the frequency ranges, that the manifestation of Being Itself has become vulnerable to potential distortions of disease and untruth. As stated above, the presence of disease, distortion of being and untruth do not represent in any way a separate source or form of being, but in fact indicate a disintegration process by which matter is at such a low vibratory rate that it is beginning to become undone as if disintegrating back into its original formless state of unmanifest and formless Being.

This is expressed as the process of fermentation and decay that is present throughout the natural world as we know it, and is likewise the source of much disease in the plant, animal and human kingdoms. In the mineral kingdom this process is seen at the heaviest end of the table of elements where lead and uranium among others become unstable at the atomic structure becoming radioactive and disintegrate further, as this material collapses into a formless state. On that level of nature these processes serve a necessary function of recycling matter through the low end of energetic frequency so it can be restructured back into a cleaner and healthier form to be reintegrated into the cycle of life and healthy existence once again.

A problem arises, however, when a Human Consciousness witnessing these processes mistakenly misunderstands them for some kind of ultimate end or reality of the Being Itself, and thus allows itself to believe in disintegration of being as the only or else most apparent outcome of Existence. This experience challenges the inner natural Tenderness of a person's Awareness with a sense of needing to harden and tighten up around a refusal to accept what is known to be unnatural in Consciousness yet appears natural to physical form and outwards expression of that inner Consciousness. When you add to that the loss of full Consciousness to our ancestors thirteen thousand years ago, and ongoing manipulations of Earth's Humanity by immoral and violent beings ever since that event, we eventually come to our present condition on Earth where a state of spiritual confusion is regarded as the norm and very few of us can boast of any degree of full Awareness about the True Nature of Reality. We even see today a school of Western secular philosophy that calls itself Existentialism, that defines existence in terms of death and decay. This is a complete misunderstanding of Reality, yet those who staunchly believe in it are often the hardest most ridged in that belief, often taking a perverse joy in spreading discouragement and a fatalistic attitude among others, as this gives them a sense of company in misery.

This kind of focus upon the lowest frequency levels of energy within the entire field of Existence and claiming that that is all that there is of Being is the product of a very low and limited awareness of Reality, and it promotes even the spread of such misery on a yet greater scale. To ask how does this occur, is to inquire into the ways in which evil works in the world, and this inquiry, it turns out, is also crucial to our understanding of our own Nature and that of Creation as well.

The concept of evil is highly misunderstood in our world and culture today. The term itself has even become politically incorrect in more new-age circles, and so it is even more necessary to define it clearly. Yet on account of complexities of our surrounding Universes and our own deep ignorance and confusion on the subject it becomes a challenging topic to discuss. Hence, I will offer a number of definitions beginning with the simpler and leading to the more complex as greater understanding of the topic is gained.

Anything that runs counter to the True Nature of oneself or Reality is problematic, although not necessarily evil on that account. There is a distinction to be made in this regard, as to whether one is acting intentionally upon oneself or upon others. In Consciousness, any distortion of dishonesty or hardness causes difficulties to ones own clear and effortless functioning as a Cosmic Being seeking to express that great intelligence in the world, and as such is not good. As long as such a distortion remains within oneself by intention and is not used in some way to effect another this condition is to be regarded simply as bad or not good. The situation changes when a person or being so harboring such a dishonesty within begins to use that distortion in order to so effect others for the sake of his or her own ends. Once there is an intention present to attempt to cause distortion in others for whatever purpose such as control or influence over them, then that intention and the distortions so used become what can be correctly called evil. This is the first and simplest definition for these discussions I can offer.

In this case distortion is being used to cause actual spiritual, if not also physical and mental harm to others, who otherwise would not so suffer such violence and abuse. To understand this well, we must recognize that distortions of Consciousness when so imposed truly are a form of abuse and violence, and this does need to be acknowledged by any more fully Conscious beings. This recognition is also important, as it offers a first basic introduction to the meaning of the concepts of the ways in which evil works in the world. Without this basic understanding we remain blind to the whole Reality and incapable of even seeing any of it.

Now I know I perhaps risk loosing some readers here, as many today consider the topic of evil obsolete or irrelevant or worse, as some who intellectually identify as "non-dualists" think that evil means duality and reject the notion as dual and therefore non-existent. I am here telling you that this is in fact a misunderstanding and not the case at all, because evil is not a separate being, but rather it is a state or style of being within the overall One Reality, and as such is not separate but simply a kind of distortion of the One. Is this by accidental design; you might ask. I do not believe so; I believe it is a part of the overall divine Will and does in fact serve the evolution of All in the greater Creation. Rather its purpose is in causing a certain effect that could not be gained by some other means. Yet as we shall see, it is still legitimate to call it evil. Let us continue.

According to John de Ruiter, as I understand him, there is immediately above our present frequency another level of existence that is inhabited by beings who have lost their natural Way, [36] and as such can not make conscious connection with their Source to access inspiration and energy. What they have learned with great skill and intelligence, however, is to mine the Earth plain, particularly humanity but not limited to humans, for energy. Over many millennia of time these beings have infiltrated and permeated our level of existence unseen and unheard to our gross senses, and thus they have remained outside of the standard range of perception for us. Over this period of time, they have become highly knowledgeable about human Consciousness, including how we react to all sorts of different stimuli, what makes us happy, sad, angry, grieve and jealous, etc.. This understanding they have used mercilessly and relentlessly to interact and interfere with us on the level of our surface bodies in ways that cause an inner tension and discomfort. In fact they cause a squeezing within our energy fields that is intended to get a negative reaction from us such that our energy is released outwards into the surrounding fields where it is free for them to pick up and absorb. In short, this is one way we are mined for our energy by these beings of limited Consciousness who have no moral or ethical qualms about doing so.

Traditionally these beings are depicted as demonic and the source of corruption and sin in the world. They are credited with inspiring much destruction and harm, such as wars, crimes and atrocities of all sorts throughout the planet and perhaps elsewhere as well. In fact all conflict and disharmony on all levels of human life, social and individual can be attributed to them and their activities.

How this works on an individual level is fairly simple. This race of beings over time has learned to permeate the very energetic fiber of this dimension such that it appears to all of us of limited awareness that this influence is a natural part of ourselves and environment, so that we simply fail to see it, until which time as we begin to see more into the fiber of Reality. When acting within the human surface bodies, such as the mental and emotional bodies these entities cause a squeezing effect that in turn creates an inner tension within those bodies, be it emotional or mental that it then hopes will create from us a negative reaction of being very uncomfortable and resisting that tension in some way. It is enough for us to simply be not all right with being so squeezed upon, even in a subtle way, for us to release energy out of our spheres into the surrounding environment, where it would be scooped up by the entity for itself. This reactive effect has been for a very long time a serious problem for all of humanity, and it is itself a major source of disease and aging that might otherwise be considered normal or to be expected.

There is however another Way of being within this situation that would prevent this serious loss of energy and create an entirely different and positive effect. If an individual could remain centered in his or her own Core and genuine knowing, such as to stay opened and softened within even while being so squeezed upon, then instead of energy being released outwardly and lost to ones self, a different sort of inner Awakening can occur where the energy is released in a way that it remains within the persons sphere, and causes the Consciousness to increase and further expand. There is no energy lost and nothing is given up to the entity that caused the squeezing in the first place. When this occurs a positive Awakening to Truth happens and instead of experiencing a draining of energy the person is more energized and enlivened by the process and a good evolution takes place that otherwise would not. [37]

So long as we are living on the Earth plain, such as it is, there is no way to avoid being so squeezed upon by this other dimension. However, if we maintain ourselves in this Way of Being that is True, than this whole situation of being squeezed in this way becomes our very process to Awakening to Truth, without the negative effects of being drained, diminished and corrupted by this destructive force. The key here is to remain non-reactive to the inner squeezing effect, which is indicated by the almost constant sense of inner tension that is brought to bear upon our conscious awareness and physical being. As stated in earlier parts of this book, this is accomplished by culturing an inner warmth of heart that is unconditional to whatever is being experienced outwardly and within the surface bodies. Of course this is far more easily said that done, yet the actual functions of doing this are contained in the overall process by which Heart, Mind and Will become Awakened, and within that context the whole actualization is effortless and totally easy. Ultimately, the fact of Ascension allows for the whole of Humanity to transcend the dimension of these corrupted beings to a level where they could never reach us again for such purposes, and from there, if it be within the divine Will, we may then be called upon to help uplift them to a spiritually true state, but that would be a holy service that some may accept to take upon themselves at some future juncture of evolution.

Cognition as Awareness and Spirit

In earlier parts of this book, we have discussed the Cognitive Process as paradigm to replace the material and sensory based Empirical Process as the primary and most accepted means of verifying scientific knowledge and Truth. In this section it is here time to look more closely into the fuller implications and meaning of Cognition and how it applies to Consciousness and Awareness as a whole. It is an important distinction to make that for this specialized use of Cognitive Process, we can not limit the term cognitive to mean or refer only to thought and what pertains to thought. As is implied although not specifically stated in our earlier discussions regarding Cognitive Process, Cognition in this context means all Awareness and not simply those involving a thought or thought process. In truth this is what makes the Cognitive Approach to knowledge so powerful. The vast majority of all our Awareness does not take place in the form of thoughts; instead it occurs on much deeper levels beneath the mental or even intuitive functions. These are Awarenesses without thoughts, and are in fact a purer form of Knowing and Cognition than the thinking mind can be relied upon to maintain.

These non-thought Cognitions are by far more powerful and reliable than the thought kind, as they are cognized at deeper levels of the entire process, closer to the Source and place of Truth within, and also because of the deeper Awareness that they themselves reflect, and as such there is little room for doubt to creep into any consideration or review of them.

When looked at in this way, Awareness Itself takes on even greater meaning, and we can begin to have a glimpse at how brilliant this whole process really is, for not only is it intelligent in a mental sense, but it is divine in Its overall scope, meaning and power. I am considering here Awareness as a movement of Spirit, as in the sense of aliveness, breath and effortless flow. In fact Cognition itself is embodied in Spirit, and Spirit also includes all of what Cognition is, for without Spirit nothing Exists nor has Being of any sort. Hence, Cognition is part and parcel to all things related to movements of Consciousness. We need look no further than Awareness Itself to recognize the power, force and effectiveness of Cognitive Process, only we must free ourselves from the limiting belief that the presence of a thought alone qualifies as a Cognition; this in fact is the least powerful and meaningful form of Cognition; the far greater elements of Cognition are actually pre-thought within the overall contexts of the movements of Awareness. This Truth is of vital significance for with it we begin to go to the root of limiting belief systems that need to be uprooted and exposed for the untruthful and problematic factors in human misery that they are. For these unquestioned and deeply held systems of belief stand in the way of all recognition of Truth that lay beyond them, thus doing more to promote limited awareness and prolonging ignorant and untrue beliefs. More is gained from our learning to trust pre-thought Awareness in terms of opening up Awareness and genuine Knowing of greater and greater Truth, than through any thought based system of understanding or learning possibly can. This Truth alone stands in the face of any Empirical approach, and reveals more than any other insight into the really limiting and problematic consequences of any strict adherence to Empirical principles in our approach to knowledge, ourselves and our world. That in spite of all seemingly practical gains of Empiricism over the centuries of modern civilization; it has come at the greatest price to humanity in terms of limiting beliefs, limiting social constructs and even limiting meaningful education, and has ultimately led humankind to the brink of extinction where we find ourselves at this time in our world.

So for purposes of this new Approach, I am using here the term Cognitive Process to refer to the pure movements of Awareness, whether thought is involved in that Awareness or not. Although in the present levels of human Consciousness this understanding of it may not yet be so critical, as we evolve and expand to greater Awareness it will increasingly become a valuable insight, and for this reason I feel a basic recognition now will enhance development through these stages in the not so distant future. Indeed, the more aware we are of these Truths now, the more our growth can be accelerated and enhanced as we move on together as a community, a species and a whole unified life essence sharing a single Cosmic connection as we in Truth do.

More Insights into Oneness

Consciousness is Unbounded. This indicates the Truth that growth in Consciousness is unending and eternal. There is simply no end to Consciousness and as such no end to our own growth, discovery process or evolution as to what we are as Consciousness. Life likewise is eternal, even as it has Its Essential Existence outside of time and space. The relative existence of the crystallized lower dimensions and the material world can not even hold a candle to this Reality, nor can it give anything but the faintest glimmer of an indication into the True Nature of these higher Realities. We are here for other reasons, and for now are meant also to finally awaken to the possibilities of such higher Truths and begin just barely our inquiry into them. For as Above so below, and the shadow world of the Earth plain during these past thirteen millennia does offer its darker indication of the brilliant worlds above it, and the present state of human civilization here offers no way out of its inevitable extinction other than the divinely Cosmic pattern of Ascension we are presently preparing for.

It is Truly an indication of the gloriousness of the supreme intelligence of this Great Consciousness of Creation that the story of this Universe can be found in this pattern of return to our True Home in higher harmonious and genuine Existence in the face of potential extinction as the only other alternative. Why else would Spirit venture so far down into crystallized matter so close to the edge of non-existence amid the actualized experiences of pain and misery and spiritual forgetfulness, but to draw up from these energetic dregs a knowledge first hand of how such low existences might be creatively included into the greater Creative Plan for Existence as a whole. In so doing the lower edges of Existence could also be phased out of existence, so that Creation could be further Unified into the higher more perfected Universes.

This is no mere speculative injunction; it is rather the wisdom of the Masters, who indicate clearly that as the lower worlds serve out their divine purpose they will be Ascended and drawn upwards to higher energetic frequencies, and the lower frequency ranges are to be emptied out and dissolved. We are indeed moving up whole neighborhoods and all! We are One, as there is only One Consciousness, and that Consciousness is all there Really Is. To paraphrase St. Augustine, Consciousness is the only Reality, and we are Real only in as much as we are in alignment with That. [38] It is all right to call Consciousness God, but we must genuinely Know that God is not some other Being separate from who we are but rather our own inner Reality and Essence. As such God is not even separate from our own moment to moment experience of ourselves and daily life. Our own daily life of waking, dreaming and sleeping is God getting to know Itself by our own ordinary experience.

As such it is not even accurate or appropriate to attribute gender to God; the Reality is completely transcendent of gender, and hence calling God He or She is misleading and promotes misunderstanding and an untrue conception of the Reality. Consciousness manifest in a male body may be referred to as He, and also the manifestation of the same Consciousness in a female body may be referred to as She, yet it is within the context of the manifestation only that any actual gender exits. Anyone may identify mentally, emotionally or intellectually as gender in a variety of ways. Still the same genderless Consciousness is simply playing a role in each case, and that role is an outward expression in the surface bodies that does have meaningful impact upon the Heart's experience of Being within Consciousness, yet still is not a part of what defines Its primary Existence as Consciousness but only as mental, emotional and physical bodies.

This being the case Consciousness remains genderless even in the midst of it giving an expression of gender. This is in the same Way that Consciousness remains totally Transcendent even in the midst of all Its expressiveness in all Ways actual and genuine as the entirety of Creation. Consciousness in expression active and manifest and Consciousness outside of expression motionless yet fully enlivened and in need of nothing are both Its states of manifest and Un-manifest Being and Existence.

The Appearance of Separation

All apparent separation is caused by identification with the "I" thought. [39] To identify with any thought at all is to be drawn up out of the Heart and into the mind. Once this occurs the Awareness is pulled out of Love and Tenderness and into a narrow identification with thoughts, feelings and preferences that immediately begins to sever the conscious and energetic connectedness with the greater Awareness of the whole and Consciousness Itself. We then begin to identify with a narrow interest and seek to preserve that interest against all other interests that are then seen as competing against one another in almost all regards. This condition of limited awareness is characterized by self centered attitude, hardness of heart and selfishness, and it is a state of ignorance and sleeping as Consciousness. There is no true union either with others, the Real Self or with the Divine. Only a sense of self-righteousness may prevail over an arrogant defiance of anything that does not support its own pre-established belief systems.

As this happens the "I" thought continues to develop into an increasingly complex form and seeks with greater energy to justify its position within the awareness and make itself necessary to the survival and success of all endeavors of the individual and his or her group. These are the beginnings of distorted patterns within the many strands of Consciousness that first emerge pristine out of the innermost Being as tender shoots of Love, Energy. Life and Sweetness. With the great gift of free will there is now the option to freely choose to allow the Being to move completely through the entire field of Consciousness as Itself, cleanly and without hindrance or simply to try something else, something that might at that moment even appear to be new. In this context the "I" thought makes great promises such as "whatever it is I can do it better," or any of an almost infinite variation of this theme. To a fully Conscious Being, these types of promises are seen through as hollow or as creative suggestions at best, but to an Awareness that is not fully conscious and largely unaware of its own status as Cosmic and powerful, these suggestions carry the capability of great interest and easily entice such a mind and heart to give credence and energy to them. Thus the false self is born vested with energy and belief and emotional power.

As has been explained earlier, patterns of distorted Consciousness require an investment of energy via personal belief in their reality in order for them to form, grow and extend out to greater areas of the Conscious being. As this occurs they grow in Consciousness like a weed or a virus infecting larger and greater areas of the Heart and Mind as well as the Will seeking to extend their new found life within the Consciousness of the being. This life is based upon the untruth that they are somehow separate and different in being from the Source of Consciousness Itself from which the very stuff of their Existence comes. The absurdity of this condition is self evident, yet within that state of limited awareness it appears compelling and equally as obvious. When awareness is centered within a distorted pattern there is simply no seeing beyond or outside of it. And this is how it goes on and on growing into ever more complex webs of interconnected separateness like a cancerous growth that will ultimately kill its host if not corrected and restored to Its pristine straightness and goodness.

Hence, as I once heard John de Ruiter say, "believing something that you do not know is true just might kill you."[40]

It is not necessarily about improper intentions, but more simply could just have to do with a misunderstanding of the Real Nature of Existence and what you are as Consciousness. Any untrue belief only promotes more areas of Consciousness to remain asleep and unaware of themselves as Cosmic and Unbounded, and as such fosters deepening the limitations of Awareness and distorted expressions of That, leading to greater harm to self and others even without a conscious intention to do so. It is simply the limitations of Awareness that are incapable of seeing the full ramifications of actions within the total interrelations of things that disable the Awareness ability to be genuinely sensitive and compassionate to all beings regardless of who, what and where they might be.

It is actually on account of this fact that the restoration of Consciousness to Its genuine and True Natural state is by Grace and this work is therefore effortless, natural and easy, and it requires no special techniques; only the genuine desire to go Home and to be Real together with an open gateway available are really needed. This Reality also attests to the illusory nature of any and all appearances of separateness of existence from Being. Illusion doesn't actually go anywhere when it is recognized; rather it merely dissolves and is gone but for a brief memory and is replaced by the restored vision of a clean and tender Reality that has also truly always been there just behind the illusion.

The Gate, the Gateway and the Gatekeeper (John 10:1-9)

When we speak of the Gate, we are speaking of the genuine pathway from relative existence into That which is of the Absolute Being-ness within. At the Core of the Heart, or the center of the Tiny Secret Space of the Heart there exists a condition even to this day of unconditional tender honesty and love that is always and forever being just as the innermost Being Is. This is the first fruit, if you will, the very first and pristine expression of innermost Being as Consciousness, that is yet outside of time and space and forms a perfect match for what the Being forever Is. As they match so precisely, there is effortless flow in and out through Consciousness of energy, intelligence, goodness and Truth between the Innermost and relative expression of the Being.

This condition of Tender Honesty, of clarity and straightness of Consciousness at the very Core of the Heart is the Gateway that allows that Consciousness that is being just as the Being naturally Is, to pass in and out of the Innermost to the relative expressiveness of the outermost and back within again freely at will without restrictions or limitations or judgment of any kind, easily, without effort or even a thought. It is the same Tender Honesty that allows Awareness to pass between dimensions and dimensional Awareness also without effort. The Gateway is that condition of Awareness that so closely matches what the Being naturally Is, that no distinction or difference can be made between them; they are being One as Essence and Being, and so they can no longer even be distinguished apart. That is the condition of being Truth as Consciousness.

A Gate is someone who is embodying That Truth fully enough to allow others to see into the Truth, so that they too can have some degree of access to That themselves. Nature is a Gate, as it is always being natural and true to itself and what it genuinely is. This is what is referred to as the "Book of Nature"; that we can read and learn from the Book of Nature as a teacher, because it embodies the Consciousness that it contains within itself so Truly and naturally and never seeks to hide an untruth or lie. Yet this occurs in nature, as it possesses no contrary ability to do otherwise, and such is capable of being nothing other than itself. Therefore, as vast as nature is, its Consciousness is still not the fullest that can be, nor is it as unbounded as that of a Master, who possesses the Grace of freedom and free will to know the Truth by choice and not merely by compulsion. Hence the Master who can see and speak and communicate freely whatever is needed to convey the Reality to those who seek That is a greater Gate than nature, and beyond that there are many levels of Mastery that distinguish among Masters, as some are still greater than others. This is not by way of competition by any means, but it is simply by way of recognition and realization for both Master and Seeker.

There are forever varying degrees of Awakening of Heart and Mind and Will, and the growth of Consciousness goes on eternally without end. Only once the ego mind is given up for good there cease to be competition, and love and cooperation and mutually shared goodness and knowledge stand to replace forever the negative tendencies of the ego mind. With this in mind we realize that the Great Ones of Heaven are in no way in competition as our darker worldly traditions might have us believe they are. Rather the mutual and unconditional Love of the divine rules the Heart and all else follows that blissful and blessed lead. The Constitution of the Cosmos is far beyond and greater than any laws and imaginings of man.

The Gatekeeper is that high Master especially appointed by the Divine Consciousness to hold that Tender position as Keeper of the Truth. It is more a function inherent within Truth Itself within that level of Consciousness whereby only Truth can enter. It is like the Ritambhara prajna (Yoga-Sutra 1.48.) of the Veda; that level of purity of Heart that knows instantly Truth from untruth even without thought or judgment. It is simply That which Knows Its own Nature so well, that It recognizes that instantly whenever and wherever It might encounter It in any way shape or form.

Differences of Intellect and Mind

In all cultures on Earth, throughout our recent history of limited Consciousness and Awareness as a darkened Humanity, we find ongoing without exception a strong and tenacious tendency to cling to our own relative understanding even in the face of what might otherwise be clear differences of surface thinking and linguistic expressions, often without anyone caring or seeking to look deeper into the philosophical or metaphysical background of each culture to more fully and truly understand the genuine meanings that are actually intended by each. This type of superficial clinging to belief systems, often while paying little attention to deeper meanings contained therein, has been used over the millennia to justify countless atrocities against our fellow human beings in the forms of wars, genocides, persecutions, bigotries and the like, even to the point of near global annihilation. Clearly these types of behaviors can not be conducted nor endorsed from the level of Cosmic Awareness that this Science of Consciousness and Pneumatology have to offer each individual and Humanity as a whole.

All such belief systems form the spiritual and psychological prison bars that we encage ourselves within, often out of fear of whatever might be existing outside those bars. In short people often become afraid of anything or any ideas that do not fit inside their system of choice, for they indicate to them that their system, into which they have vested their entire identity, may not be as complete or totally accurate as they have decided it must be for them.

As such I must recognize that even this volume, which is not at all intended to be offered nor received as a belief system, could be interpreted as one by anyone who is still living within his or her intellect or mental thinking capacity. The very message of this Pneumatology is one of Transcendence of surface bodies, of identifications with the body, ones family and ethnic group and heritage, with anything at all to do with relative existence even. In the words of Teihard de Chardin, we are here as Consciousness, Spiritual beings having a human experience. [41] It is not that belonging to such groups in the relative scheme of things is bad, but when they are believed in so fully in any kind of an ultimate sense they become our prison walls in that they block the free flow of our own True Nature as Consciousness to be Cognizant and consciously Aware of our True Cosmic status. This is just the basic and very tangible consequence of belief in anything that is not consistent with our True Natural Self and hence untrue or out of alignment with our Innermost Being. As is stated in biblical scripture, "a house divided upon itself cannot stand." (Mark 3:25) So it is with the house of Consciousness that we, each one of us, is.

As is typical with distorted patterns, they are conceived in deception. Whereas they may openly state their objective as one thing, their actual effect is most often the exact opposite, and so it is with belief systems that claim to exist to promote connections with like minded people, yet for the price paid for that smaller connection is a disconnection from the far greater Cosmic whole. It begins with the acceptance of labels, and it continues to the complete identification with that label and the group it represents to the exclusion of all else that does not agree or conform to it. Now there is a division of us and them; now we are stuck with choosing sides in a superficial conflict of words and ideas that are more about expressions and styles of life and work and have nothing to do with genuine substance or the deeper more True matters of Existence and Consciousness that are in Truth common to us all.

What the old metaphysicians called "accidentals" are not worth fighting over. One can wear blue and another grey; we can each speak a myriad of different languages, and still Know in our Hearts, Minds and Wills that we are forever One Consciousness sharing a common Existence outside of time, space and causality. The colors of skin are of no greater or deeper meaning than the color of clothes; the many languages of different religions, as beautiful as each may be, are to be enjoyed individually for what they are and express in themselves and never are meant to be set apart and against one another for some superficial and misguided ego driven agenda.

Cognitive Process in Light of Unity and Oneness

The direct realization of Unified Awareness as the genuine Reality of all Creation, such as described here as the Cognition of the Consciousness of Creation as One and whole and the entirety of All That Exists and has Being is Itself a Transcendent Reality that is both beyond thought, feeling, emotion, intuition and form of any kind. This direct realization of Oneness as Reality has an ultimate and absolute impact upon the meaning of Knowing and is therefore of utmost importance to the Cognitive Way and Process; such that all lesser forms of knowing become obsolete, unnecessary and by far inferior. The Empirical Process is but a mere shadow in a dimly lit world of confusion and uncertainty with little hope of knowing anything whatever by comparison. This is not some vague speculation; it is really more like a comparison of the forms and Consciousness of an earthworm and a whale. Even this distinction may not be great enough to suggest the very great differences between what has been the ordinary or average conscious Awareness of men and women of our recent past ages and the Unbounded Awareness that we move into when we actually become ourselves as Consciousness fully awake and alive to the Reality of ourselves, Existence and the Innermost Being in Tenderness and Honesty and fearless commitment to what we Know to be Truth.

What Oneness tells us, among many others, is that the Knower and the Known are also One. The Cognition gained by direct Awareness in what we already are as Consciousness is none other than an aspect or perspective upon our Real Self and not anything hitherto imagined as separate or in any way different from that Divine Self. How else could it be when there is nothing else apart from that? It also needs to be understood that it is one thing to simply say and read this upon a printed page; it is however a totally new Reality for us to have that direct experience in a timeless transcendent moment that Knows and experiences directly for Itself, by Itself and of Itself. Certainly this occurs by Grace, and still there is no separation, as Martin Buber put it, between I and Thou. [42]

In this realization the free flow of Love becomes like a tsunami in Its movement through and between all beings. Such a person experiences others as aspects of him or her Self merely in other forms that are themselves illusory. It is the Consciousness that matters in that it is Consciousness that determines and defines the Reality. This is not a new reality, because it is how Life itself exists in all times and places, but actually the experience is new for us just newly Awakened to it. This tsunami of Love is the Life blood of the Cosmos flowing through the arteries of Creation being and doing Life everywhere. So for us in this context it becomes a new living Reality, one that redefines for us our Way of Being in a new and yet for us familiar world to engage with and explore. Likewise we get to genuinely live out the two ultimate commandments of the Christ, to Love God, the One Reality, with our whole and entire Being, for there is likewise nothing that is not That, and also to Love All as Self and God, for again there is Truly nothing that is not That.

The Divine Joy of it, the pure Bliss of all of it is simply unspeakable. It is the realization of an interaction with the One True Self in all forms and aspects of the One Consciousness, and All in the context of ever new and beautiful discovery, ongoing and without end. In this higher state of Consciousness ascension becomes easy; we rise like a helium balloon to the stratosphere of Creation and Universes for all weights and burdens are removed from the Reality of Love that flows so effortlessly and naturally through the Unboundedness of infinite Awareness.

That which is Known directly is Known by and through the True Self, and as such the whole of Creation both conspires to make everything known and stands in affirmation of that so Cognized for the good and edification of all of Life, out of Love, Tenderness and Goodness alone. By this Way there is nothing excluded or left out; this tsunami flow of Love sweeps up All as it moves leaving nothing behind and "no stone unturned". It is a lovely expression of the Love and Light and Touch of Creation getting into every corner and particle of Creation to the exclusion of not the tiniest particle of Being and Creation anywhere.

Love as Unifier of Creation in Consciousness

In the Vedic Literature the term Soma is used on both an individual and Cosmic level. On the individual level it refers to what Maharishi calls "the product of perfect digestion," [43] so that when physiology is functioning in total balance digestion is producing everything the body requires to maintain a state of perfect health. Thus Soma holds the body together in balance, health and at a level of very high functioning. On a Cosmic level, Soma serves a very similar purpose supporting the highest levels of functioning and keeping the Universes in balance and harmony within themselves and relative to each as necessary for the perfect health of the Being of Creation as a whole. This function serves the highest good of all parts and aspects within that Creation including ourselves and the Universe we find our existence in and know.

Within the Human Consciousness as well, Soma allows for this free flow of energy that promotes perfect harmony and functioning among all aspects of the surface bodies and higher faculties of Heart, Mind and Will. In so doing Soma provides for the opening of the Heart and Its fullest expansion and Awakening, which in turn leads to all other expansion and inner opening. From the Vedic point of view, this free flow of Soma is experienced within Consciousness as Love, that is That which enables Awareness to transcend all limitations of thought, space and time and to bring into manifestation the fullest and most complete Will of the Creator. It is Love as this

Way of Being that can be known as unconditional Tenderness amid all conditions of existence, that keeps all of Creation consistent with Its True Nature and maintains us also in the Way of Truth that is so central and indispensable to our own Awakening, evolution and Ascension.

There is a fascinating relationship between Love and Awareness, for they mutually feed and nourish one another. As Awareness of Truth grows it draws us unto greater Love for all that is Known, and likewise as Love grows it so invites greater Awakening and Awareness out of the pure joy of the Reality coming more fully into Awareness. It is the win - win of Creation; that leads ever onwards toward greater fulfillment of True destiny and divine purpose. This is so much of the profound joy of Cosmic Awareness and full Awakening of Consciousness. It is in my humble opinion the ultimate motive of Creation Itself; that so much Real joy can not be contained without giving birth to such a huge and powerful expression of Life that Transcends all boundaries and is far more diverse and vast than the conscious thinking mind can ever begin to comprehend.

Thus it is this ever expanding Love as unconditional Tenderness and purity of Heart that first allows for the Heart's great Awakening and in the same action draws all Awareness into the Devotion to Truth and divine Awareness of Oneness of all Reality. This event allows for both an Awakening to an already ever present Reality, and also it really is creating a new Reality at the same time. This new Reality is in the Consciousness of the now fully enlivened human who knows clearly now the merging into Oneness of All Existence and Consciousness. It is as if God, Itself were reborn anew each time another human being Awakens to Reality, and this is in Truth an aspect to the Reality of what is actually occurring as this new Awakening happens.

The fulfillment of Creation that occurs in the fullest Awakening of the Human Consciousness is such an edification to the whole of Being that even the greatness of God is thus increased. The individual Consciousness realizes Itself as immortal, eternal and unbounded, and in this realization adds Its own immensity to the already eternally existing immensity of the whole Consciousness of Creation. In that moment suddenly this appears to be the ever ongoing process and purpose of all creative function and the very nature of Creation, recreating this divine Being endlessly and from what appears also to have had no beginning. It is both childlike and fully mature; it contains easily within itself the entire range of active and potential being in a single realized and Awakened Consciousness with which to touch and engage all of Creation.

Truth as God

Mahatma Gandhi was a great proponent of Truth. He is quoted as saying, "Many people, especially ignorant people, want to punish you for speaking the truth, for being correct, for being you. Never apologize for being correct or for being years ahead of your time. If you're right and you know it, speak your mind. Even if you are a minority of one, the truth is still the truth." [44]

There are philosophical systems that propound an Absolute Truth and also claim to know It. Other philosophies say no, there are only relative truths. Still others will deny any so called truth at all, saying that relative truths do not qualify as such, that because what is truth for one is not true for another there can be no Truth at all. I am here to tell you that all such belief systems are mistaken and full of problems. They are as stated earlier spiritual prison bars meant by a diabolical intention to entrap us within the confines of our limited minds and mental awareness, so that if it were possible, we might never awaken as Consciousness to Reality and unbounded Awareness.

We must always remember that whatever we believe in we give the power of our unlimited Consciousness to, and in so doing we actually enslave ourselves to that belief or the system to which we attach ourselves. Also there is a fundamental dishonesty to allowing yourself to believe anything at all that you do not actually and genuinely Know to be True. This is the act of believing in a lie, and it is the birthplace of distortions within Consciousness that carry the ultimate price of spiritual amnesia, unconsciousness and ill health on all levels, not only physical but mental and spiritual as well.

In light of this we recognize the meaning of Honesty of Consciousness that goes right to the Core of a persons Being and extends out from there into all aspects of what he and she is as Consciousness to allow for the fullest expression in Tenderness and Openness of all that the person is as Consciousness. In this state you realize there is room for all kinds of differences on the mental and intellectual levels, and that these will certainly make possible a great many variations and styles of expression and ways of looking at Reality, even when seen by any number of people all of whom are being Honest and Awake as Consciousness.

One of the many problems with dishonesty is that it cuts us off from the deepest levels of our own Cognitive Process and makes it impossible for us to access that level through which Reality and Truth can be realized. In short dishonesty is ignorance; whereas Honesty of Consciousness gives us direct access to that deeper Awareness that can actually access our genuine Knowing within. In religious terms Honesty of Consciousness is a state of Grace, and dishonesty causes a barrier to Grace. Dishonesty is thus sinful in its effects upon Consciousness. We do not need to make a big deal of this, nor is it good to create a guilt trip around it; only it is important to make a note of it and then to keep that in perspective. We do need to realize the True implications of what we are being as Consciousness in order to fully Awaken to Truth and then to become One with That, and this point is critical to the Awakening Process and to our overall health as well.

Hence, when we speak of Truth, we must Know that what we are talking about is not meant to be a relative or personal thing that we can own or reshape or possess in some way. That which is True is not dependent upon you or me or anyone else; that which is True is independent of all beings, places, times and conditions of mind, body or heart. When we speak of Truth, that which is worth Awakening to, we are speaking of That which is beyond the relative Universes of this Creation and in fact the Author of them. It is accurate to Know Truth as that to which all Existences belong and not the other way around.

The clear implications of this is that it is we who belong to Truth, and not that Truth belongs to us. When we say, "my truth" we are referring to that which we need or want to be true for our own agendas or personal reasons. While it may be important to acknowledge these, it is even more important to know that these are not the Real Truth, which is universal for all and not in any way dependent upon personal wants and needs. The distinction to be made here is not mental or emotional, but it is deeper down at the Core level of the Heart, which has no wants and needs but only Knows what Is and what is Truth. To live for wants and needs, to live for your own truth is to live in the surface bodies, the mental, emotional, volitional or even the intuition. So doing keeps you out of the Real Heart that genuinely knows, and in so doing binds you to these thoughts and feelings without a genuine Tenderness of Heart. This also is not the Honesty of Consciousness of which I speak.

Genuine Honesty of Consciousness is rooted at the Core of the Heart, deeper than any surface body and at the base of individual Consciousness Itself. It is a commitment to the Real impersonal Truth, that is the Heart's first Love and Devotion. Such profound Honesty roots out all personal agendas and will not allow them to stand in the face of what is genuinely known as True. There are no stories here, no drama and no using others or even what is known as True to get anything at all. You will not seek to distort another being for the sake of getting them to do or give you what you want or think you need. You will not seek to take energy from others either for a personal gain that in any way harms them or leaves them diminished. There is only the Tender and Honest response to what is genuinely known as Truth in each situation and moment for as long as we are awake, aware and active as Consciousness in the context of this world.

Part VII

CONCLUSIONS

How to Live in a World Truly and Cleanly

Tenderness speaks for Itself; Honesty speaks for Itself; total devotional commitment to Truth as first Love as well speaks for Itself. To Be in the Way of Being that is True is the greatest state of being a human being can aspire to in this life. This inner weakness of Being within is Real strength without in the world. The weaker and more Tender we are willing to be within, the greater our genuine strength in the world. Although this may appear as a paradox to the intellect; it is also a genuine Truth that the Heart being pure and clean within actually knows. [46]

It is no small thing for anyone living in this world as it has been for thirteen thousand years to learn how to Honestly live and be at Home here in the midst of all the spiritual confusion and pollution that we encounter on a daily and moment to moment basis. These conflicts can not be avoided, yet they need not be allowed to distort what we are being within ourselves, nor need they be allowed to make us sick or miserable with ourselves our relationships nor anything else for that matter. This does not mean there would be no pain nor displeasure; that is another matter which we will come to soon, but it does mean we cannot be made against our own will to take these pressures in such a way as to turn us into something that we are not. Dishonesty is not an option for the Truth, nor is it an option for us if we truly Be and remain in Truth no matter what.

The Way of Truth

In the First Part of this book the question was asked as to where are we regards our present only partially conscious state within this greater Cognition of Divine Consciousness into which we are continuously growing. Now we can have another look at this Way of Being that is True, that so matches what this Cosmic Being Is and see just how even in a less than fully conscious state we still can Be within our innermost Core as this Being so naturally is, that It can then move through us so freely and thoroughly that for us Consciousness is raised to a level where It can begin to gain greater direct insights into the Cosmic Being Itself, thus growing and sharing in the realization of Yoga and direct Union with That One and Whole Consciousness of Creation.

We have already touched upon many of the basic qualities of this Way of Truth, such as unconditional Tenderness, Honesty of Heart, willingness to accept any Cognition of what is genuinely known to be True and to let go of any and all of our cherished notions as they are revealed as untrue. This process of letting go of newly recognized untruths is one of inwardly dying to untruth and the ego, and is akin to a kind of Fire of Truth burning through whatever can be burned within, as a flame of True Self that burns up the non-self as it moves through Consciousness purifying all there that is not clean, honest or is in any way distorted.

This process within may feel more or less comfortable or dis-comfortable depending upon our attitude, understanding and degree of willingness to accept and give ourselves into the process. Also the depth at which Consciousness is being purged is a factor how we experience the relative effects of it. For our own part, we do nothing actively within this process at all except to Tenderly allow it out of a pure love for what we do know to be True. This inner Willingness to be Real within itself begins the natural process by the Grace of what Consciousness Itself Is, and as it progresses Willingness turns into Devotion to the Truth, which in turn gradually leads into Oneness of Being. [46] Grace and the Nature of Consciousness Itself are the only Real driving factors in this totally natural process. Our part is to simply recognize and become Cognizant of what little we do Know to be True and then to give ourselves over to That for love and goodness. As beings of free will, we have the power to stop this process at any time by simply saying no to it, or to allow it to continue with ongoing trust and acceptance of what we know.

These basic principles form the foundational essentials of the Way. There is much more to it, and far more that can be said in specific terms to specific questions and experiences, but here I am drawing a broad picture with an eye to begin this discussion.

Grace and Karma in Unity

For at least two thousand years in the West there has been an ongoing argument among philosophers and theologians of what is regarded as the problem of Grace and Merit. Early Christian sects were divided greatly over this issue on theoretical terms that colored the very Cosmology of the age. It grew to a head with the debates between the bishops Augustine and Pelagius that ended in a most unfortunate divide between the two camps that; although it has softened somewhat has not been resolved truly even to this day. I feel the time has come to put this issue to rest once and for all with a more complete recognition of the Truth and how Reality is actually experienced, manifest and brought to fulfillment in Consciousness and therefore in Creation.

Since the introduction in the West of non-Christian religions of Asia in the earlier and mid 20th Century the Sanskrit term Karma has become more familiar and better understood, and serves as a more complete stand in for the term Merit, which I think is too limited relatively to do justice to this broader understanding and concept of the ways of all action as they intercept and interrelate to the fullest meanings of Grace overall. I would like to present here the simple Cognition for consideration that in Reality these two are so interwoven and concurrent that they Truly can not be separated in any Real sense, and that to do so is purely intellectual and mental, as in a play on words that has long been confusing the issue to the detriment of us all.

Grace, of course, is classically defined as a gift freely given, which is neither earned nor is it deserved. Karma as interpreted from the Sanskrit and Vedic philosophy primarily means Action as relative to Creation. As in the Karma Mimamsa system of Hindu philosophy, Karma is not only individual but is also Cosmic, and thus it includes the very Action of Creation Itself. In this regards everything that Creation does is also Karma, but on the greatest of Cosmic levels. Hence, in this perspective the Actions of the Creator are also Grace as well as Karma. The Act of the Giver of Grace to offer freely Its divine Gifts is thus an Action making it also Karma; the Act of the receiver of this same Grace accepting It as an Act of Willingness and Openness to that Truth must also be a Karma, just as it is a Grace to be so Open and Able to receive. On this level of pure Act there can be no distinction between these apparently two functions of Being, as in the Coincidence of Opposites of St. Nicolas of Cusa and the Reality of Being Itself upon that Transcendent level.

We humans in our minds can make a division of everything, as we have done in every conceivable way during these millennia of darkness, yet it truly is time to be done with it now, and to fully drop into our Hearts, which Know and can resolve these arguments of words and distinctions that have meaning only in the mind that has separated itself from its Heart Core and thus claims to know something on its own without any real basis in genuine Knowing.

How are we to distinguish between the Actions of God and man? The implications of the Oneness of Consciousness must also be carried to this field of Action and recognized as having Its place within the Cosmic scheme of Creation for the good and well being of all. It is not rocket science when you think of it, but I'd add that it does make rocket science possible, as it makes all things possible. It is simply the Truth of what Is.

I do not state this Cognition in this way to make light of the great minds that have debated and fought over these concepts for so long; only I present this as an invitation to any and all who genuinely seek to know the Truth to look into this consciously themselves and see what is there to be seen. As with the Real acceptance of any Grace you must remain truly open to that Grace to actually receive it whenever it is Actually given. That is your part of the Grace and your part of the Action. It is Consciousness being conscious on both ends, so to say.

It is no longer possible for us to remain asleep as Consciousness and expect a higher Consciousness to do everything, while we doze and do nothing; a real spiritual maturity requires us to at the least be Awake to ourselves as Consciousness and to genuinely seek to match that greater Consciousness that is so dearly trusted to run the whole Creation with our Way of Being within. This is not beyond us; it is Truly within our potential as Human Consciousness to be so responsible and Actualized in this metaphysical sense; that we can become active participants in our own Being and in our own part within the greater Cosmos.

This is the Reality of Grace and Karma as One, as I believe it to look like in Realization. As we grow in Union and Yoga with the Divine, we grow also in the recognition of the fullness of these Blessings. As Human Beings act consciously our actions become more and more in alignment with the full Goodness and Grace of the Consciousness of Creation, and this makes our Actions Grace, and Grace becomes the Actualization of Creation. There can be no longer any division between the Creation's Act, Its Grace and our Act and our Grace. Unity is Unity; Oneness is Oneness. There is no longer any exception nor exclusion.

The Christ The Buddha and God Talk

Contemporary Christians most often seem obsessed with God talk; they talk and talk about God, and fair enough the tradition clearly states that "God is the only Reality..." [45] Some Western students of Buddhism I have found are fond of quoting the Buddha as saying, "We do not need to talk about God." I find this expression fascinating. What a blessed time and place we live in this world today, where these two teachings would come face to face in front of us to reconcile into One Truth that gives meaning and power to both.

Throughout this look at our new Pneumatology, this Science of Consciousness, we have been focused here upon Consciousness as the One Reality. The Consciousness of Creation therefore as Holy Spirit is God as That. In this Christian context it is simply not possible to not talk about That, because of the Nature of the Reality of It. We certainly do not have to use the word God; It can be called by so many other names; although in the highest sense, as in Vedic and Biblical scripture as well, That Reality is also known as "The Nameless One," as all verbal names that can be given That fall short of Its greatness and majestic Being. Words after all are only words, vibratory entities that actually reflect in some aspects the actual vibratory qualities of that which they are intended to depict or name. Hence, ultimately all words point back to That Source of language Itself, which is also the Source of everything that can be so indicated by language in actualization and in potentiality. Recognizing this can allow those who adhere to the traditions of Christ to relax more into the talk without getting hung up on and need to use specific words in describing That. One particular obsession that comes to mind is the habitual reference to God in the masculine gender, when the Reality can be no such thing. That which is Transcendent is likewise Transcendent of gender, and so no such label can truly apply, yet traditions persist in forcing this masculine image of God upon Humanity as if it were the Truth, which it clearly is not. In this volume about Consciousness as Spirit, I plainly avoid all such use of these references of God as He and Him, for this important reason. It Truly is not a mere matter of semantics; rather it is vital to free our inner Consciousness of the many misconceptions that these misguided references impose upon our deeper Cognitive process that distort what we are as Consciousness and our perception of ourselves and our worlds.

There is much more that can be said about this in its proper context, but here I am limiting my discussion to the broader topic of God talk relative Christian and Buddhist understandings of the topic and speaking from my own more Christian orientation.

How are we to interpret this statement attributed to the Buddha that, "We do not need to talk about God"? I would suggest considering its many implications through this process and seeing all in context of the fullness of Consciousness, which is the way all scripture is to be interpreted in the Truest sense, anyhow.

First we recognize as always we are dealing with imperfect translations of ancient texts, and again this is all the more reason indicating the necessity to pass all such statements through our deepest inner Knowing before attempting any interpretation. The Consciousness that we are is in need of nothing, and this Truth is first and foremost to be recognized and honored

Cognizant of the Reality that Truth can not be genuinely and
honestly approached from a position of need; therefore we
are not to speak about God out of need or neediness, and are
admitted to speak of God and Truth and Consciousness best
from within our own Knowingness and the genuine Honesty
of Tender Straightness that brings us into alignment with that
Knowingness, and from here we can speak or not, and if we
speak we are at least doing so out of Truth and Real integrity.

So often in our modern times when people talk about God
it really is done out of a sense of necessity, that somehow so
doing makes them a good something or other, whether that
be Christian or anything else we'd care to identify with, and
without that talk we would not be living up to that identification
and belief system which we are buying into. These are the
problems and barriers we set up for ourselves against any
Real Knowing. Once we have accepted the belief system we
also set up the requirements of acceptable talk according to
the preconceived notion of the belief, which is not based in
any real knowing of our own. Such talk then, based upon
belief without a genuine depth of Knowing is fundamentally
dishonest; even if what is said is actually True, for the person
speaking it is out of integrity. Hence in this fashion we are best
to not talk about God, but rather it is important to Cognize first
and then speak when it is True to do so. That is not needing
to speak about God. It is really letting God speak for Itself as
and when It Will, as in using yourself as the mouthpiece and
form in context of surface expression. In the words of Lao Tzu
from *Tao Te Ching*, "Those who know do not speak; those who
speak do not know." The True Way is to allow Knowing Itself

278

to speak, as It does in Tenderness without interest in personal gain or agenda. For the Knowing Itself does have a Love of being Known that is itself interwoven with the Essence of Life and Being-ness.

Truth is Independent and Without Ownership

As has been stated earlier, no one owns the Truth, but rather it is Truth that owns you. So long as anyone is holding onto ego there is a tendency to want to own or feel entitled to be owners of what we know or hold as true. This is just what ego does by its nature. It is a thief by nature by assuming that it owns whatever it identifies itself with. [46]

No one, however, owns Truth, as Its existence is independent of anything we may think, feel or know about what It Is. That said, we must be free to speak of what That is, as it becomes True and important for us to do so both in context of our own growth and of those around us. This is not speaking out of need, but out of Willingness to be of service and Love for Truth. Consciousness is whole and complete onto Itself and in need of nothing, yet It is made manifest as Creation. What then is Its purpose; what is It trying to achieve by this ultimate Expression of Being and Unbounded-ness made perceptible unto Itself as all living and conscious things?

There is an inherent tightness, clinging and grasping with any ego identification that tends to squeeze upon whatever it is wanting or needing for whatever reason. Consciousness that is being straight, honest and clean, being True to Its nature does not do this. Such a clean Consciousness simply rests in Its knowing of the Truth with an open hand. What is true to remain will remain; what does not belong there will float away of its nature and can not truly be held onto regardless. Nothing stolen nothing lost.

Likewise in speaking about Truth it also does not belong to us. The Truth I am explaining here is not my truth; rather while the specific expression given it here may be my expression, the Truth spoken of belongs to no one but Consciousness Itself. Thus we all can speak about the Truth as we experience and Know That, but we can not truly put our name on it. It does not belong to any of us; it is we, each one of us, who belong to It. We each have a name in our identified state, yet Truth is the Nameless One, and outside of that context, we have no meaning or connection to That. Recognizing that we see once again how humility is home. The Mind is humbled before the Heart, and the Heart is humbled before Truth its first Love and highest Good.

Relationship in Truth

When the Heart is Awakened there is a natural pull of Being towards relationships. This unique kind of pull is not born of wants and needs but rather it is born of the innermost Being's own innate tendency to express Its Essence in a fuller flowering of manifestation. Hence the relationships that evolve from this kind of pull tend to be based upon Truth and a True Way of Being within, without the more common tendency to use the relationship to get something that is otherwise wanted or needed for some mental, emotional or physical reason. [46]

When this is the case that relationship is based in Truth, it takes on a very different meaning and color than relationships based on other aspects of surface body conditions and personality. There is a deeper spiritual connection that is shared where all involved come together in a common place within the Being Itself; this is a common centering that is shared and offered freely between participants to the extent that all are Awake as Consciousness and so able to be aware of this connectedness. In such cases the relationship itself becomes an arena for Truth to reflect back and forth between partners and serves the important role to accelerate the growth and Self discovery of all involved. It is a great service that each partner does for the others while also being advanced in the same way themselves.

So how does this type of Truth relationship develop and who can participate in it? First off, relationships of a True and deep nature are only for those who are already Home and Awakened inside as Consciousness. That is the most basic prerequisite of all; a Heart that is asleep is not capable of seeing itself or another in anything other than a dreaming and groggy sort of way. Such a Heart will only be able to serve the ego sense and the belief systems of the mind, and thus will be stuck in a want and need cycle of satisfaction and dependency. This is a relationship based in mind and ego and can only continue so long as it is getting from the relationship whatever it is envisioning that it wants and needs. As soon as there may be an interruption in the flow of these satisfactions the person will not be able to be intimate any longer with another. Such a relationship is without a spiritual foundation and if it withstands the test of time and endures, generally it is because of a relatively stable codependency that outer circumstances are supporting.

A relationship based on Truth, however, will not be so vulnerable to outer circumstances, yet the partners involved will be far more vulnerable in a Real way to one another. This is because their connections go so much deeper where both must be totally Honest and Real with themselves and be so willing to share and reflect back to the other what is genuinely happening for them in their Core. When people are this Real with each other there is a timeless quality to relationship that can span eternity. There is a power behind it that has a genuine life of its own that can uplift all partners to higher frequencies of energy and dimensions by virtue of their common resonance and polarity flow that builds between them and expands with each growing expression of the love that penetrates through them all.

Such relationships can exits on many different levels and maintain a Transcendent quality by virtue of their status within the Being Itself. True Love finds Its fulfillment here in a bonding that not even death can separate. It is the Spirit's capacity to Unite all as One that knows no limitations or boundaries of space, time or concept. The Reality speaks for Itself; the Love presents Its own Life as One eternal and immortal Being; the Heart so Awakened knows what It is Being. The only proof is in the direct experience of That singularity of Being with another Being who is unique yet none other than One's own True Self. The rationale of the mind is boggled by the Reality of the Heart, yet it is Real and experiential to anyone so Awakened as Consciousness.

Masculine and Feminine
Energies Relationship

There are throughout Creation differing types of energies, as has been discussed on various levels already. The unique interplay and relation between what are known as masculine energy and feminine energy, which are not to be construed as duality, have a vital role in the functions of life and relationship that is important and timely here.

Wherever there is a flow of energy there is a motion from one pole to another that involves a completed circuit, as in a current that completes this movement and is reabsorbed into the opposite pole. If the polarity is intact, that energy will then return to the first pole and the flow will continue back again to its ground, over and over. In context of the male and female this flow follows some similar parallels. Generally speaking the masculine energy is electric, while the feminine is magnetic. This means that the electric energy of the male is drawn to the magnetic energy of the female, which grounds or completes the circuit. In what we would call a healthy relationship a polarity is created by the love frequency or bond of Being between them, which allows for the free return of energy to the electrically charged male, and the circuit repeats. A truly healthy relationship is one where there are no short circuits or energy leakages within this polarity, so that this flow of energy naturally builds between these partners, and both are uplifted and mutually energized by and in context of their relating together. The masculine energizes the feminine, who in turn reenergizes the masculine and so on.

Such a smooth and mutually healthy energetic flow is a natural harmony that is likewise dependent upon all partners' Honesty of Consciousness, and is the blessing of relationship based upon Truth and Tenderness between all involved. As has been pointed out in the previous segment, any dishonesty of Heart in either or both partners will also disrupt this polarity and cause energy to drain away from the relationship, and both partners will generally feel the effects of this, as the relationship will not serve to nourish and revitalize them, as it would more naturally if this energy were remaining within the polarity of their relating together.

This being the case, we can begin to see into the Reality of this vitally important link of Honesty of Consciousness and relationship based in Truth and the pure love of Being both for Itself and for each other in context of relating within that arena.

Importance of Proper Understanding

What we have witnessed in contemporary society and Western civilization as a whole over the entire course of history that is available to us is that the price of misunderstanding can be dire. Even our most deeply assumed beliefs in aging, disease and death are the results of deep seated misunderstandings, which I propose are present within our subconscious minds as the result of profound manipulations to which we, as our own ancestors, were subjected to by beings of a lesser moral character. It is testament to the immense creative power of the Human Consciousness that we manifest for ourselves so vividly in our own lives that which we believe in so fully and without question or doubt that we assume the truth and reality of them as a matter of course. Our collective, seemingly universal, experience of the aging process, disease and death is only the most powerful case in point, but there are many others that could also serve as examples of how we are all collectively bamboozled into our lives of limitations, fears and all the difficulties associated with limited awareness and self-deprecating belief systems, none of which are Essential to who and what we are as Consciousness.

No such limiting belief or affectation is True to the Consciousness of Creation, and as That is what we likewise are, there is no Truth to these limitations for ourselves either; only we have to give power to what is Real alone and stop these long standing patterns of self abuse, denial of Truth and being something that is unreal. Hence the return to the Way of Truth is so required and necessary.

Fact is the whole process and condition of untruth and ignorance can be characterized as a simple misunderstanding of our Real Nature, yet it is our own Consciousness that gives that misunderstanding power over us by virtue of the belief we place in it. Truly we are sovereign beings with inherent freedom to live as we Truly are or to live within the prison bars of our own making. Manipulated as we have been to believe we can only live within these sets of prison bars we have lost sight of what life would be without them or even how to restore ourselves to such a pure and genuine state of Being-ness. That also is what this book is about.

In the final analysis an inner clarity of vision and straightness of understanding of Truth Itself relative to our dimensional experience and expression are the keys to a joyful, fulfilled, peaceful, harmonious and spiritually enlightened life, society, world and beyond. The peaceful cooperation of all life everywhere is our Natural state of affairs in True relationship within the overall Consciousness of Creation. We are all part and parcel of That making us all One. Any disharmony within the whole must be symptomatic of some kind of disease in the Whole. For the sake of possibility we must acknowledge this, yet that being the case it becomes our conscious responsibility to seek to be agents of cure rather than agents of disease. This must always guide us towards the role of peacemakers and resolution finders. The war maker is acting out the disease; while the peacemaker is being the cure and the healthy influence.

Seen in this light the war maker is inherently dishonest and distorted as Consciousness. No amount of rationalization or mental arguing can effect this basic fact. The Truth that violence in all forms for whatever reasons the mind, that is divorced from Heart, can come up with is rooted in dishonesty, delusion, distortion of Consciousness, untruth and unreality.

There is no moral war; there is no just war; there is only rationalized violence on a massive scale, pitting brother and sister nations against themselves for the private interests of the privileged and powerful who can muster command of the requisite military forces to do so.

This being the case there is no further excuse for wars of any kind. As Humanity Awakens to Its own greater Reality, the Way of Tender Honesty is destined to prevail over the egotistical self-centered ways of the dishonest and criminal mind of the ignorant confused and self-deluded. Those who would make war are unfit for the responsibilities of positions of authority; those who can not see the Unity by virtue of Awareness of all life can not be trusted with the fate of living things in the balance. It is not rocket science; it must be as obvious as the sun in the sky. We are One; we respect the One; we honor the Life that This represents and is embodied by; we Love That for It is the Source of all that Is including ourselves; we do not make war against ourselves, no matter what the appearance or location of origin in the Universe of that Being.

Truly as we have witnessed and experienced, the consequences of misunderstand of our Real Nature are severe. Yet the converse of this is also True, as with the joyous effects of the Reality of our Being when lived within harmony, honesty and tenderness. Without our destructive addictions and misunderstandings the Reality of our Being-ness will have little to block Its shining presence to emerge as creative expressions, inventiveness and the highest good for man and woman everywhere. Universal peace, prosperity, abundance, good health and longevity are to be the Reality of All. The Body of Creation is growing, evolving and becoming more healthy, and we are to be among the witnesses of that.

Evolution of Creation on All
Levels Simultaneously

Creation evolves with the Creator. As all dimensions coexist parallel and simultaneously, so too do all parallel Universes evolve and grow in a kind of coordination together as a whole, for in Reality they do not exist separately from one another but together as a larger energy exchange and within the single Consciousness of Creation. The recognition of this Truth is crucial to the Awareness of Unity and Oneness. It is more than simply an intellectual assent, but rather an inner conviction born of genuine Knowingness of Reality. This is beyond "faith"; it is a direct Awareness from actual experience of an inner nature cultivated by clarity and Truth of vision and understanding.

What happens with us in our world and within our own lives effects all of Creation, and likewise whatever happens anywhere else on any dimension whatever effects us here in our lives and world as well. To thoroughly Know this and understand how these interactions actually work and to Know the phase of development Creation is going through at any moment is to Truly Know God, and to Know That as both the Body of Creation and Its Consciousness.

These Cognitions connect us directly in Awareness with the fullness and depth of Creation and make clear for us the highest Good in all interactions with our environment and our fellow beings. In Vedic terms there is a condition of celibacy inherent in this view of the Cosmos. Celibacy is here defined as a state of being within where the life force is always directed upwards. It does not as in the common Western usage refer to a state of refusal of marriage or to engage in any sort of sexual activity with a beloved, but it does indicate a constant Self Referral or Inner Wakefulness to what is Known to be Truth within, such that you are constantly being informed by what is genuinely Known to be True and in each moment responding to That in all interactions with the world and fellow beings. This Inner Way of Being that is True by Its very Nature keeps you in a state of Real celibacy, due to Its constant referral to the highest Good within as your Source of response to all things.

Living Oneness and Unity in this is the fulfillment of the genuine meaning of celibacy in this Real sense. It is a natural state of Knowing and responding in Tender Honesty to the Known as Truth in Tenderness living as you through you and for you in the world. All things are known and responded to according to the Way, and as John de Ruiter puts it, "Tenderness gets to live instead of you." [46] Tenderness in this context is meant as the Real Self, and this is opposed to the ego or "I" thought, the you that you think you are, which of course is only a thought and could never be a stand in or replica of Consciousness and all that That Is. Just as no concept can ever be what Consciousness Is; no idea of "I" could ever be a Real indication of what is genuinely Real. A creation of mind and thought process is not to be confused with the Source of Mind or thought, nor is it to be mistaken for the Source of Knowing.

When we realize Consciousness as One and Creation as a single living Being, it becomes quite clear that evolution is nothing like we've imagined it to be in a universe of separate species, various eco-systems, endless types and patterns of living things somehow co-existing in an amazingly diverse world. Yes, the world is diverse, and eco-systems create niches for all manner of species to find their relative places in which to flourish, and yes, they also co-create a balanced energetic-physical system that mutually supports itself as all of them, as all of it. As has been repeated so often, it is all interconnected as are all the cells of a single body and all the stars in a single galaxy and all the galaxies that combine to form the mysterious thing we call a Universe, and beyond that even are all these co-habitating Universes of the still greater Creation.

As below so above; just as the growing body grows as one, so does Creation grow, evolve and discover Itself as Its own divine manifestation of all Consciousness within It. In this divine process nothing is excluded, nothing wasted, nothing even left to chance, and this points also to the greatness of the Gift and the mystery of who we are as Consciousness. The possibilities Truly are endless; the prospects for development and evolution of civilization without end transcend anything imaginable to our Awareness today. What is life on higher dimensions? What is Knowable and Known to civilizations so conscious of their unbounded origins that they exist constantly in the direct knowing of themselves as the totality of Consciousness?

These are not mere speculative or rhetorical questions; they are quickly becoming the pressing inquiries of our times. To fully Conscious Humans they are to be the defining moment that gives meaning and purpose to their life's quest. It is time we set our life force looking upwards to the Reality into which we are meant by Creation to move and to see into our own True Nature enough to see in that our quest to Awaken in Creation everything we ourselves are so meant to Be.

The Invincible Nature of Reality

Truth as Reality and Reality as Truth are interchangeable terms; they are to be regarded as one in the same. I believe it is good to have multiple terms whenever they so fit, as this adds to the richness of understanding on so many levels. Invincibility applies to Truth as it does to Reality. What does invincibility mean, and what can be the implications of Truth and Reality as invincible?

What genuinely Is is Real. What is being Real in its Being is also being True. What is True can not be made untrue by a lie or anything that is being unreal. Only the lie and what is being unreal have stolen energy from somewhere it had become available to it in its efforts to make itself into an alternative to the Real and create a deceptive life of its own separate from and distinct from the Real. This is a distorted pattern being unreal, pretending to be something that it is not. In the Sanskrit term, it is Maya or illusion presenting as if it were Real. In classical Western terms, the Maya simply Is not.

Whatever is being unreal or in an unreal state is destined to decay and dissolution, because its energy is always finite. It has disconnected from its infinite Source, and is distorting itself into being something it "Is not." This applies to all forms of Consciousness that have this capacity to choose to be unreal, something that they are not.

Of course this capacity to choose applies only to the Human Consciousness and also to a higher order of Angelic Beings who also are Graced with the Free Will to so choose. It is the partially conscious human, however, who makes the choice to use that freedom to be unreal, and yet this also is by design.

Because Holy Spirit, the Consciousness of Creation is all inclusive of everything that exists in Creation, nothing can ever Truly be separated from That in any Real sense. The feeling and belief anyone may have of being separated or disconnected indicates a loss of direct Awareness of That only, for the very presence of life is itself that connection which is felt to be missing.

Nevertheless, the dense material existence of 3rd dimension can make this sense of separation appear most convincing in the ordinary states of dreaming and waking Consciousness. It is therefore necessary that careful and deliberate focus is placed to keep Awareness in its natural and restfully alert state. This means on so many levels, right living, right eating, exercise and spiritual practice with the proper guidance and instruction. It is a common mistake made today that so many think they can form these vital practices on their own as a matter of course or nature. True that the right practices when found will also be found to be natural, but to leave such important matters to chance in the present polluted state of our world's environment is asking for trouble and disillusionment. It is the long standing wisdom of both East and West that the teacher of Truth is needed to ensure success and a happy outcome in all cases.

Still that which is eternal and infinite by its very nature is the possessor of Invincibility Itself. Worlds and even Universes are created and dissolved on a constant basis. [47] It is Consciousness that is neither created nor dissolved that is without limit and boundary that both Knows and is Known; it is both that which is known as well as the One who Knows. In this context even the concept of Invincibility is illusory. What is being overcome is itself an illusion, an aspect of the Maya, that which Is not. As it never existed, the appearance of any conflict or challenge to the Infinite was never even Real. It was only an appearance for the benefit of a denser Consciousness that was temporarily disabled, if you will, from directly seeing into the Reality, and as such it took this appearance of separation seriously and believed in it.

Invincibility is simply telling us that what is Real will prevail over that which is being unreal. How else could it be? Time is on our side; evolution is on our side as it were; after all it is Creation Itself which is evolving as us all, and that leaves nothing out or unaccounted for. We are One; we are One Creation, One Being, One Life and One Spirit. There is really no other Consciousness other than this One whole Spirit whose Creation is all that Is here knowable for us.

We Do Not Make What Is Truth

Just as a lie can never alter what is True, so too Truth remains independent of our wants and needs. Anything we would make true can not be True. We do not make what is True; only we discover the Truth to ever greater and deeper degrees. That which is True has always been True; we discover through Tender Honesty of Consciousness and surrender to that which we genuinely know to be That. "My truth" is relative, changeable and only indicates what I would want or need to be true in order for me to have what I want. [48] While this may be satisfying to the ego, and may even be reflective of the good to some extent, it does not Awaken you to Reality and to Truth Itself. It only awakens you to what it is you are wanting to be true. If what you are wanting is untrue, you are actually awakening to an untruth. There is an arrogance and dishonesty implied in this, as it calls for a bending of truth to your own will, which is further distorting to what you are as Consciousness.

Yet it is natural for the Being to Desire; this is what motivates and gives rise to Creation Itself. The genuine Desire of the Being is that clean and straight pattern of Creation by and through which all action and manifestation emerge from the Being. Such genuine Desiring is not born of need or want; there is no ego in it; only it is the genuine manner of expression of the pure Consciousness of Creation, and hence we call it the Will of God or the Creator. When individual ego is transcended there is an Awakening of the Will such that your own will merges with the Will of the Cosmic Creator, so that individual Will becomes the pure expression of That. It is the fulfillment of the prayer, "Not my will, but Thine be done." In other words, Divine Will becomes your will, as your will surrenders itself into That. It is the pure and voluntary process of Devotion transforming into Oneness. It is the transparency of the ego to That which is Real for the pure Love of what you Know is the True Way to Be.

The being of untruth is one who refuses this transformation for the sake of being what he or she is wanting to be rather than what is True and Real to Be. It is a profoundly difficult pattern of distortion that can lead one into this sort of state. It is like the addict who believes he can get it right and somehow make the addiction work for him, yet all the while it is killing him in ways he refuses to see. Ultimately he will either hit rock bottom and he will see the need for change, or the addiction will kill him.

The world is yet currently inhabited by many of these beings of untruth, some of whom still hold onto positions of power and influence and who continue in their attempts to make of the world what they personally want it to be; even at the cost of its destruction and so much more. At this delicate stage of human evolution only the Divine Will stands between us and their diabolical plans, yet That alone must be enough for without It the power of ego would overcome Tenderness and the Way of Truth, which it can never do.

It must be clear at this point that evolution is inevitable; we can not help but evolve no matter what. It is in the simple principle of change, as in change is inevitable and unstoppable, but the question is what is this change; what are we becoming. The Reality is that if what we are being in our Core is True, if our Way of Being in That is True, then we are evolving into Truth and becoming a being which is more and more Real and True. If on the other hand our way of being at the Core is untrue and not Real, than you evolve into something distorted. The stakes are that high; the question of what is it do you wish to become, True or untrue, is that important. At the same time there is no escaping or avoiding the issue; you either evolve into the Real or unreal, the True or untrue. You become as Consciousness something clean and straight, Tender and Honest or as Consciousness you become unreal and untrue, distorted and twisted. [48]

Ultimately, this is the value of Free Will; as Consciousness the choice you make to be Real or not leads you to one or the other. There are no other alternatives to this.

Beauty as Reality

The great ancient Greek philosopher Plato identified the Beautiful as a Transcendental. In this context a Transcendental is something which emerges directly from the Transcendent Being. Aristotle and others before him identified three Transcendentals, which are Goodness, Oneness and Truth. By including Beauty among these, Plato was confirming the intrinsic Beauty of the nature of the Being Itself and thus identifying the other three as also Beautiful by virtue of their intrinsic nature. Goodness is Beautiful, as is Oneness and Truth as well, and likewise each of these are intrinsic to Beauty in the same way.

With this we realize that Consciousness that is being Real and is awakening to Truth, Goodness and Oneness is also awakening to Beauty and Itself becoming more Beautiful as it so becomes increasingly realized and Awakened. Conversely, if any of these Transcendentals are lacking so too to that extent would all the others. They are in fact not separate, but simply serve as categories for our understanding of the Being and how to perceive It among ourselves and in the world. The Being is Itself imperceptible to mind and intellect, but It is knowable only within Consciousness as the Heart, the faculty of Knowing. Recognizing this we become Cognizant of the Eye to See and the Ear to Hear the imperceptible Word of Truth that the Master of Truth can show and speak.

Final Conclusions and Afterthoughts

We are living in a world in the midst of a great transition occurring on so many levels simultaneously it boggles the mind and awareness. As the operational frequencies of our world rise and lift us all with them right out of our familiar 3rd dimensional realities, so do the entire operational modalities of that reality become obsolete, inefficient and increasingly untenable. We witness this today as institutional breakdown, environmental breakdown and social disturbances of all sorts.

The good news is that just as the previous dimensional energies dissolve beneath our feet, so do the next phase of energetic frequencies move into place to support those new modalities that can replace the old; thus the new solutions for these problems besetting us by the collapse of the old are presenting themselves even as part of the same process that is breaking down the old ways. An optimistic view of our world at present, yes, but we are ever to remember that Creation is not self destructive, nor is it wasteful or angry, but rather Creation is evolving and growing and we along with it as part and parcel of all that Is. We are here for a reason, and that reason is our collective destiny.

When we consider Creation as a single whole, living, breathing Being as an entity unto Itself endowed with Consciousness of all that is within Itself, we are confronted with the Cognition of ourselves in Union with That All as well. This realization follows naturally once we've accepted this type of relationship with our Universe as Real and knowable within our own Heart. Consciousness is everything, and we are That. There is no escaping this inevitability, and it is high time we stopped trying to be something that we imagine might be somehow greater, more important or more special than That, just to be able to say, "I did it my way!"

Some may say that this view of ourselves is too arrogant; that it is some kind of sinful pride to see oneself as more than a grain of sand in a Universe full of stars; how can something so insignificant as we be so boastful in the face of such a vast Creation, so large and so much bigger than you and me? Yet we are told by scripture that "The Kingdom of Heaven is within you." Still the analogy of Indra's Web as it comes to us from Vedic scripture reveals the holographic nature of Creation; that the whole is contained in every grain of sand, in every particle of matter and light and energy. Truly, the Kingdom of Heaven is everywhere present without exception, see it or not, believe it or not. Truth is Truth; Reality is Reality; Nature is Nature, and the real arrogance is in believing that what we choose not to believe is not Real.

We are to believe only what we genuinely Know in our Hearts to be Real. We are to remain Tenderly open to anything and everything we do not so Know the Truth of until its Reality can be so confirmed within our Knowingness. These are the hallmarks of the Way of Truth; unconditional Tenderness, Openness, Honesty of Consciousness and steadfastness, the total willingness to keep hands off the Heart no matter what is passing through it as feelings, emotions and events. It is a trusting of the divine Grace in all things and Ways It works in our lives.

To what end does this flow; in what manner does this Way of Being lead us into the highest Union with Reality? How does Tender Honesty cure everything and restore Consciousness to the full brilliance of Its Divine status? To this I say, try it and see for yourself. Take no one's word for it, but follow the inner

Truth within your own Heart, for That is the only way you can move towards genuine Realization; no one can do this for you; we must each embrace our inner Knowing in Tenderness and Honesty and from that beginning Grace, Beauty and Truth begin to take over as we allow and lead us Home by Their and our own Nature. So It Is; so It has always Been, and so It Will ever Be.

Acknowledgements

It is truly a daunting task to list and adequately give credit to the vast cast of Great Ones who have influenced my own personal growth and understanding over the course of a life time of study and practice. Several have been named through the course of this text as mentors and whose speech and writings served more directly as contributors to this thinking and insight. Mentors such as Maharishi Mahesh Yogi, Sri Sri Ravi Shankar, Sri Bhagavan Ramana Maharshi, Sri Nisargadatta Maharaj, Martin Buber, John deRuiter. Also the thinking of Wayne Dyer, Neale Donald Walsh are ever present influences that are with me constantly. Special mention must be made to Drunvalo Melchizedek and Almine for their important insights into ascension and higher states of Consciousness. Beyond these there is the infinite sea of Masters, living and ascended, who informed as they are by the great Sat Guru, the Holy Spirit and Consciousness of Creation Itself, are both too numerous to mention; named and unnamed, they stand as the great beacons of Light and Inspiration outside of time and space, yet ever present within the fabric of Awareness that embraces all of sentient Life, there for the asking as the light of the sun, moon and stars and air of our breathe.

In this endeavor I acknowledge that I am standing upon a mountain of Divinity to peer above the wall of division and illusion, and thank God for the gift to be able even for a moment to look at what lies beyond the remaining veil towards the new millennium into which we are now just beginning to embark. The little bit of roughness we may now encounter will soon be quickly forgotten amid the joy of our new realization of Heaven upon Earth. If this volume can serve in any small way to Awaken those looking for these answers during and after this transition I will consider my efforts well rewarded and successful. In Truth, God is the author of this book; I am only Its scribe.

Thank you for reading and considering and for growing into the Truth of Yoga and Union with the All. The Grace of the Almighty Be with you always.

References

PART I

[1] John Hagelin, Ph.D., <u>Consciousness & Physics Part 1: Discovery of the Unified Field</u>

[2] Almine. <u>www.spiritualjourneys.com</u>

[3] Mahrishi Mahesh Yogi. <u>Science of Being and Art of Living</u>, pp. 29-35

[4] William Shakespeare. <u>Julius Caesar</u>

[5] Merriam Webster Dictionary

[6] Heisenberg's uncertainty principle: That the Consciousness of the observer alters or has an effect upon that which is observed. "The more precisely the position is determined, the less precisely the momentum is known in this instant, and vice versa." 1927

[7] Ewert Cousins, <u>Bonaventure and the Coincidence of Opposites</u>, p. 15

[8] Sri Nisargadatta Maharaj. <u>I Am That</u>. A Collection of 101 dialogues between The Maharaj and his students.

[9] www.MantrasonNet.com/Indra'sWeb

[10] Maharishi. <u>Love and God</u>, pp. 42-43

PART II

[11] Maharaj, <u>I Am That</u>

[12] John de Ruiter. <u>Unveiling Reality</u>

[13] Maharishi. <u>On the Bhagavad-Gita: A New Translation and Commentary, Chapters 1-6</u>, see Bibliography

[14] Maharishi. Courses and Lectures, Maharishi Channel and u-tube

[15] Benedict Groeshel. <u>Spiritual Passages</u>, p. 160

PART III

16   Ingram Smith. <u>Truth is a Pathless Land</u>. General reference is here made as suggested reading.
17   Maharaj. <u>I Am That</u>
18   Maharishi. Lectures

PART IV

19   Maharishi. Lectures
20   Drunvalo Melchizedek. Drunvalo.net and u-tube references
21   ABOVE
22   ABOVE
23   Dr. Steven Greer. DisclosureProject.com
24   ABOVE
25   One such large pyramid exists submerged off the western tip of Cuba in the Gulf of Mexico.
26   Greer. DisclosureProject.com
27   Drunvalo. Drunvalo.net and u-tube references

PART V

28   Drunvalo. Drunvalo.net and u-tube references
29   ABOVE
30   ABOVE
31   ABOVE
32   Hagelin

PART VI

33   Jung, Carl. <u>Psychology and Alchemy</u>, see Bibliography
34   Maharishi. <u>Maharishi Mahesh Yogi on the Bhagavad-Gita</u>
35   Greer. DisclosureProject.com
36   John de Ruiter. <u>Unveiling Reality</u>
37   ABOVE
38   St. Augustine.
39   Maharaj. <u>I Am That</u>
40   John de Ruiter. Lectures
41   Teilhard de Chardin, <u>Divine Milieu</u>

[42] Martin Buber. <u>I And Thou</u> . General reference is here made as suggested reading.

[43] Maharishi. <u>Maharishi Mahesh Yogi on the Bhagavad-Gita</u>

[44] Mahatma Gandhi. <u>Complete Writings of Mahatma Gandhi</u>

PART VII

[45] St. Augustine.

[46] John de Ruiter. <u>Unveiling Reality</u>

[47] Maharaj. <u>I Am That</u>

[48] John de Ruiter. <u>Unveiling Reality</u>

Bibliography

Almine. www.spiritualjourneys.com

Cousins, Ewert H. Bonaventure and the Coincidence of Opposites, Franciscan Herald Press, Chicago, 1978

de Ruiter, John. Unveiling Reality, Oasis Edmonton Inc., Edmonton, 2000

_____, www.johnderuiter.com

Greer, Dr. Steven. www.thedisclosureproject.com

Groeschel, Benedict. Spiritual Passages, Crossroad Publishing Co., New York, 1983

Jung, C.G. Psychology and Alchemy, Routledge and Kegan Paul, London, 1953

Maharaj, Sri Nisargadatta. I Am That, Chetana (P) Ltd., Bombay, 1973

Maharishi Mahesh Yogi. Love and God, MIU Press, Livingston Manor, New York, 1973

_____. On the Bhagavad-Gita: A New Translation and Commentary Chapters 1-6, Penguin Books, 1967

_____. The Science of Being and Art of Living, MIU Press, Livingston Manor, New York, 1966

Melchizedek, Drunvalo. www.drunvalo.net

Smith, Ingram. Truth is a Pathless Land: A Journey with Krishnamurti, The Theosophical Publishing House, Wheaton, Ill., Madras, London, 1989

The Nag Hammadi Library in English, James M. Robinson (gen. ed.), Harper and Row Publishing Co., New York, 1973

Printed in the United States
By Bookmasters